Florence Eveleen Elenore (Olliffe) Bell

ChamberComedies;

A Collection of Plays and Monologues

Florence Eveleen Elenore (Olliffe) Bell

ChamberComedies;
A Collection of Plays and Monologues

ISBN/EAN: 9783744768610

Printed in Europe, USA, Canada, Australia, Japan

Cover: Foto ©Andreas Hilbeck / pixelio.de

More available books at **www.hansebooks.com**

CHAMBER COMEDIES

A COLLECTION OF PLAYS AND MONOLOGUES

FOR THE DRAWING ROOM

BY

MRS HUGH BELL

LONDON

LONGMANS, GREEN, AND CO.

AND NEW YORK: 15 EAST 16th STREET

1890

PRINTED BY
SPOTTISWOODE AND CO., NEW-STREET SQUARE
LONDON

CONTENTS

[1] Reprinted from 'Temple Bar,' by permission of Messrs. Bentley.

[2] Reprinted from 'The Woman's World,' by permission of Cassell & Co., Limited.

L'INDÉCIS

COMÉDIE EN UN ACTE.

PERSONNAGES.

PAUL IMBERT   .   .   .   (35 à 40 ans).
ALINE DELAROCHE   .   .   (veuve, 28 ans).
LOUISON   .   .   .   .   (femme de chambre).

SCÈNE.—*Le salon de madame Delaroche. Au fond, bureau, avec ce qu'il faut pour écrire. Au premier plan, une petite table à ouvrage. Un canapé, des sièges, etc.*

Louison (introduisant Imbert). Si monsieur veut entrer—je vais prévenir madame.

Imbert. C'est bien, c'est bien. *(Se ravisant)* Non, ne la prévenez pas, je voudrais plutôt lui faire une petite surprise.

Louison. Très bien, monsieur. Alors, je ne préviendrai pas madame ?

Imbert. Mais si . . . mais si . . . la surprise pourrait lui être désagréable . . . enfin, faites comme vous voudrez.

Louison. Bien, monsieur !   [*Elle sort.*

Imbert (seul). Décidément, il n'y a pas de plus grand tourment que l'indécision ! je ne peux pas arriver à savoir ce que je veux . . . je suis dans la situation la plus embarrassante, la plus terrible dans laquelle puisse se trouver un homme de mon âge, éperdûment amoureux d'une jeune et charmante veuve. Oui, je suis amoureux ! cela au moins je le sais—amoureux au point de demander en mariage celle

B

que j'aime. Mais par quelles angoisses, ô dieux ! ai-je passé
pour en arriver jusque-là ! et de dire qu'après tout, après
avoir pris cette décision surhumaine, j'ignore encore à
l'heure qu'il est, si ou non j'ai formellement demandé la main
de la belle madame Delaroche ! Cela vous semble bizarre,
n'est-ce pas ? c'est pourtant vrai. Voici comment la
chose s'est passée. J'ai fait la connaissance de madame
Delaroche à Trouville, l'été dernier, sur la plage, où
elle était toujours très entourée, très recherchée—ce
qui du reste n'avait rien d'étonnant, elle est toujours
si aimable pour tout le monde ! c'est l'unique défaut
que je lui reproche, celui d'être trop avenante, trop
charmante envers les gens ennuyeux—et Dieu sait s'il s'en
trouve, des ennuyeux, sur la plage de Trouville ! comme,
du reste, partout ailleurs. Le vicomte de Ravignan, par
exemple, ce grand lieutenant de cavalerie—quel benêt !
D'abord, je ne peux pas souffrir les militaires. Je sais bien
que cela n'est pas bien porté en France à l'heure qu'il est,
de ne pas aimer les militaires : mais que voulez-vous—je
suis comme cela—je ne peux pas les voir, non, je ne peux
pas les voir ! et le souvenir de ce Ravignan, toujours
assidu, toujours empressé auprès de madame Delaroche à
Trouville, me crispe les nerfs rien que d'y penser. Mais
enfin, il n'a pas besoin qu'on s'occupe de lui en ce moment,
pauvre garçon, puisqu'il est en garnison de province, et que
madame Delaroche, depuis trois mois qu'elle est rentrée à
Paris, n'a pas paru trop obsédée de son souvenir . . . tandis
que pour moi, pendant ces trois mois, elle a été parfaite—
j'ai fréquenté son salon, je l'ai rencontrée dans le monde,
j'ai appris à la connaître, et je commence enfin à entrevoir
que je suis amoureux comme un garçon de vingt ans, et que
je n'ai plus qu'à demander sa main. A qui m'adresser ?
elle est orpheline . . . elle a bien un frère, à ce qu'il paraît,
au Brésil—il colonise. C'est un peu loin ! il n'y a donc qu'à
elle-même que je puisse faire ma demande, cela est évident.

Eh bien, après avoir pris cette résolution, j'attends encore une semaine, pendant laquelle je pèse le pour et le contre. Enfin, hier soir je retrouve madame Delaroche dans le monde, à un bal au ministère—nous passons une soirée délicieuse . . . je sens que nulle autre femme ne pourra compléter mon existence . . . je rentre agité, heureux, tenant à la main une précieuse relique de ma bien-aimée, un carnet qu'elle avait laissé tomber. Je passe une nuit blanche . . . je compose une lettre d'une éloquence persuasive . . . le matin, je cours moi-même la jeter à la poste. Une fois la lettre partie, j'espérais reprendre mon calme—me retrouver tranquille, digne, attendant de pied ferme la décision de celle que j'adore. Aucunement ! une fois la lettre partie, mes angoisses me reprennent de plus belle . . . je recommence mes discussions avec moi-même . . . je me représente le refus accablant qui m'attend peut-être . . . bref, je me dis qu'il serait plus prudent d'attendre encore vingt-quatre heures, et je me précipite dans le bureau de poste, pour réclamer ma lettre à l'employé. 'Comment, monsieur ! me répond-il d'un ton bourru—vous ignorez qu'une lettre une fois jetée à la poste ne peut pas être réclamée ? elle ne vous appartient plus ! — Comment, elle ne m'appartient plus ? — Non, monsieur, non ! elle ne vous appartient plus. — Quoi ! la lettre que je viens d'écrire est là, devant mes yeux, et je n'oserais pas étendre la main pour la prendre ? mais puisque je vous dis que j'ai changé d'avis depuis que j'ai écrit cette lettre, que vous allez vous rendre complice d'un malheur, oui, d'un malheur irréparable si vous persistez à l'expédier ! — Mais, monsieur, c'est pour expédier les lettres que je suis ici, ce n'est pas pour confesser le public ! me répond-il impatienté : si e malheur qui vous menace est aussi grand que cela, envoyez une dépêche pour dire que vous avez changé d'avis—elle arrivera encore avant la lettre !' Oh, quels insolents que ces employés de bureau ! je sors furieux, la rage dans l'âme —j'arpente le boulevard pendant une demi-heure—je me

Aline entre, une corbeille à ouvrage à la main.

Aline (surprise). Monsieur Imbert ! la bonne surprise ! Y a-t-il longtemps que vous êtes là ? on ne m'avait pas prévenue.

Imbert. Madame . . . quelques minutes seulement . . . mais le temps m'a paru long sans vous, comme toujours.

Aline (souriant). Vous êtes trop aimable.

Imbert. Quelle charmante soirée hier au ministère, n'est-ce pas ?

Aline. Charmante, en effet, une soirée tout à fait agréable. A propos, pendant que j'y pense—est-ce que je vous aurai confié par hasard un petit carnet que je tenais à la main ?

Imbert. Non, madame, non, vous ne me l'avez pas confié.

Aline. Alors, mon dernier espoir est perdu.

Imbert. Vous ne me l'avez pas confié, mais vous l'avez laissé tomber en sortant de la salle, et j'ai eu le bonheur de le ramasser. Le voici, je vous l'apportais.

Aline. Comment, vous avez eu cette prévoyance ? Je vous remercie mille fois—je tenais beaucoup à ce petit carnet, que mon père m'a donné . . . en rentrant j'ai voulu y chercher une adresse, et c'est en m'apercevant que je ne l'avais plus que j'ai tout de suite pensé à vous.

Imbert. Je regrette de vous l'avoir rendu alors, car vous auriez eu l'occasion de penser à moi chaque fois que vous vouliez chercher une adresse.

Aline. Mais il me semble que cela ne serait pas bien flatteur pour vous—c'est plutôt un rôle d'almanach Bottin que celui de preux chevalier que vous vous attribuez là !

Imbert. Je ne demanderais pas mieux que d'être votre Bottin—toujours près de vous, à la portée de votre main.

Aline (riant malgré elle). Je vous demande pardon de rire, mais vraiment, cette comparaison est par trop prosaïque !

Imbert (*vexé*). En effet, oui. (*A part*) J'ai voulu la toucher, elle se moque de moi !

Aline. Souhaitez plutôt d'être un mince volume de poésies, que je tiendrais à la main.

Imbert. C'est cela, oui, un volume de poésies remplies de pensées tendres et délicates, dont chaque page respire le sentiment et l'amour.

Aline. Oh ! comme vous dites cela bien ! c'est charmant—vous êtes un poète manqué !

Imbert (*interdit*). Manqué, madame !

Aline. Je voulais seulement dire que vous auriez dû vous consacrer à la poésie, que vous vous êtes mépris sur votre véritable vocation.

Imbert (*flatté*). Mon Dieu, madame, pour ce qui est de la vocation, j'ai bien la prétention de me consacrer un peu à la littérature, comme tout le monde au jour qu'il est—je fais quelquefois des vers, de la prose aussi . . . quelquefois je n'en fais pas—voilà mes moments vraiment inspirés !

Aline. Comment, vous écrivez ? vous êtes auteur, et vous avez la modestie de ne pas vous déclarer ?

Imbert. Mais, madame, jusqu'ici ce sont les éditeurs qui ont eu de la modestie pour moi, et qui m'ont empêché de réclamer l'attention du public . . . d'ailleurs, pour moi, la poésie est plutôt une amie, une confidente, qu'un moyen de réclame.

Aline. Oh, que c'est beau, que c'est généreux ce que vous dites là ! Ainsi, pour vous la poésie est uniquement un moyen d'épanchement ? dans les moments d'émotion peut-être . . .

Imbert. Justement, madame, oui, vous me devinez . . . dans des moments d'émotion, comme tout à l'heure, par exemple, une métaphore à l'aile hardie s'échappe de mes lèvres . . . voilà comme je suis.

Aline. Oh, vous n'avez pas idée à quel point cela m'intéresse de pénétrer ainsi dans les secrets de l'inspira-

tion poétique ! Et vos écrits ? C'est peut-être dans les
moments de solitude qu'un morceau fugitif s'échappe de
votre plume.

Imbert. Oui, madame, oui : c'est cela.

Aline. Ne me ferez-vous pas voir une fois quelque
chose que vous aurez écrit ?

Imbert (à part). Hélas, que trop ! Si je saisissais cette
occasion pour lui dire——

[*On entend sonner. Imbert tressaille, il regarde la
porte avec inquiétude.*

Aline. Qu'avez-vous, monsieur Imbert ? vous paraissez
inquiet ?

Imbert. Mais, madame, j'ai cru entendre des pas, puis
un coup de sonnette.

Aline. Eh bien, quand cela serait ? Ce n'est probablement que le facteur, qui passe ordinairement vers
cette heure-ci.

Imbert (inquiet). Le facteur ?

Aline (surprise). Mais, mon cher monsieur, qu'avez-
vous donc ?

Imbert (cherchant). Madame, vous me voyez confondu . . .
je vais vous expliquer la chose . . . c'est très singulier . . . c'est
plus fort que moi . . . mais depuis ma plus tendre enfance j'ai
toujours eu la plus profonde antipathie pour les facteurs.

Aline (surprise). Pour les facteurs ?

Imbert. Pour les facteurs, oui, madame (*parlant
rapidement*). Il y a de ces exemples, qui sont parfaitement
bien connus dans le monde de la science, de ces antipathies
natives, inexplicables, contre lesquelles la raison ne peut
rien . . . ainsi, il y a des personnes qui ne peuvent supporter
la vue d'une araignée—il y en a d'autres chez qui la présence
d'un chat produit une crise de nerfs . . . eh bien, moi aussi
j'ai des antipathies comme cela, et je vous affirme que la seule
pensée que je viens peut-être d'entendre les pas d'un facteur,
encore invisible pour moi, sur le palier de votre apparte-

ment, me cause un malaise inexprimable, qu'il m'est extrêmement difficile de vaincre.

Aline. Voilà un fait tout à fait singulier—vous devriez
en faire part à l'Académie des Sciences.

Imbert. C'est vrai, on pourrait trouver cela intéressant.

[*On entend un bruit de pas, puis deux coups de sonnette.*

Aline (souriant). Rassurez-vous, on a sonné deux fois ...
ce n'est pas le facteur, ce sera probablement une dépêche.

Imbert (vivement ému). Une dépêche ! Ah !! ...

[*Louison entre avec une dépêche.*

Aline. Vous voyez, j'ai eu raison—voilà une enveloppe
bleue.   [*Louison sort.*

Imbert. Une enveloppe bleue ! Ah ! [*Il jette un cri.*

Aline. Mais qu'avez-vous ? encore une antipathie ?

Imbert. Madame, je vous conjure de me pardonner ...
je sens que je suis complètement ridicule, mais je vous
avouerai que—que—je ne peux pas supporter le bleu ! (*A
part*) C'est ça, j'ai trouvé !

Aline. Le bleu ? vous n'aimez pas cette couleur ?

Imbert. Non seulement je ne l'aime pas, mais je ne
peux pas la supporter.

Aline. Comment faites-vous alors, vous qui vivez sous
le ciel bleu de Paris ? Voilà une antipathie qui doit être
assez génante.

Imbert. Du tout, madame, du tout ... à Paris il y a
bien de quoi regarder dans la ville, sans lever les yeux plus
haut—si je veux regarder le ciel, je n'ai qu'à aller à Londres,
où il est toujours gris.

Aline (souriant). Au moins je puis vous ôter la vue de
cette dépêche. (*Elle la tient à la main, derrière le dos.*)
Là, vous voilà calmé, je l'espère ?

Imbert (très nerveux). Oh, tout à fait, absolument ...
je suis extrêmement calme.

Aline (le regardant). Vous faites bien de me le dire !

Imbert. Pourquoi ?

Aline. Parce que je vous trouve, au contraire, excessivement agité.

Imbert. Mon Dieu, madame, vous allez me trouver très arriéré—mais je vous avouerai que, malgré le nombre de dépêches expédiées par tout le monde aujourd'hui, malgré notre emploi constant du fil électrique à chaque instant de la vie, je n'ai jamais pu m'habituer à voir arriver un télégramme sans en ressentir une vive émotion.

Aline. Est-il possible, au jour où nous sommes ? Eh bien, voyez, au contraire, combien je suis esprit fort, moi ! je reçois cette dépêche, je la tiens à la main avant de la lire, avec un calme absolu—elle ne me cause pas la moindre émotion.

Imbert. Mais, madame, vous ne songez pas que ce chiffon de papier dont vous parlez si légèrement peut contenir la nouvelle d'un désastre effroyable—que les quelques paroles sinistres que vous y trouverez vous apprendront peut-être quelque accident, quelque malheur arrivé à une personne qui vous est chère . . . qui sait ? un télégramme est capable de tout ! en le tenant à la main on se sent parcourir toute la gamme des possibilités humaines !

Aline. Mais vous avez l'imagination illimitée, monsieur Imbert ! quand je vous disais que vous devriez vous faire poète ! Voyons, pour vous rassurer je vais ouvrir cette dépêche alarmante, et vous verrez qu'il n'y aura pas de quoi vous inquiéter—vous n'y trouverez pas cette nouvelle foudroyante qui, selon vous, nous attend !

[*Elle ouvre la dépêche.—Imbert la regarde avec inquiétude.*

Imbert (*à part*). Mais puisque je sais à l'avance que je vais être foudroyé, j'ai bien le droit d'être inquiet, il me semble !

Aline. Mais c'est incompréhensible—c'est un énigme ! . . . je n'y comprends rien.

Imbert (*troublé*). Vous n'y comprenez . . . rien ? . . .

Aline. Absolument rien.

Imbert. J'espère au moins que mes prévisions se sont trompées, et que ce n'est pas une mauvaise nouvelle qu'on vous envoie ?

. *Aline.* Une mauvaise nouvelle ! mais ce n'est pas une nouvelle du tout ! écoutez plutôt—' *Prière pas ouvrir ma lettre arrivant aujourd'hui* '—Voilà tout ! vous conviendrez que cela est mystérieux.

Imbert (agité). En effet . . . très mystérieux . . . oui ! Est ce que vous auriez déjà reçu la lettre dont il est question ?

Aline. Mais puisque je ne sais pas seulement de qui elle est, cette lettre, j'ignore si je l'ai reçue !

Imbert. Il me semble qu'elle doit être de la même personne qui vous a envoyé le télégramme.

Aline. C'est évident ! mais quelle est-elle, cette personne inconnue ? elle n'a pas même pensé à signer la dépêche !

Imbert (vivement). Comment, la dépêche n'est pas signée ?

Aline. Mais non, elle n'est pas signée—je ne comprends pas cela, car il y a ordinairement tant de formalités à remplir.

Imbert. C'est cet employé distrait qui n'a pas pensé à regarder ! (*se reprenant*) je veux dire, cela arrive quelquefois.

Aline. Enfin, inutile de nous en préoccuper davantage . . . je n'ai qu'à attendre l'arrivée de la lettre, qui me donnera la clef de l'énigme ! (*Se ravisant*) Mais non, puisque je ne dois pas l'ouvrir ! et, au fait, comment saurais-je laquelle je ne dois pas lire ? faudra-t-il que je me prive d'un des plus grands plaisirs d'une femme, celle de recevoir et de lire ses lettres, à cause de cette malheureuse dépêche ? par exemple, ce serait trop !

Imbert (inquiet). Mais, madame, que comptez vous faire alors ?

Aline. Ce que je compte faire ? c'est tout simple : je compte tout bonnement ouvrir et lire chaque lettre que je reçois pendant toute la journée d'aujourd'hui ! s'il y en a dont le contenu n'est pas pour moi, tant pis—je le regrette, mais ce ne sera pas de ma faute.

Imbert (à part). Grands dieux ! que faire ? je ne peux cependant pas rester ici . . . ce serait terrible ! (*Prenant congé*) Madame . . .

Aline. Mais non . . . restez . . . restez encore un instant - nous n'avons pas causé du tout. Ces antipathies, ces dépêches arrivant à tout propos ont gâté notre conversation !

Imbert (distrait, inquiet). Madame, je ne demande pas mieux . . . seulement, je crains d'être indiscret . . .

Aline. Pas le moins du monde. Asseyez-vous là, et racontez-moi vos impressions de la soirée d'hier. La marquise de B * * * comment la trouvez-vous ? elle avait une bien jolie toilette hier, n'est-ce pas ?

Imbert (distrait). Charmante, oui, jolie toilette . . . elle est très bien, la marquise.

Aline. Et madame de K * * * comment l'avez-vous trouvée ?

Imbert. Comme toilette, voulez-vous dire, ou comme femme ?

Aline. L'une et l'autre, puisque la toilette d'une femme montre ce qu'elle est elle-même.

Imbert. Eh bien, franchement, je vous dirai que j'ai trouvé la toilette un peu tapageuse.

Aline. Ah ! vous voyez ! et la femme aussi, n'est-ce pas ?

Imbert. Cela, je ne l'ai pas dit . . . mais enfin, madame de K * * * je la trouve fatigante . . . elle a trop d'esprit, elle parle trop, elle a des idées, des lubies . . . je n'aime pas les femmes qui ont des idées.

Aline. Merci ! si vous ne recherchez que les femmes nulles ! Il faut avouer que vous êtes bien peu flatteur aujourd'hui !

Imbert. Oh, madame ! vous donnez à mes paroles un sens bien défavorable . . . je voulais seulement dire . . . que —que—— [*On entend un coup de sonnette.* Ah, mon Dieu !

Aline. Qu'avez-vous ?

Imbert. Je craignais seulement, madame, que ce coup de sonnette n'annonçât quelque visite, qui me priverait du plaisir de causer avec vous en tête-à-tête.

Aline. Oh, il ne vient guère de visites à cette heure-ci, avant trois heures — ce n'est pas comme a Trouville, où les visites pleuvaient toute la journée, vous rappelez-vous ?

Imbert. Si je me rappelle ! je crois bien ! et ce grand dadais de Ravignan, qui arrivait toujours avec son air de commander une charge !

Aline (riant). Mais oui, il était impayable, Ravignan ! Savez-vous que j'ai cru l'apercevoir hier aux Champs-Elysées ?

Imbert. Comment, il est ici ? mais qu'est-ce qu'il fait à Paris ? je le croyais en garnison à Tours !

Aline. A Tours ? non — son régiment est à Orléans, mais cela revient au même.

Imbert. Sauf pour les Orléanais, que je plains de tout mon cœur ! Pourquoi abandonne-t-il son poste alors, pour venir à Paris ?

Aline. Mais c'est qu'on lui aura donné un mois de congé, voyons ! Je ne sais pas pourquoi vous lui en voulez tant, à ce pauvre garçon !

Imbert. D'abord, parce que je le trouve insupportable !

Aline. C'est déjà une raison . . . et après ?

Imbert. Après . . . oh, il y en a bien d'autres, je vous assure !

[*Louison entre avec une lettre, qu'elle donne à Aline.*

Aline. Ah, voilà une lettre ! c'est convenu, n'est-ce pas ? je les ouvre toutes ! ainsi . . . (*Elle brise l'enveloppe.*)

Imbert. Je suis perdu ! (*il regarde Aline à la dérobée*) elle a l'air étonné, elle rit, elle se moque de moi !

Aline. A-t-on jamais rien vu de pareil ?

Imbert. Ah !

Aline. Mais c'est de la folie !

Imbert. De la folie ?

Aline. Mais oui, de la pure démence ! Comment, se poser en prétendant ! une connaissance de bains de mer !

Imbert (à part). Décidément, je suis perdu ! je n'ai plus qu'à me retirer. (*Haut*) Madame . . . veuillez pardonner à mon indiscrétion . . . je vous ai fait une visite d'une longueur déraisonnable . . .

Aline (riant). Mais non—restez encore un instant, trouvez-moi l'explication de cette lettre ridicule !

Imbert (à part). Ridicule ! Le mot est un peu fort. (*Haut*) Mais, madame, la lettre, il me semble, doit contenir elle-même son explication—le malheureux qui l'a écrit a pensé peut-être que—que—il ne vous était pas absolument indifférent . . . la bonté que vous avez eue pour lui l'a sans doute encouragé à vous ouvrir son cœur . . .

Aline. La bonté que j'ai eue ! Voyons, je n'ai pas été meilleure pour lui que pour les autres ! vous le savez bien vous-même, qu'au fond je suis de votre avis—je le trouve insupportable.

Imbert (saisi). De mon avis ! Insupportable ! De grâce, de qui parlez-vous donc ?

Aline (étonnée). De qui je parle ? mais de Ravignan, évidemment !

Imbert (de plus en plus mystifié). De Ravignan ? Comment—cette lettre——

Aline. Est de lui, certainement ! je croyais vous l'avoir dit tout d'abord. De qui donc voulez-vous qu'elle soit ?

Imbert. Madame, je ne le savais pas . . . je me le demandais . . . d'un inconnu, peut-être, de quelque infortuné dont la triste situation, le peu d'espoir auprès de vous ont éveillé ma pitié, ma compassion.

Aline (riant). Mais cet inconnu, cet infortuné, c'est tout bonnement Ravignan, qui, parce que je lui ai accordé quelques valses au casino, parce que je lui ai donné une po'gnée de main à la gare, se croit en droit de me demander ma main !

Imbert. De demander votre main ! Ravignan ! . . .

Aline. Mais oui ! l'histoire est divertissante, n'est-ce pas ? C'est très mal de ma part de vous l'avoir dit . . . mais je n'aurais vraiment pas pu me priver d'en faire la confidence à quelqu'un. Vous ne trahirez pas le secret, n'est-ce pas ? Je puis compter sur vous ?

Imbert. Madame, je serai d'une discrétion à toute épreuve, je vous assure.

Aline. J'en suis convaincue. Je voudrais bien vous montrer la lettre—c'est un chef-d'œuvre ! mais ce serait bien mal, n'est-ce pas ? Cependant (*elle relit la lettre*) . . . tiens ! voilà un post-scriptum que je n'avais pas vu. (*Riant*) Oh ! que cela lui ressemble ! c'est lui-même ! 'Si vous me permettez, madame, de vous annoncer ma visite pour cette après-midi, j'ose espérer que vous voudrez bien me faire l'honneur de me recevoir.'

Imbert. Comment, il va venir ici ! Il ne manquait plus que cela!

Aline. C'est le plus correct des hommes . . . vous voyez, il ne me fait pas une visite sans m'envoyer un document à l'avance pour me prévenir de son arrivée. Tout ce qu'il fait est compassé, réfléchi—je suis sûre que s'il se trouvait empêché par cause ou autre de se présenter, qu'il m'enverrait une dépêche pour m'annoncer un quart d'heure de retard ! Tiens ! j'y songe ! Cette dépêche ! . . .

Imbert (*troublé*). Cette dépêche . . . madame ?

Aline. Vous ne voyez pas de qui elle est?

Imbert (*de plus en plus ahuri*). Mais si, madame . . . mais si . . . en effet . . .

Aline. Cette dépêche ne peut être que de Ravignan !

Imbert. Comment, la dépêche est de Ravignan aussi?

Aline. Evidemment, ce ne peut être que lui qui l'a envoyée !

Imbert. Ah, très bien ! mais c'est une mine de documentation alors que ce garçon !

Aline. Oh, que cela lui ressemble encore ! Je vois d'ici ce qui est arrivé ! (*s'échauffant peu à peu, à mesure qu'elle parle.*) Il lui a fallu d'abord trois mois pour se décider à m'envoyer cette lettre—puis, la lettre expédiée, il s'est ravisé—il a pensé qu'il lui fallait encore trois mois de réflexion, sur quoi il a envoyé le télégramme, pour m'empêcher de lire la lettre—eh bien, je vous dirai que je trouve cela un procédé assez peu galant, et qui certes n'est pas fait pour gagner les cœurs.

Imbert. Mais, madame, je vous ferai seulement observer qu'après tout ce n'est peut-être pas lui qui a envoyé——

Aline (*impatientée*). Comment donc ! il n'y a que lui pour faire des bêtises pareilles !

Imbert. Ah . . . permettez . . .

Aline. Du reste, je vous supplie de ne point prendre sa défense à présent, vous qui l'arrangiez d'une si belle façon tout à l'heure ! d'autant plus que ce serait absolument inutile, car je vous affirme que pour rien au monde je ne lui pardonnerai ce qu'il a fait aujourd'hui envers moi. Il n'a qu'à se présenter ici—il verra comme il sera reçu ! ou plutôt comme il ne le sera pas—un homme capable d'agir de la sorte ne remettra plus les pieds chez moi.

Imbert (*à part, s'essuyant le front*). Que vais-je devenir, mon Dieu, que vais-je devenir ?

Louison entre.

Louison. Madame, c'est monsieur le vicomte de Ravignan, qui demande si madame veut bien le recevoir.

Aline (*sèchement*). Non.

Louison (*surprise*). Madame ne le reçoit pas ? (*A voix basse, se rapprochant d'Aline*) Monsieur le vicomte est là . . . dans l'antichambre . . .

Aline (très haut). Dites-lui que je n'y suis pas—que je regrette bien de ne pas y être.

Louison. Bien, madame.   [*Elle sort.*

Imbert (à part). Quelle situation, mon Dieu ! comment sortir de là ?

Louison rentre.

Louison. Monsieur le vicomte fait dire à madame, qu'il repassera plus tard, pour voir si madame veut avoir la bonté de le recevoir, et qu'il aura en tous les cas l'honneur d'écrire à madame ce soir.

Aline. C'est bien.   [*Louison sort.*
Un bon averti en vaut deux ! Je suis vraiment ridicule de me fâcher pour si peu, au lieu d'en rire ! mais, aussi, convenez que ce personnage s'est conduit à mon égard d'une façon quelque peu singulière.

Imbert. C'est possible, mais enfin . . .

Aline. Mais enfin ! demandez-vous s'il vous serait jamais venu à l'idée de faire vous-même ce qu'il a fait ! non, n'est-ce pas ? vous reconnaissez que vous en seriez tout à fait incapable.

Imbert (de plus en plus embarrassé). Madame, je ne dis pas . . . mais cependant . . . voici comment je m'expliquerai la chose, moi. Le pauvre garçon, follement amoureux de vous ——

Aline. Follement ? où prenez-vous cela ? dites plutôt méthodiquement, flegmatiquement !

Imbert. Soit, comme vous voudrez—mais amoureux enfin, n'importe comment, se décide à vous écrire. Il envoie la lettre, puis il réfléchit trop tard que la parole écrite ne serait peut-être pas assez convaincante, assez irrésistible—il vous envoie donc une dépêche pour vous dire de ne pas ouvrir cette lettre, qu'il ne croyait pas digne de plaider sa cause, puis il est accouru ici pour se jeter à vos pieds.

Aline (riant). Qui n'ont pas voulu de sa prostration ! je suis vraiment fâchée d'avoir fait échouer cette belle combinaison ! mais que voulez-vous ? je n'ai pas, comme vous, l'imagination d'un poète—jamais je n'aurais pensé à reconstruire de mon propre fonds le travail qui, selon vous, s'est opéré dans le cerveau de ce pauvre vicomte ! du reste, je ne l'aurais jamais cru capable d'une passion comme celle que vous lui attribuez.

Imbert. Mon Dieu, madame, ce n'est qu'une hypothèse, une supposition que je pose là . . .

Aline. Evidemment, mais cependant je crois qu'elle est juste . . . je commence même à regretter mon peu de courtoisie . . . j'ai envie de lui écrire un petit mot aimable, pour lui faire mes excuses, et lui dire que je le recevrai demain. Cela ne m'engage à rien, après tout.

[*Elle se dirge vers la table à écrire, au fond.*

Imbert (à part). Ah, je suis allé trop loin ! si cette lettre est envoyée, le vicomte viendra tomber ici, et il en résultera une explication des plus embarrassantes pour moi. Que faire, cependant ? je ne peux pas laisser la responsabilité de ce malheureux télégramme à mon rival . . . ce ne serait pas d'un galant homme . . . il faudra bien que j'en aie le cœur net, et que je fasse mon aveu. Mais cependant, l'idée de me sacrifier pour cet espèce de lieutenant m'est souverainement déplaisante ! aussi, pourquoi est-il venu se fourrer à Paris en ce moment, pour m'embrouiller toutes mes affaires ? Il aurait bien mieux fait de rester à Orléans. Charmante ville, Orléans . . . il y a des (*cherchant*)—des—séminaires . . . des archevêques . . . des statues de Jeanne d'Arc, quoi ! toute espèce d'agréments de province, enfin !

Aline (se levant). Voilà . . . je vais dire qu'on lui porte ce billet . . . cela me réconciliera avec moi-même.

Imbert. Mais, madame . . . un instant . . .

Aline (surprise). Qu'est-ce que c'est ?

Imbert (hésitant, confus). Madame, c'est peut-être très

c

indiscret ce que je vais vous dire là . . . mais la confidence que vous avez daigné me faire m'encourage à penser que vous ne m'en voudrez pas . . .

Aline (de plus en plus surprise). Mais parlez—qu'y· a-t-il donc ?

Imbert. Est-ce que vous auriez . . . c'est-à-dire, vous n'avez pas, n'est-ce pas, l'intention d'accueillir favorablement la demande de monsieur de Ravignan ?

Aline (riant aux éclats). Mais non, voyons ! Pour qui me prenez vous ?

Imbert (soulagé, à part). Grâce à Dieu ! (*Haut*) Mais alors ne craignez-vous pas que ce billet aimable ne fasse renaître en son cœur des espérances . . . qui n'en seront que plus cruellement déçues ?

Aline. Vous croyez ?

. *Imbert.* J'en suis sûr.

Aline (réfléchissant). Je ferais peut-être mieux alors de ne rien lui envoyer—d'attendre seulement qu'il repasse ici.

Imbert. Je crois en effet que c'est ce qu'il aurait de plus prudent.

[*Aline déchire la lettre, jette les morceaux, se remet à la petite table au premier plan, et reprend son ouvrage.*

Imbert (pendant ce temps, à part). Voilà au moins du temps de gagné . . . il s'agit maintenant de me tirer d'affaire. Ah, maudite dépêche, va ! Aussi, pourquoi faut-il qu'on vous plante un bureau télégraphique à chaque coin de rue, pour entraîner les passants à leur perte ? C'est inique, cela ne devrait pas être.

Aline (riant aux éclats). Non, vraiment . . . cette his- oire est trop drôle ! Certes, quand j'ai aperçu Ravignan hier, qui arpentait les Champs-Élysées, guindé, correct, comme d'habitude, jamais je ne me serais doutée que nous passerions cet après-midi à nous occuper de lui !

Imbert. C'est vrai qu'il n'en vaut pas précisément la peine!

Aline. Et cependant . . . savez-vous? il me plaît aujourd'hui plus qu'il ne l'a jamais fait . . . car, si les choses se sont passées comme vous le dites, cette histoire de lettres, de télégrammes, quoiqu'elle soit, bien entendu, absurde et ridicule au possible——

Imbert (à part). Mille fois merci.

Aline. Montre cependant qu'il n'est pas toujours aussi impassible qu'il en a l'air . . . que, sous l'influence d'une véritable émotion, lui aussi est capable de se troubler, de se laisser porter à des mouvements naïfs et passionnés, qui font preuve d'un cœur sensible et aimant.

Imbert (joyeux). Comment, madame! vous vous sentez alors portée à l'indulgence, à des dispositions favorables envers celui qui a pu agir de la sorte?

Aline. A des dispositions favorables, non . . . à l'indulgence, oui . . . mais rien de plus—le pauvre Ravignan ne saurait m'en inspirer davantage.

Imbert. Ah! je n'y tiens plus, madame . . . vos paroles m'encouragent à vous faire un aveu que je ne peux plus retenir . . . celui qui vous a envoyé ce télégramme, c'est moi—moi-même, et non pas Ravignan!

Aline (se levant vivement). Comment! que dites-vous? c'est vous?

Imbert (avec une agitation toujours croissante). Oui, madame, oui—oui! c'est moi! moi, qui, ainsi que vous l'avez bien dit, suis absurde, ridicule, mais naïf et passionné aussi . . . moi qui ai eu de ces mouvements qui font preuve d'un cœur sensible et aimant—moi qui vous aime follement, qui vous adore, qui vous ai écrit une lettre que je n'ai pas crue capable de vous persuader, qui vous ai ensuite envoyé une dépêche pour vous prier de ne pas l'ouvrir, et qui su enfin accouru ici pour plaider moi-même ma cause, et implorer à vos pieds votre miséricorde!

[*Il se jette aux pieds d'Aline.*

Aline.   Décidément, il faut être poète pour savoir se tirer d'embarras avec des figures de rhétorique ! mais qu'est-ce qui me prouvera que toutes vos déclarations de tout à l'heure ne sont pas également dues au souffle de l'esprit poétique ?

> *Louison entre avec une lettre—Imbert s'en empare vivement, et la donne à Aline.   Louison sort.*

Imbert.   Voici ! cette lettre vous le prouvera, j'espère . . . et si, après l'avoir lue, vous doutez encore de moi, accordez-moi seulement le temps, madame, je saurai bien vous convaincre de la vérité de mon amour !

> *Louison rentre.*

Louison.   C'est monsieur le vicomte de Ravignan qui demande si madame veut bien le recevoir.

Aline.   Faites entrer.   [*Louison sort.*

Imbert (inquiet).   Comment, vous le recevez ?

Aline.   Mais oui—à nous deux nous saurons bien l'éconduire !

> [*Elle tend la main à Imbert, qui la baise avec transport.   On baisse vivement la toile au moment où le vicomte est censé entrer.*

A CHANCE INTERVIEW

COMEDIETTA IN ONE ACT.

CHARACTERS.

COLONEL PERCEVAL.   LADY ROCKMOUNT.   A MAID.

SCENE.—*Mrs. Greville's drawing-room. Books, &c., on table; clock on chimney-piece.*

Maid (showing in Colonel Perceval). I will tell Mrs. Greville you are here, sir. She is dressing.

Col. Perceval. Dressing?

Maid. Yes, sir. She is going to a ball.   [*Exit Maid.*

Col. Perceval. Dressing to go to a ball, at this time? Why, it is only twenty minutes to ten. She will be two hours too early—unless she means to dance a *pas seul* before the other people come. What a bore that she should be going out just this evening! It never occurred to me that that was likely, as her daughter is away and she has no one to take.   [*Enter Maid.*

Maid. Mrs. Greville will be ready in a quarter of an hour, sir. She is sorry to keep you waiting.

Col. Perceval. Oh, pray tell her not to hurry. It doesn't signify in the least.   [*Exit Maid.*

Col. Perceval. Not signify indeed! It does signify most particularly. That was one of the idiotic things one says by way of saying something. Well, I must just make up my mind to wait patiently for another quarter of an hour. After all, when I wrote to Mrs. Greville saying that

I would look in this evening about ten o'clock, she probably
didn't grasp the fact that I should appear twenty minutes
earlier—how should she? After all, I can't expect her to
be as anxious as I am for the interview—and yet—report
says—— Report is a fool! (*Walks about the room: reflects.*) I don't like it. I don't at all like having these
additional twenty minutes for reflection! and it is very odd
that, though I have had the last six months to consider the
situation, it has never presented as many aspects as it is
suddenly developing at this moment. It is a foolish plan,
an embarrassing plan, for a man to have to come and ask
formally for the hand of his future bride. In fact, I had
no idea how embarrassing it would be. It is tremendous—
quite tremendous! It is absurd, I admit, to be so agitated.
Here am I, an Indian officer of some renown, if I may be
permitted to say so, trembling, positively trembling, at the
thought of asking for the hand of little Mary Greville, to
whom I used to bring sugar plums fifteen years ago—quaking at the idea of an interview on the subject with her
mother, dear, mild Mrs. Greville, with whom I used to dine
every Sunday before I went to India. Yes, I must admit,
I am as foolishly agitated as I was that day when I went
to Kate Vernon's house on a like errand, and found Lord
Rockmount's carriage at the door—that well-appointed
brougham, which I verily believe was as powerful an advocate of his suit as Lord Rockmount himself. But what is
the good of reviving these memories? Lady Rockmount,
I dare say, has been happy—and, as she has lived in London
and I in India, our paths have, fortunately perhaps, lain
apart. When I returned a year ago I heard she was in the
country, in mourning for her husband. Well, well! her
image has faded from my heart now, and another has taken
its place—I can afford to smile at the infatuation of my
youth. Yes, Kate was delightful to be in love with,
certainly—exactly the woman to be in love with, but per-

haps, after all, not the woman to marry. As a wife she might be less satisfactory. Now Mary Greville—dear little Mary! so gentle, so sympathetic, so domestic, so exactly the kind of woman to find smiling at one's fire-side—always the same, no moods, no flightiness—a woman who would be sure always to think her husband right! that is my idea of married happiness. Whereas Kate!! (*Smiles at the recollection.*) No one could expect that of her, certainly. No one could imagine that she would be always the same, with her impressionable nature vibrating to every passing wind of fancy, 'full of tears, full of smiles,' an endless variety of aspects—now full of brilliancy and wit, now of tender melancholy. Heigho! Well (*rousing himself*), that was years ago, and now is now, to-day, another time altogether—mustn't mix them up! (*Walks about.*) Not ten minutes to ten yet! I'm sure that clock must want regulating—its short hand doesn't know what its long hand is doing. It must be at least a quarter of an hour since the maid came in. Extraordinary how many quarters of an hour it takes women to dress! It has been calculated, I believe, that a woman spends one-fifth of her life in doing her hair. No wonder she doesn't succeed in doing much else. Hark! I hear some one coming. (*Listens.*) No, that is not Mrs. Greville's voice, surely—that gentle little woman never spoke in those ringing tones! [*Maid opens door.*

Lady Rockmount (speaking outside). Yes, I know I am much earlier than I had meant to be.

Col. Perceval (starts). What! That voice——

Lady Rockmount (still outside). Tell Mrs. Greville that I had a box for the opera sent me, and I thought it might be pleasanter to give up the ball, as it is so hot to-night. (*Enters.*) So I came early on the chance of her being ready. But it doesn't matter at all. I shall be quite happy waiting.

Maid. Yes, my lady. [*Exit Maid.*

Lady Rockmount. Colonel Perceval!

Col. Perceval. Lady Rockmount !

Lady Rockmount (recovering herself). This is a most unexpected pleasure.

Col. Perceval. It is indeed.

Lady Rockmount. How long is it since we have met ? Six years—seven years ?

Col. Perceval. More like ten, I'm afraid.

Lady Rockmount. Ten ! Is it really ? Ah, I have such a shocking memory ! I never can remember things.

Col. Perceval (aside). A most enviable gift !

Lady Rockmount. But what an extraordinary coincidence that we should meet here ! Ha ! ha ! It makes me laugh to think of your face of utter stupefaction when I walked in. I don't wonder. I was just as amazed to see you. You were the very last person in my thoughts at that moment.

Col. Perceval (aside). I wish I could say the same !

Lady Rockmount. I was to call for Mrs. Greville, to take her to Lady Silverton's ball—then a box turned up for the opera, and as I am very tired, having been to a *matinée* and two 'at homes' since luncheon, I thought it would be pleasanter to give up the ball.

Col. Perceval. I see.

Lady Rockmount. So I came round earlier, on the chance of Mrs. Greville being ready, but apparently she is not.

Col. Perceval. No. She will be ready in a quarter of an hour, so the maid tells me.

Lady Rockmount. A quarter of an hour ! Oh, well, that is not very long. We can endure existence for that time, I dare say. What has brought you here to-night ?

Col. Perceval (embarrassed). Oh, nothing. I am here casually—that is, I have a sort of appointment with Mrs. Greville—a half-appointment at least—and—and——

[*Pauses.*

Lady Rockmount. Then a half-appointment, I presume, is when one person comes and the other doesn't ?

Col. Perceval. The fact is, I had no answer from Mrs. Greville. I wrote to tell her I should be here at ten——

Lady Rockmount. And then for greater security you came on beforehand to announce your arrival ! for it is only five minutes to ten now, and I am sure you have been here at least a quarter of an hour.

Col. Perceval. What makes you think so ?

Lady Rockmount. Because I know exactly what a man looks like who has been waiting impatiently—I could tell by your expression when the door was opened.

Col. Perceval. Yes, I've no doubt I looked uncommonly like a fool—I feel like one too.

Lady Rockmount. Do you ? I am so sorry ! I've been told it is a horrid sensation.

Col. Perceval (desperately). I think I won't wait any longer now, Lady Rockmount—it will be very good of you to give a message for me to Mrs. Greville, to explain that —that—I have had to go away. You will tell her how it is.

Lady Rockmount. Certainly, if I knew. How is it ?

Col. Perceval. Would you say that I have suddenly recollected an appointment I am obliged to keep—with— with—a man at the club, and that I hope to be more fortunate another time ?

Lady Rockmount. To be more fortunate ! you mean that another time you won't remember it ?

Col. Perceval. No, no, I don't mean that—I mean——

Lady Rockmount. You mean, that when you found you had to wait in the company of some one else, and that some one your humble servant, your fortitude was not equal to the occasion, and you fled, leaving the unwelcome interloper in possession of the field, to explain your absence as best she can ! Ha ! ha ! Very well, I will tell her, never fear.

Col. Perceval. Lady Rockmount! You attribute sentiments to me——

Lady Rockmount. Now, now, my good friend! I am not as blind as a mole, nor do I share its propensity for burrowing to the foundation of things—neither do I go to the other extreme, like a fly, which I believe can see in every direction all round its head at once, more or less: but this much of vision I have, that when something is standing bolt upright in my path I am conscious of its existence— I can see it is there!

Col. Perceval (preoccupied, looking at door). Very observant of you; you show an acquaintance with natural history which is most edifying! It is a fly, you say, that can see all round it?

Lady Rockmount. Yes: the common house fly, I believe. We cannot wonder, therefore, that it should be a little flurried and undecided in manner sometimes, for I find even my limited powers of vision occasionally somewhat bewildering.

Col. Perceval. I've no doubt you must, if they carry you astray in the way they have this morning.

Lady Rockmount. Carried me astray? in what way? They have carried me straight to the point, I assure you. I have grasped the situation already in all its bearings.

Col. Perceval (aside). The deuce you have!

Lady Rockmount. I come in casually to wait for Mrs. Greville, and find you here, in an even greater state of agitation than a man is generally in when he is being kept waiting, which is saying a good deal! So I perceive at once that you must have something very important to say to your hostess. [*Col. Perceval is going to interrupt her: she stops him.*] No, no, my dear friend! it is of no use your telling me you haven't—it would not carry conviction at all! And, as I am sure Mrs. Greville would rather listen to what you have to say than to the last act of the ' Afri-caine,' which is really a very dull affair—with that upas tree on all the time, and the rest of the characters gradually collapsing round it—by far the best thing is that I should retire gracefully—which I shall be very glad to do, for I am tired out already—and leave you in possession of the field, to have your chat with Mrs. Greville—your momentous interview, I mean !

Col. Perceval. No, no—I could not think of such a thing. I assure you that what I have to say to Mrs. Greville will keep quite well till another time.

Lady Rockmount (smiling satirically). In—deed !

Col. Perceval. I will go away and leave you with Mrs. Greville, to go to the opera together.

Lady Rockmount. No, no—it is too absurd ! you shall not go, *I* will.

Col. Perceval. No, I wouldn't make you go for the world—*I* will.

Lady Rockmount. Certainly not—I couldn't allow it. After all, you came here first.

Col. Perceval. Yes, but you came in second! I mean——

Lady Rockmount. Ha! ha! Your mind has run into its usual channel, the sporting one. The winning-post, then, is Mrs. Greville ? Curious race this, in which the competitors arrive first and the winning-post comes in afterwards.

Col. Perceval. You are pleased to be very light-hearted, Lady Rockmount—I am sorry I cannot stay to enjoy a good laugh with you.

Lady Rockmount. You obstinate man ! You shall not go, I declare ; but stop—— (*With a sudden idea*) Why should either of us go ? Why should we not both remain ?

Col. Perceval (taken aback). Why not ? Because— because——

Lady Rockmount. Because you would rather not have me there when you are asking Mrs. Greville for her daughter's hand.

Col. Perceval. Lady Rockmount ! You certainly do jump to conclusions in the most rapid way.

Lady Rockmount. Now, now—take care what you are going to say ! remember the story of Tommy. Tommy said, ' I have no father nor mother : yet I am not an orphan.' What was Tommy ?

Col. Perceval (exasperated). How should I know ? I never guessed one of those things in my life. His great-grandson, I suppose !

Lady Rockmount. Ha! ha! no. The answer is, Tommy is—a liar ! The word is forcible, I admit, for polite society— but it expresses the desired meaning, which is a great thing. So let Tommy be a warning to you, and don't contradict me when I tell you you have come here for a momentous interview. Well, I will help you.

Col. Perceval (staggered). You ?

Lady Rockmount (calmly). Certainly. Does that surprise you ? Why shouldn't I ?

Col. Perceval. Only—because—because——

Lady Rockmount. Because you think that kind of thing is better done *à deux* ? Quite a fallacy, I assure you. Nowadays everyone helps on these occasions : the father helps, the mother helps, the daughter helps herself—often to a very desirable morsel, ha! ha !

Col. Perceval (with an effort). Lady Rockmount, you must forgive me if I say that these pleasantries are a little painful to me. I am, as you have guessed, in a situation of peculiar delicacy.

Lady Rockmount. Come, come, don't let us exaggerate the horrors of it. It isn't so very peculiar, you know, after all. Every man I know goes through it once a month on an average, till one day he does it so successfully that there is no occasion to repeat the experiment—in other words, he proposes to some one who accepts him, and there is an end of it ! and of him too, as far as his friends are concerned.

Col. Perceval (trying to speak with dignity). Your knowledge of the world, I know, is great, but it is apparently so vast that it is unwieldy. I must beg to tell you that this is the first time in my life that I have ever found myself in what you consider this very ordinary, commonplace situation, but which appears to me, a—an—unsophisticated Indian officer [*Lady Rockmount smiles*], a somewhat momentous crisis. You must forgive me, therefore, if I am more agitated by it than other of your more accomplished friends.

Lady Rockmount. My dear friend, you are positively scathing in your wrath ! I feel crushed—I assure you, absolutely crushed to the ground, and am only able to lift my head for one last expiring glance at the phenomenal person before me, who has actually reached the age of—thirty-nine, shall we say ?—without ever having risked his fate on a woman's caprice. [*Col. Perceval turns away impatiently.*] Do tell me how it happened, as they say in the ' Arabian Nights.' You know the ' Arabian Nights'? No? A pity—such pleasant reading ! though I always wonder why it is necessary in them when some personage in the story—a street porter, let us say—who turns out to be the one-eyed son of a king, or more frequently the son of a one-eyed king—it comes to the same, for these things are generally hereditary—[*Col. Perceval smiles in spite of himself*]—I wonder, I was going to say, why, when they are asked why they are found on a pyramid, or in a harem, or some other unexpected place, they have to begin their recital fifteen years back in order to explain.

Col. Perceval (aside). How she does run on ! Still the same ! (Aloud) Don't be afraid—I have no intention of inflicting my very unromantic life and adventures on you. My father was not a king.

Lady Rockmount (with an assumption of the deepest interest).   Indeed ?   You surprise me.

Col. Perceval (checking himself).   You will only laugh at me, I know—you are not at all as 'helpful as you promised.

Lady Rockmount.   On the contrary, I feel eminently helpful, I assure you—and I can render you my assistance with conviction, for I never heard of anything more suitable than the step you are going to take.

Col. Perceval.   Suitable ?   I hate that expression.

Lady Rockmount.   Why, I can't think of any other that better expresses my meaning ! it is all so natural, so exactly what everybody expected.

Col. Perceval.   Horrible !

Lady Rockmount.   You come back from India after a long absence, and find the daughter of your old friend, General Greville, grown from a child into a charming woman, thrown constantly into your society with the intimacy of long friendship.   What more obvious than that you should end by falling in love with her ?

Col. Perceval.   Oh, don't !   It makes me feel as if I had had nothing to do with it !

Lady Rockmount.   Well, really, we have not much to do with these things after all—we are the creatures of circumstances, more or less.   That is not a strikingly original statement, I know, but it will bear a good deal of repetition.   It makes one feel very small to reflect occasionally on the way one's destiny is determined.   You are asked out to a dinner where you would have met your fate— you have a headache and decline to go.   You miss your train because your cab is slow, and hear afterwards that half the passengers have been killed in an accident.   Your neighbour puts a piece of carpet on the pavement for his friends to walk on, and you use it to break your leg over instead. Somebody forgets to post a letter for you, and so your burning declaration of love remains for months in his greatcoat pocket—or, on an evening when fate is more propitious to you, you unexpectedly meet with a female friend whom chance has brought to your support and help. Ha! ha! Now do you agree with my doctrine? Has my eloquence convinced you?

Col. Perceval (uneasily). Oh, certainly—no doubt! only, don't think me very rude—I feel somehow as if I could do it better alone.

Lady Rockmount. Oh, don't slight my powers as an advocate; you wound me in my tenderest point. You admit that I have some command of language, don't you?

Col. Perceval. Oh, certainly, certainly! no one could doubt it.

Lady Rockmount. More command, perhaps, than you have?

Col. Perceval. Yes. Oh, incontestably.

Lady Rockmount. Well, then, it is clear that Providence, or fate, or chance, whichever brought me here to-day, did so for the express purpose of coming to your rescue! and never shall it be said that I refused my aid to a timid monosyllabic friend.

Col. Perceval. Thank you, thank you very much. (Aside) This is too absurd! What shall I do? The situation is becoming horrible. It is no use. I don't feel now as if I could speak to Mrs. Greville to-day.

Lady Rockmount. Now, then, let us prepare for our exordium. Oh, this is most interesting—this is exactly what I enjoy.

Col. Perceval. It is a good thing somebody enjoys it.

Lady Rockmount (gaily). Now, what shall we say when Mrs. Greville comes in?

Col. Perceval. Oh, this is fearful—it is outrageous—

it is impossible ! Lady Rockmount, I am very sorry, but I really cannot do it.

Lady Rockmount (surprised). Cannot do what ?

Col. Perceval. I cannot stay—I really can't. I will write to Mrs. Greville. You know what a shy and awkward creature I am. As I told you, I am not accustomed to this kind of thing, and I couldn't do it for the first time with an audience—I positively couldn't.

Lady Rockmount (looking at him reflectively). But now do tell me how you have managed to preserve your pristine simplicity ! Is an officer's life in Calcutta absolutely the same as that of a maiden in an English village ? How is it that you have escaped the temptations of matrimony unscathed ? Do tell me ! Was it prudence, coldness, or the force of circumstances ?

Col. Perceval (gloomily). It was mainly, I suppose, the force of circumstances, again bearing out your favourite theory. I will tell you, though I shall be laughed at for my pains. I have not escaped so unscathed as you imagine from the sufferings which beset the susceptible. In my youth, when I was not as wise as I am now, I fell deeply, hopelessly in love with a young girl I knew. I thought she returned my affection, for it was easy to be misled by her manner—sweet, bright, sympathetic, fascinating, women adored her, men were at her feet. Why should I have flattered myself that she should choose me from among the crowd of competitors, to reward me with the priceless gift of her hand ?

> [*Voices outside. Lady Rockmount, who has been listening pensively, starts up.*

Col. Perceval. There is Mrs. Greville ! I had forgotten her ! What time is it ? Good heavens ! it is past ten !

Lady Rockmount (recovering herself). And your exordium ?

Col. Perceval (half to himself). What shall I say ?

Lady Rockmount (maliciously). And yet you seemed extremely fluent just now. Well, don't let us be absolutely silent when she comes in—let us be talking about something! [*As door opens Lady Rockmount speaks loudly*]—and whatever you may say about the Primrose League——

[*Door opens. Col. Perceval standing with his back to it, trying to recover himself.*

Enter Maid.

Maid. Mrs. Greville is so very sorry to keep you waiting, my Lady—she will be ready in a quarter of an hour.

Lady Rockmount. Oh, pray tell her not to hurry—it doesn't matter in the least. I have plenty of time.

Maid. Thank you, my Lady. [*Exit Maid.*

Col. Perceval. Another quarter of an hour! that makes the third within the last twenty minutes. But this one is more welcome than the others were.

Lady Rockmount. A quarter of an hour! Then you have time to go on with that delightful tale.

Col. Perceval. No, no—why should I? After all, it is not worth hearing—it is a most foolish story, of no value or interest to anybody but the owner.

Lady Rockmount. Nay, nay! you must go on with it.

Col. Perceval. I was not in a position to marry—I could not ask her, of all people in the world, to share comparative poverty—when my fortunes suddenly changed. I got an appointment in India, which at once altered my position. For three days I was unable to go to her, as I had to go to Scotland to see a Cabinet Minister who was at Balmoral. On my return I found I must sail in two days. I went off at once to see her, but when I reached her door there was a carriage drawn up in front of it.

[*He pauses.*

Lady Rockmount (lightly). Well, what then? How

did that impede you? It was not, I presume, driving up
the steps to the hall door?

Col. Perceval. It stopped me because I knew the
owner! and not only that, but I knew also for what
purpose he was in that house, for the night before we had
walked home together from the club, having a smoke, and
he had then told me that he was in love—that he was going
to propose—to—to the girl I also loved. I said nothing: I
did not return his confidence. Foolishly, idiotically secure
as I thought myself, I let him, as I thought, rush on
his fate—but ah! the result was very different from my
expectations!

Lady Rockmount. What! did she not refuse him?

Col. Perceval. Refuse him? Ah, you know well
enough that she did not.

Lady Rockmount. I?!!

Col. Perceval. Yes, you, who, after playing with me
and torturing me for two months, were content to dismiss
me with a thought, without a regret!

Lady Rockmount. What! You were still in England
that day when Lord Rockmount came, and you were content to turn away from the door when you found he was
in the house, without making an attempt to discover what
had happened?

Col. Perceval. No indeed—I did make the attempt. I
came next morning again to the house, full of hope and
confidence, but it was then I found how fatal my pro-
crastination had been to me, for in the street I met Mrs.
Storey, who stopped me to tell me, with evident satisfaction,
that she knew for a fact that the girl I loved was engaged
—engaged to him, whom, fool that I was! I had calmly
left in possession of the situation the day before! I left
London that night, and sailed for India next day.

Lady Rockmount (starting up). Mrs. Storey told you
that? She knew, then, that you were still in London! False,

wicked, perfidious woman! She knew that if I were engaged it was her doing, for she had told me, two days before, that you had unexpectedly received an appointment, and had suddenly left for India, unmindful, as I thought, of me, of everything but your ambition. What was I to do? Lord Rockmount, I knew, was the best and most chivalrous of men. I thought you were gone, that I was abandoned, deserted, miserable! Oh, Philip, you know the rest!

Col. Perceval. Kate, my dear Kate! that I should have been so blind, such a fool as to throw away the happiness that lay within my grasp! You were not false to me, then—it was not your manner, your dear entrancing manner, that deceived me!

Lady Rockmount. Deceived you! You were capable of thinking I had deceived you! I have an entrancing manner, no doubt, but it was hard on me that you should have been so ready to think the worst of me at once.

Col. Perceval. But didn't I tell you that I don't understand how to manage these things? You won't believe what an unsophisticated creature I am. If it had not been for the blessed chance of meeting you here this evening I should have gone down to the grave believing you heartless.

Lady Rockmount (smiling). And didn't I tell you that we are the creatures of circumstances? If that carriage had not been drawn up before my door you would have come in—or if you had not met Mrs. Storey in the Square next morning everything would have been different.

Col. Perceval. Yes: but if, on the other hand, that opera box had not been sent you, and you had not come in here early to fetch Mrs. Greville, things might have been more different still.

Lady Rockmount. Oh, yes, no doubt things might have been worse.

Col. Perceval. Ah, Kate—my darling!

Lady Rockmount. Yes, yes—but there is no time for

all that now. The question is, what are you going to say to Mrs. Greville?

Col. Perceval. By Jove, yes! What am I to say to Mrs. Greville? Oh, I will say that I want to go to the opera too—that—that—I adore Meyerbeer—that I worship the Africaine!

Lady Rockmount. Come, come, I am afraid she will hardly believe that you wanted to see her in order to tell her you were passionately in love with—the Africaine!

Col. Perceval. Very well, then, you had better tell me what I am to say—you have so much more command of language than I, you know.

Lady Rockmount. I am not so sure of that, after all! you have improved wonderfully in that respect within the last quarter of an hour.

Col. Perceval. Yes, it is the last quarter of an hour that has done it! I shall always love Mrs. Greville for taking so long to dress.

Lady Rockmount (listening). Here she is, though, this time—she is ready at last.

Enter Maid.

Maid. Your carriage is here, my Lady, and Mrs. Greville is just ready.

Lady Rockmount. Very well, we will go down.

[*Exit Maid.*

Col. Perceval. Really, the amount of emotions that maid has caused me to-day by coming in and out!

Lady Rockmount. See what it is to have a guilty conscience!

Col. Perceval. I admit I would rather face a jungle tiger than Mrs. Greville at this moment! Do you know, I think I will not come with you to the opera?

Lady Rockmount. But remember how you adore the Africaine!

Col. Perceval. Yes, yes—but all the same it would be better if you went *tête-à-tête* with Mrs. Greville, and told her that—that——

Lady Rockmount. That—what ?

Col. Perceval. That we are engaged.

Lady Rockmount. Engaged, are we ? I had not understood that.

Col. Perceval (staggered). What ? Ah, Kate, Kate, you are laughing at me ! be merciful to me after all you have made me suffer !

Lady Rockmount. I declare that nothing has been said about our being engaged. . We have talked about the past— we have sentimentalised over bygone memories, lamented over lost opportunities : that was all, I think.

Col. Perceval (hotly). Yes, and why ? Because you would not let me say all I was burning to utter—say the words that for ten years have been waiting on my lips— that I love you, I adore you, that the whole strength of my life is in the love I bear you—that my one dearest hope is to call you my wife ! that for you I am ready to—to——

Lady Rockmount (trying to conceal her emotion). To face Mrs. Greville to-morrow morning with an explanation ! Ha ! ha ! I wish you joy of that moment !

Col. Perceval. Ah, Kate! if I am but sure of you I am ready to face anything. One word from you will be enough to make me dauntless.

Lady Rockmount. One word—ah, Philip ! that one word is—Yes. [*Col. Perceval seizes her hand.*

Lady Rockmount. I hear Mrs. Greville on the stairs.

Col. Perceval. I don't care. I am afraid of nothing now.

Lady Rockmount (going out, followed by Col. Perceval). Come, then, you shall put us into the carriage—and I will take Mrs. Greville to the opera, and tell her how fate brought us together here to-day to have a Chance Interview !

Curtain.

THE WRONG POET

CHARACTERS.

THE POET SERAPHIN.	MRS. VERNON.
CAPTAIN SEYMOUR.	LADY ROCKVILLE.
MR. GORE.	MRS. DODSON.

SERVANT.

SCENE.—*Mrs. Vernon's drawing-room.*

Mrs. Vernon (reading). Oh, what delightful poems! How perfect in substance and form! This indeed is true poetry! And to think that to-day, perhaps, I shall see the gifted one who wrote them—that he will come in here—into my drawing-room!—that I shall, perhaps, hear from his lips some undying sentiment, such as those over which I have been gloating in his latest volume, the 'Sobs of the Soul'! I wonder if he will really come? Captain Seymour and Mr. Gore undertook to bring him, to tell him of my enthusiasm and admiration. What will Lady Rockville say when she hears he has been to see me? She will tear her hair out with envy and vexation! and well she may, for Seraphin is not the sort of tame poet to be found on every hearthrug. No: to have him in one's house is a privilege indeed, and belongs only to the elect. [*A ring at the bell.*] A ring! If it were he! Quick—where are the 'Sobs of the Soul'!

> [*She takes the volume and appears absorbed in it as the door opens.*

Servant (announcing). Lady Rockville.

Mrs. Vernon. Good heavens! That woman to-day, of all days!

Enter Lady Rockville.

Mrs. Vernon. My dear Lady Rockville, how delightful!

[*Exit Servant.*

Lady Rockville. How kind of you to say so! It is a shame to disturb you when you are reading so comfortably.

Mrs. Vernon. On the contrary. Do sit down.

Lady Rockville. You are very studious to-day. What is your book?

Mrs. Vernon. Can you ask? It's the latest volume published by Seraphin, 'Sobs of the Soul.'

Lady Rockville. Oh, yes! the 'Sobs of the Soul.' How beautiful it is! so touching, so stirring—I positively adore poetry.

Mrs. Vernon. Indeed? I did not know it.

Lady Rockville (surprised). Didn't you? But, my dear friend, surely you know what a frenzied musician I am? that I breathe and exist only for music—that I live for nothing else?

Mrs. Vernon. Yes, yes. I remember you have told me so more than once.

Lady Rockville. Well, when one is as musical as that poetry is included.

Mrs. Vernon. Well, it doesn't seem strange to me, of course, that anyone should care for poetry. It's my passion, a positive mania.

Lady Rockville. That's just like me for music. I wander at will in a world of my own.

Mrs. Vernon. Just like me too. I wander in a world of my own, far removed from the echoes of everyday existence.

Lady Rockville. Really? It's quite odd to see how alike we feel. I only long to be out of reach of the echoes of vulgar existence: the commonplace everydayness of things repels me. My mind would ever be taking wing towards the empyrean.

Mrs. Vernon. Exactly ! so would mine. I often have that feeling.

Lady Rockville. I dream of music and musicians—of nothing else absolutely. Oh, by the way, I am going to have a great and most enviable treat next week. Staccati, the great composer Staccati, has promised to come to my house, and he is not to be met with everywhere, I can assure you.

Mrs. Vernon. Oh, really? I thought he was. I thought he was very anxious to go into society since he has been taken up by two or three people, who are beginning to make him a reputation.

Lady Rockville. You are under an entirely mistaken impression, I assure you. He goes hardly anywhere, though with his great fame it is often difficult to remain secluded.

Mrs. Vernon. I am expecting some one who is really difficult to get. Of course he is far above Staccati, or anybody else in the present day.

Lady Rockville (annoyed). And who is that, may I ask ?

Mrs. Vernon. The poet Seraphin.

Lady Rockville (excited). The poet Seraphin ! What ! do you mean he is coming here to see you ? Do you know him, then ? .

Mrs. Vernon (embarrassed). Yes, yes—that is to say, I have written to him. He knows that he can rely on my unbounded sympathy and admiration.

Lady Rockville. I must say I should like to see him. When do you expect him ? Do you think there is any chance of his coming to-day ?

Mrs. Vernon. I don't know—at any rate I shall be delighted if you will stay on the chance.

Lady Rockville. Oh, how kind of you ! I shall be delighted, I need not say.

Mrs. Vernon (aside). There's nothing else to be done, I suppose.

Lady Rockville. Oh, I shall quite appreciate the privilege of meeting him, I assure you. You must remember that my soul is as sensitive, as ready to vibrate to every impulse, as your own.

Mrs. Vernon (aside). I must say I like that!

Lady Rockville. No—I am not like Mrs. Dodson, who would have no more emotion at meeting the great Seraphin than—than——

Mrs. Vernon. Than the great pyramid.

Lady Rockville. Exactly! not so much. What a commonplace woman she is! prosaic to a degree!

Mrs. Vernon. Indeed she is. Just imagine, the other day, when I went to see her, she talked to me the whole time about her children's education.

Lady Rockville. Heavens, how deadly! That's just what that sort of woman does talk about—no poetry, no imagination.

Mrs. Vernon. There's a ring at the bell.

Lady Rockville. Seraphin himself, perhaps.

[*Mrs. Vernon takes the ' Sobs of the Soul' into her hand hastily.*

Lady Rockville (loud, as the door is opened). Oh, it is too beautiful! Don't stop reading for a moment, dear friend, pray. [*Servant announces Mrs. Dodson.*

Lady Rockville. Oh, that woman at this moment!

Mrs. Vernon. What shall we do?

Enter Mrs. Dodson. Exit Servant.

Mrs. Dodson. How do you do, Mrs. Vernon? Are you quite well?

Mrs. Vernon (shaking hands). Quite well, thank you, and you?

Mrs. Dodson (shaking hands with Lady Rockville) Oh, I am perfectly well, of course—I always am.

Lady Rockville (aside).   Oh, the coarse fibre of such a nature !   [*They sit down.*

Mrs. Dodson.   What a beautiful day !

Mrs. Vernon.   Yes, very.

Mrs. Dodson.   It was a little cool in the morning. Were you out then ?

Mrs. Vernon.   No.   I never go out in the morning.   I devote it to the earnest and intense study of my favourite authors.

Lady Rockville (smiling).   To one especially, I imagine.

Mrs. Vernon.   Yes, one above all.

[*Taking up the ' Sobs of the Soul.'*

Mrs. Dodson.   What a pity to stay in the house when it is so fine !   I was out nearly two hours this morning in Kensington Gardens, with baby.

Lady Rockville (aside).   I knew that baby would come into the conversation before long.

Mrs. Vernon.   Oh, I should consider that a deplorable waste of time.   I prefer to raise and transfigure my intelligence by absorbing the great works of the masters of literature.

Mrs. Dodson.   What is the work you have been reading this morning ?

Mrs. Vernon (reverently).   The ' Sobs of the Soul.'

Lady Rockville.   By Seraphin.

Mrs. Dodson.   Seraphin—let me see, I know that name, I think.   He's a poet, isn't he ?

Mrs. Vernon.   A poet !   *The* poet—the greatest poet of modern times.

Mrs. Dodson.   Oh, really—I must read some of his verses when I have time, then.   Just now I'm busy covering the dining-room chairs.   You've no idea of the time it takes. I've been to every shop in London.   I want rather pale red.   Don't you think that will be pretty for the dining-room ?

Mrs. Vernon (bored). I dare say, yes. We have red in our dining room.

Mrs. Dodson (interested). Oh, have you, really? I wonder if it is the red I want. Might I see it? Perhaps it is the colour of my dreams.

Lady Rockville (aside). Dreams, indeed! Yes, her dreams are of dining-room chairs, and nothing else.

Mrs. Vernon. Certainly. If you would like to see the colour of our dining-room I shall be delighted to show it to you. Will you come too, Lady Rockville?

Lady Rockville. I shall be delighted. [*They go out.*

Enter Servant, followed by Mr. Gore and Captain Seymour, the latter in disguise.

Servant (announcing). Mr. Gore, Mr. Seraphin. (Looking round) Oh, I thought Mrs. Vernon was here, sir. I'll go and tell her.

Mr. Gore. No, no, don't tell her—we'll wait here. [*Exit Servant.*] I'm not sorry to have one moment more to combine our plans.

Captain Seymour (anxiously). Are you sure she won't know me?

Mr. Gore. How on earth should she know you in that get-up? You look like Shakespeare, or Beaumont and Fletcher, or somebody of that sort.

Seymour (anxiously). Do you think she'll take me for Seraphin?

Gore. Of course she will, you donkey!

Seymour. My conscience is beginning to smite me.

Gore. Nonsense! We did all we could to make Seraphin come, and as he wouldn't we've brought somebody else instead. She'll be just as pleased.

Seymour. And suppose Seraphin were to change his mind, and suddenly appear while I am here?

Gore (laughing). Then there will be two ! Don't you be afraid : he won't come. He told me so, point blank. He hates society, he hates being adulated, and, above all, he would hate to come and see an adoring lady whom he does not know, and who would overwhelm him with senti- mental chatter about things she does not understand. No, Seraphin will not come here, you may be sure.

Seymour (laughing). I must say this is very funny. I'm dying to hear what she'll say to me.

Gore. I'll tell you what would be still funnier, a still better joke, and that is that after you have retired I should appear, also personating Seraphin.

Seymour. How would you get yourself up, then ?

Gore. I have the very thing. I have in my rooms, just over the way, a costume of the time of Louis XIV. of France, in which I went to a fancy dress ball the other day. As soon as you're gone, I appear. While I'm here you go to my rooms and change your things : I follow you there and do the same, and then, in our ordinary attire, we come back here to make a formal call, and apologise for not having been able to bring Seraphin.

Seymour. That really would be excellent, I must say— only——

Gore. Only what ?

Seymour. I still feel rather conscience-stricken.

Gore. Your conscience is perfectly ridiculous. Mrs. Vernon has brought it on herself.

Seymour. Yes—she deserves it, I must say.

Gore. Very well, then, that's settled. I'll go back to dress and wait for you in my rooms. You sit there near the table, the 'Sobs of the Soul' in your hand. That's right—most poetical ! You're certainly more unlike Seraphin, who looks like a lawyer's clerk, than anyone I've seen for a long time. There ! they are coming—I must fly !

[*Exit Gore.*

Enter Mrs. Vernon, Lady Rockville, and Mrs. Dodson.

[*Mrs. Vernon starts as she sees Seymour sitting by the table.*

Mrs. Vernon. Oh, I beg your pardon.

Seymour (getting up and bowing). Madam, you expressed a wish to see me here. I was told you desired to make the acquaintance of the poet Seraphin. Behold him.

Mrs. Vernon. Oh, how can I thank you for the great favour, the great honour you have shown me? I hardly hoped for so much gracious condescension.

Seymour. It is but seldom that I yield to the importunity of my admirers—I pass my life in profound seclusion. When, however, I come across one who can breathe in the lofty regions which I inhabit, I am willing to stoop to brief communion for a space.

Mrs. Vernon. Oh, how condescending!

Lady Rockville. How affable!

Mrs. Dodson (aside). How frightfully conceited!

Lady Rockville. Pray, dear Mrs. Vernon, introduce me to the greatest of our poets.

Mrs. Vernon (aside). She must always come to the front somehow. [*To S.*] This is Lady Rockville, one of your heartfelt admirers.

Lady Rockville. If I may say so, my nature is as sensitive, as impressionable as that of Mrs. Vernon.

Seymour (aside). Indeed! (*To Lady Rockville*) I congratulate you most deeply. (*To Mrs. Vernon*) It must be your excessive sensibility which attracts that of others.

Mrs. Vernon (flattered). I think it must be—at least that's how I account for it.

Seymour (turning to Mrs. Dodson). And is this friend of yours also one of the chosen?

Mrs. Vernon. Of the chosen?

Seymour.   I mean, does her soul also respond and vibrate to each impulsive emotion ?

Mrs. Dodson (stiffly).   I can't say that it does.   I don't respond, and I don't vibrate.

Seymour.   Oh, I pity you then—I pity you indeed ! But, alas ! everyone cannot be equally gifted.

Mrs. Vernon.   Naturally.

Lady Rockville.   That is obvious.

Mrs. Dodson (aside).   Upon my word !

Mrs. Vernon (to S.)   You see, there lies your immortal creation, the 'Sobs of the Soul,' my favourite volume, the inseparable companion of my solitude.

Seymour (taking the book).   Ah ! indeed ! you are right.   There are beautiful things in the 'Sobs of the Soul' —beautiful things.   Tell me, which is your favourite sob ?

Mrs. Vernon.   Amid so much perfection it is indeed difficult to make a choice, but it seems to me that the one that is entitled 'A Seventh Love' is still more transcendent than the rest.

Seymour.   'A Seventh Love ?'   Yes, you are right, perhaps, to choose it : it is transcendent—it flowed from my pen, complete, in one gush of inspiration !

Mrs. Vernon.   Oh, what a sentence ! How magnificently said !

Lady Rockville.   It is worthy of the author of the 'Sobs of the Soul' !

Mrs. Dodson (aside).   It is, indeed.

Mrs. Vernon (to Seymour).   I have another favour to ask you.

Seymour.   A favour ?   Speak : it shall be granted.

Mrs. Vernon.   There is a portrait of you at the beginning of the book.   I long to possess your precious signature, written by your own hand underneath.

Seymour (aside).   A portrait ?   By Jove !   That won't

do. (Aloud) The only thing is, that this portrait is so un-like me.

Mrs. Vernon. It is true it is not very satisfactory. The fact is, the dress and the beard make such a difference.

Seymour. Yes, that's true. As to my costume, I must apologise for coming to you in my workaday clothes, straight from my writing-table. It is one of my fancies that I can only write verse when I am dressed like Shakespeare. We men of genius are often like that. Wagner could only write in a pink dressing-gown.

Mrs. Vernon. I think it is a most delightful play of fancy.

Lady Rockville. So do I.

Mrs. Dodson (aside). They are all three mad, I believe.

Seymour. No, no, I really cannot sign that portrait. You must allow me to send you a better one, one that will remind you more of one whom you have so kindly welcomed.
                                    [*He puts out his hand.*

Mrs. Vernon. You are not going already?

Seymour. I must indeed. Immortality summons me ; posterity awaits me without—in a figurative sense, of course. Farewell, then, Mrs. Vernon. The Muses be with you. (*To Lady Rockville*) With you, also, Lady Rockville, since you, too, respond and vibrate. (*To Mrs. Dodson*) To you, madam, I hardly dare to utter the same wish.

Mrs. Dodson. You are quite right, thank you. I should not at all like the Muses to be with me : they would disturb my household arrangements too much.

Seymour. Ah, again I pity you—I pity you indeed ! (*To Mrs. V. and Lady R.*) Farewell, then, my sisters of the soul.   [*Exit Seymour.*

Mrs. Vernon (with a sigh, to Lady Rockville). Well, my dear friend, what do you say to that ?

Lady Rockville. My dear, he's tremendous—over-whelming.

Mrs. Dodson (aside).   Overwhelming, indeed !

Mrs. Vernon.   Well, I must say it is something to be proud of to have had Seraphin in one's own house.

Lady Rockville.   It is, indeed, most enviable.

Mrs. Vernon.   Such urbanity ! such condescension !

Lady Rockville.   And how affable he was to me, too ! 'My sisters of the soul !' What a glorious title !

Mrs. Vernon.   Glorious, indeed.   I felt myself transported into the ether.

Lady Rockville.   And you, Mrs. Dodson ?   What do you think of it ?

Mrs. Vernon.   I'm afraid we needn't ask.

Mrs. Dodson.   Well, since you ask me, I think it a mistake to make the acquaintance of men of genius.   One can't help being disappointed.

Lady Rockville.   It seems to me, on the contrary, that that man is the very quintessence of his books.

Mrs. Vernon.   Poetry and inspiration breathe in every word he utters.

Mrs. Dodson.   Well, I must confess I would rather he had been a little less conceited, a little more modest.

Mrs. Vernon.   Modest ?   My dear Mrs. Dodson ! that really is too much to expect.

Lady Rockville.   How can a man of genius be modest ?

Mrs. Vernon.   Since we realise how great his genius is, of course his greater intelligence must realise it incomparably more.

Mrs. Dodson.   I should prefer that he should pretend not to see it.   Good-bye, then, Mrs. Vernon, and thank you very much for your advice about my chairs.

Mrs. Vernon (aside).   Is it possible that at this moment she can think of chairs ? .

Mrs. Dodson (smiling).   Do you expect many other great men to-day ?

Mrs. Vernon.   To-day ?   No, I think not.

Lady Rockville. Next week I expect Staccati at my house.

Mrs. Dodson. Staccati? I don't think I know that name. Who is he?

Lady Rockville (aside). What an extraordinary woman!
[*A bell is heard.*

Mrs. Vernon. There is another ring!

Mrs. Dodson. Perhaps it is the Poet Laureate.

Servant (announces). Mr. Seraphin!

Mrs. Vernon (goes hastily to door). I wonder why he has come back?

Enter Gore in costume of the time of Louis XIV.

Lady Rockville (aside). What can this mean?
[*Gore bows.*

Mrs. Vernon (embarrassed). I think there must be some mistake—to whom have I the pleasure of speaking?

Gore. To a poor poet, madam, a wretched scribbler whose name you may perhaps have heard—the poet Seraphin.

All (together). The poet Seraphin!

Gore. No other. Seraphin, author of the 'Sobs of the Soul,' a trifle unworthy of consideration.

Mrs. Vernon. I don't understand—I think there must be some mistake. The poet Seraphin has just left us.

Gore. What! Some one has dared to take my name?

Lady Rockville. Your name?

Gore. My name, certainly. I am the poet Seraphin.

Mrs. Vernon (still hesitating). But then how does it happen——

Gore. You don't believe me, I see. Just as you please, of course. If you prefer to believe in some impostor who has apparently been to see you—— [*Goes towards the door.*

Mrs. Vernon (stopping him). One moment. I am really very sorry—this is the most extraordinary situation.

E

If I only knew—if I dared to ask you for some sort of proof. . . .

Gore.   Proof, madam ! My proofs are in my writings, in my inspiration.   I will tell you, however, that I received a note from you this morning couched in the most flattering and appreciative terms, and begging me to come and see you.

Mrs. Vernon.   What ! *You* received my letter, the one which I sent yesterday by post to the poet Seraphin ? You are really the person, then, for whom it was meant ?

Gore.   Apparently, since it was delivered to me.

Mrs. Vernon.   But oh, who can have come here instead of you ? I have received and welcomed an impostor !

Gore.   So it would appear. But it doesn't surprise me— it was probably some enemy, whose envy tried to bring discredit on me by investing me with his own unworthy personality.   What was he like ? Was he simple and modest, like myself ?   I dare say not.

Mrs. Vernon.   I can't say that he was very modest.

Lady Rockville.   If anything, I should say rather the reverse.

Mrs. Dodson (aside).   Yes, I should say the reverse !

Mrs. Vernon (to Seraphin).   Oh, will you ever forgive me for doubting you, for the terrible mistake I made when I first saw you ?

Gore.   Since you recognise your fault so generously, I can say no more—but come, let us leave this unpleasant subject. Tell me something of your literary tastes, which are admirable, I believe.

Mrs. Vernon (pleased).   Oh, you are too kind. I try to understand, that's all.

Gore.   That's a great deal, when you try to understand the right thing.

Lady Rockville.   I, also, try to understand.

Gore. Oh, indeed ! I congratulate you. (*Smiling, to Mrs. Dodson*) Do you also try to understand ?

Mrs. Dodson. No, I'm afraid I don't.

Mrs. Vernon (aside). She'll spoil everything. (*Hurriedly showing him book*) This is my favourite volume, the ' Sobs of the Soul.'

Gore. Oh, oh ! really—you are too good, indeed.

Mrs. Dodson (aside). Come, I like this Seraphin better than the other, at any rate.

Gore. And which is your favourite piece, may I ask ?

Mrs. Vernon. ' A Seventh Love,' I think.

Gore. ' A Seventh Love '—really ! It is my favourite too.

Mrs. Vernon. I am so glad to find I have chosen rightly ! and now I wonder if you would do me a favour ?

Gore. I am grateful to you beforehand for asking it.

Mrs. Vernon. It is to write your name under your portrait, the frontispiece of this book.

Gore (aside). A portrait ! That's awkward. (*Aloud*) Oh, really, this portrait, taken in my youth, is so unlike me. It's the portrait of an unknown Seraphin, who had written nothing, who had not even his present slight claims on your regard. If you will allow me, I will send you the next edition of my poems, which will have a better portrait.

Mrs. Vernon. It's true that this one is not very like you.

Gore. No, no. For one thing, I dressed differently at that time—since I have consecrated myself in earnest to the immortal art of poetry, I always dress in the costumes worn by the masters of the past, in order to remind me that I must endeavour to tread, however unworthily, in their footsteps.

Mrs. Dodson (aside). Oh yes, I like this Seraphin much better than the other.

E 2

Gore. I fear I must go now, Mrs. Vernon. I am most grateful to you for your kind welcome.

Mrs. Vernon. It is I who feel grateful for the honour you have done me in coming here.

Gore (bowing). No, it is I who am honoured, I assure you.   [*Exit Gore.*

Mrs. Vernon. Well, that was extraordinary, I must say.

Mrs. Dodson. I don't suppose it often happens to any-one to receive two Seraphins in the same day.

Lady Rockville. Who could the first have been ?

Mrs. Vernon. One of his enemies, I should think, as he suggested. Imagine daring to assume the immortal name of Seraphin !

Lady Rockville. And to carry it off with such an air too !

Mrs. Vernon. I will admit now that I thought him somewhat self-satisfied, though I did not like to say so.

Lady Rockville. So did I.

Mrs. Dodson (aside). And so did I!

Mrs. Vernon. It certainly is a bore to have received the impostor so well.

Lady Rockville. After all it does not matter much, as you have had the honour of receiving the real Seraphin all the same.

Mrs. Vernon. Yes, indeed, that is something to have lived for. It consoles one for everything. [*A ring.*] There is somebody else !

Mrs. Dodson (aside). Perhaps it's a third Seraphin.

Servant (announcing). Mr. Seraphin !

All. Seraphin ! ! !

Enter Seraphin, plainly dressed in a frock coat, &c.
Exit Servant.

Seraphin (bowing stiffly to Mrs. Vernon). Mrs. Vernon ?

⌐ ⌐nink you were kind enough to ask me to come and see you.

Mrs. Vernon (bewildered). I think there must be some mistake——

Seraphin. My name is Seraphin.

Mrs. Vernon. Seraphin ! ! No—this time it is too much ! even a woman's credulity has its limits.

Seraphin. What ? ! !

Mrs. Vernon. Seraphin, the poet Seraphin has just left this room—I beg, therefore, that you will cease this practical joke, which can have no other object than to insult me.

Seraphin (furious, but controlling his passion). Madam, it is not you who are being insulted here ! but your sex protects you—I will say no more. I will only add that my name is Seraphin, that I came to gratify the burning desire you expressed to see me, and that I will now leave your house, never to re-enter it. I am much indebted to you for your courtesy and welcome.   [*Exit Seraphin.*

Mrs. Vernon. What can all this mean ?

Lady Rockville. I don't understand a word of it.

Mrs. Dodson. It's showering poets to-day ! I never saw anything like it.

Enter Seymour and Gore hastily, dressed in their own clothes.

Gore (breathless). I must apologise to you, Mrs. Vernon, for rushing into your room in this way, but what have you been doing to Seraphin ?

Mrs. Vernon. Seraphin ! !

Gore. Why have you turned him out of your house ?

Mrs. Vernon (faintly). Turned him out ?

Gore. Yes ! we've just met him on the stairs in the most raging, the most tearing passion. We tried to find out what was the matter, but he rushed past, uttering curses like a madman.

Mrs. Vernon (with a shriek). You met him on the stairs ! What, it was really Seraphin ?

Seymour. Of course it was !

Gore (feigning surprise). Who else should it be ?

Seymour. There's his portrait—you only have to look at it to see it is the same person (pointing to book open on table).

Mrs. Vernon (looking at it). Yes—it is himself !

Lady Rockville. It is indeed !

Mrs. Dodson (aside). No mistake this time !

Mrs. Vernon. Oh, miserable woman that I am ! Seraphin has been into my house, and I have insulted him and turned him out !

Mrs. Dodson. ·And rapturously welcomed the Wrong Poets !

Curtain.

THE PUBLIC PROSECUTOR.

PLAY IN ONE ACT.

(Suggested by Boisgobey's ' Crime de l'Opéra ')

CHARACTERS.

JEAN DARCY, the public prosecutor.
PHILIP DARCY, his nephew.
ALINE, Philip's wife.
DORA LARIVIÈRE, a widow.

SCENE.—*Aline's drawing-room, Boulevard Malesherbes, Paris. Philip, Aline—Ph. reading newspaper, Al. working.*

Al. How absorbed you are in your book, dear Philip !
[*Ph. does not answer.*

Al. (aside). How extraordinary it is that when a man is reading anything he must needs give his whole attention to it ! Women are not like that at all. (*Aloud*) Philip !

Ph. (starts). I beg your pardon, darling—did you speak to me ?

Al. (smiling). Speak to you ? Of course I did ! I have been chatting with you for the last quarter of an hour.

Ph. Oh, indeed—it must have been rather a one-sided conversation ! I always thought it took two to chat, but apparently I was mistaken.

Al. Well, what am I to do if you will go on reading ? I can't sit silent for ever, can I ?

Ph. Most certainly not, I should say from experience.

Al. A pretty state of things it would be if we were

each to sit in a corner of the room with our heads wrapped in a newspaper, buried in fusty politics.

Ph. I am ashamed to say that it was not a political subject that was interesting me so deeply just then.

Al. What was it, then ?

Ph. It was this celebrated trial that is exciting all Paris so much—the murder that took place at the Opera, you know.

Al. That is the case that your uncle is trying to unravel, is it not ?

Ph. Yes—but I fear that this time even his penetration is at fault—for once the Public Prosecutor is baffled.

Al. Poor uncle John ! It will be a great blow to him. His whole heart is wrapped up in his profession—he has not a thought for anything else.

Ph. (dubiously). H'm—I am not so sure of that! He has found a fresh subject of interest lately, in the shape of the fascinating Madame Larivière, who is acquiring an influence over him which no woman has ever had before.

Al. You don't mean to say that you think there can be a question of his marrying her ?

Ph. I cannot tell—he is only 55 after all, and though I admit that I have known instances of men marrying at an earlier age than that, still I should not like to make any rash prophecies about his remaining a bachelor till the end of his days.

Al. Well, I must say Madame Larivière does not altogether inspire me with confidence. She is too—too——

Ph. (maliciously). Too pretty ?

Al. No, no, Philip—you always think women are jealous of each other. It isn't that at all. But she certainly seems to have a kind of manner which——

Ph. Which men think delightful and women call bad style, eh ? I know ! ha, ha !

Al. You always laugh at me, Philip, as if I were so

foolish. I know much more of the world than you think, I can tell you.

Ph. I've no doubt of it, my darling. But don't be too worldly and clever, please. I like you best as you are, simple, unworldly, and trustful—and, joking apart, I am quite ready to agree with you that perhaps your instinct about Madame Larivière is right, and that it is a pity that a man in my uncle's position should show himself constantly and conspicuously alone in public with a charming widow.

Al. Well, well—it is not our business, I suppose.

Ph. No, it is not—and at any rate it would not come with a very good grace from me to persuade my uncle against any possible marriage—for since, if he dies unmarried, I am his acknowledged heir, he would certainly think I was preaching for my own parish, as the proverb says, and dissuading him from marrying for my own interest.

Al. At any rate he will not be able to think of marriage until this case is settled.

Ph. No, and it does not seem likely to be concluded just yet. They have most ingeniously got up to a certain point in their discoveries, but now they have arrived at a blank wall. Oh, how I wish I could find out something! Fancy, Aline, the joy of suddenly getting on to the clue! There is no career in the world that appears to me as entrancing as that of the judicial investigation in a case of this kind—playing a game of chess blindfold against the whole of society, and at last succeeding by mere force of patience and ingenuity in winning the match. Ah, whatever my uncle may say slightingly of my talents in that direction, he will find them out some day, never fear.

Al. I hope so, dear Philip, since you wish it—but I can't help thinking that it would be nicer if you did something else. There is a ring—who can it be, at this time?

Ph. It sounds like my uncle's voice.

Door opens hastily.   Enter Darcy.

Al.   What, uncle !

Darcy.   Yes, you may well be surprised—I have come early this morning.

Al.   Well, we are delighted to see you—will you not sit down ?

Darcy.   No, thank you : I am afraid I have not time.

Al.   And how is the case prospering ?

Darcy (preoccupied).   Oh, very well.

Ph.   Very well ?   Then are you on the track ?

Darcy.   No, no—I was not thinking of what I was saying—it is not prospering at all.

Ph. (to Al.)   He is farther gone than we thought !

Darcy. (to Al.)   I think you know Madame Larivière ?

Al.   I have seen her—but I have not yet made her acquaintance.

Darcy.   Indeed ? how does that happen ?   I have met you constantly in the same places.

Al. (confused).   Oh, it is because—because—I have not yet had an opportunity of being introduced to her.

Darcy.   That obstacle, I hope, will soon be removed —you will oblige me very much, Aline, if you will go and call upon her.

Al.   Call upon her, uncle ?

Darcy.   Yes, call upon her—why not ?

Al.   Because—I don't know her.

Darcy.   But if you are only going to make the acquaintance of people you know already, it seems to me that your circle of friends will not have much chance of increasing.

Al.   Besides, she might wonder at my going to see her.

Darcy.   Not at all—she is the most accessible person in the world.

Ph. (aside). I have no doubt of it.

Darcy. She would receive you with open arms, I am sure.

Al. Very kind——

Darcy. And I feel assured that, when once you know her, you will like her as much—as—as—everyone else does.

Al. Does everyone like her very much, uncle?

Darcy. All those, that is to say, who do not allow themselves to be unjustly prejudiced—she is a person of unusual intellectual gifts.   [*Ph. bows assentingly.*

Darcy. Of rare personal charm. [*Al. bows assentingly.*

Darcy. Of the warmest heart possible——

Al. That is delightful.

Darcy. Full of sympathy and kindness——

Ph. (smiling). It is something quite new to hear you, uncle, showing so warm an interest in anyone, or anything, outside the sphere of your profession.

Darcy. Yes, it is new, I dare say—everything is new when it is done for the first time, and yet everything must have a beginning at some time or other. I don't know why I, more than any other man, should, when I meet with a type of perfect womanhood, remain insensible to her charms.

Ph. But are you quite sure, dear uncle, that in Madame Larivière you have found that type?

Darcy. Sure—of course I am sure! Have I not been describing her to you, and do you mean to tell me that is the description of an ordinary woman?

Ph. No—certainly not—only——

Darcy. Only—what?

Ph. (embarrassed). Only—that you may perhaps be prejudiced in her favour by the interest you appear to take in her.

Darcy. Prejudiced! . . . if there is any prejudice it is not on my side, let me tell you!

Al. Dear uncle, the only reason we are perhaps seeming not to sympathise with you sufficiently is our anxiety for your welfare.

Ph. You see, of course everyone knows the world's opinion of Madame Larivière is——

Darcy (interrupting him). I beg your pardon—*I* don't know it—I don't wish to know it.

Ph. But, uncle, surely, before forming a friendship seemingly as close as this you ought to hear——

Darcy. I want to hear nothing. I believe, as I have said, that Madame Larivière is the type of what a woman ought to be—and I have asked her to be my wife.

Ph., Al. (together). Your wife !

Darcy. My wife, yes—so, you see, it is rather late for criticism. I asked her last night if she would share my life, and she consented. Does that surprise you ? I don't see what there is so utterly preposterous in the announcement, I must confess.

Ph. Certainly not, uncle—certainly not.

Darcy. I am not as young as I was, I must admit— but all the more, therefore, my choice is likely to be guided by rational judgment rather than by youthful impulse— and, after all, it is no reason, because I have been a bachelor so long, that I should remain so to the end of my days—why, bless me—it seems to me that being single is a very good reason why I *should* marry !

Al. Oh, certainly, dear uncle—certainly.

Darcy. Oh yes—you may say certainly—but I can see very well that you think me an old fool !

Al. I assure you, dear uncle——

Darcy. Well, let me tell you that I am not, then— nothing of the kind !

Ph. We are quite ready to believe it.

Darcy. I am not quite so sure of that—you are a pair of most sympathetic confidants, I must say !

Ph. You know that everything which interests you interests us.

Darcy. That, I dare say, is possible—even people without much sympathy can be moved to feel a pecuniary interest in other people's affairs !

Ph. (angrily). Uncle ! [*Aline lays her hand on his arm.*

Darcy. There—there—you need not fly into a rage. I only meant that if you are not a fool you must know that my marriage will make a certain difference to you—after all, I don't blame you for resenting it—each man for himself, I suppose, in this egotistical world.

Ph. Uncle, you wrong me most grievously if you think that my opposition has anything to do with my own interests—and since you have made up your mind to the decisive step, all I can now do is to wish you happiness and joy, which I do from the bottom of my heart.

[*Holds out his hand to Darcy.*

Al. And so do I.

Darcy. Thank you, thank you, my children—I believe it—you mustn't be angry with me—I am hot-tempered, I dare say. And now, the only thing that stands in my way is this wretched case—as long as it continues I am bound hand and foot to the law courts, and dare not absent myself for a single day in case anything fresh should appear.

Al. How far have you got now ?

Darcy. As far, and no further, as we were three weeks ago—viz. that we have ascertained that the murdered woman, Fanny Duval, was visited in her box during the evening by another woman, closely veiled—they seem to have had an excited and angry interview—no one saw the visitor depart—she probably succeeded in slipping away unobserved. At the close of the evening, Fanny Duval was found dead in her box, with a wound in her chest close to the heart—a small dagger was lying by her side—nothing more is known.

Ph. I only wish I could prove my good wishes by helping you to a discovery.

Darcy (smiling). Well, why don't you? why don't you employ these famous aptitudes for the career that you are always talking of, and put us on the track of this?

Ph. Ah, you may laugh at me, uncle—but I will do it.

Darcy. Just listen to him! well, well! it is a good thing to be self-confident! no—you have no turn, believe me, for criminal investigation, but we will find you some other path of distinction, never fear—in fact—but no, I will not say anything about that yet. Good-bye, my little Aline—now remember you are going to be a good, kind, sympathetic niece.

Al. I will do all I can, dear uncle.

Darcy. Good-bye, Philip, my boy.

Ph. I am coming with you.

Darcy. Not to the courts, my boy, please!—if you are going to carry on this discovery business, it must be on your own account, and quite unofficially—it would never do to have the authorities imagine that I am employing my nephew as a sort of amateur detective.

Ph. No, uncle, I will not go to the courts with you, yet—I will bring no descredit on you, never fear.

Darcy (laughing, going out). Well, Aline, I hope you believe in this husband of yours as much as he does himself! (*To Ph.*) You will let me know, then, when you have made this famous discovery? will it be within the next hour?

Ph. (laughing). Quite possibly.

Darcy. Ha, ha! The sooner the better, as far as I am concerned, remember!

[*Exit Darcy. Ph. runs back to kiss Aline.*

Al. Oh, do take care of yourself, Philip—don't be murdered too!

Ph. Not if I can help it—if I am I will let you know ! Silly child !—I shall be back this afternoon. [*Exit Phil.*

Al. (alone). It is all very well to laugh at me, and call me silly child—but all the same I can't bear his going among murderers and people of that kind ! What an extraordinary mania it is, wanting to know who has done these things—it is much nicer not to know, I think ! but then Philip says women do not understand. Dear Philip ! I wish it were time for him to come back—how long has he been away ? [*Looks at clock.*] Dear me, I am afraid only about three minutes as yet. How nice it is to be married, and in love with one's husband ! Poor uncle ! I dare say he feels very lonely sometimes. It is hard he should not marry if he likes—but yet what a pity he should just fix on such a horrid woman ! I can't be sure she is horrid, of course—but one can't help feeling inclined to dislike people before one knows them. And to think she is going to be my aunt ! What am I to do about going to see her ? I shall have to do it, I suppose—but I really don't feel as if I could.

Enter Servant with a letter.

Al. Is there any answer ?
Serv. No, Madame. . [*Exit Serv.*
Al. What a peculiar writing ! I wonder whose it is ? it is not the writing of anyone I know, or I am quite sure I should recognise it. It is beautiful, certainly—so clear and legible, and yet not in the least stiff—perhaps the best thing would be to look inside ! ! [*Opens letter—looks puzzled —turns to signature—starts.*] 'Dora Larivière' ! what, can this be her writing? I should not have thought so. (*Reads*) 'Madame, I venture to write to you, although I have not the pleasure of knowing you yet—we have met often, but as strangers. Let us become friends now—it would be a real and deep happiness to me. I have told the bearer not to

wait for a reply to this letter—I will come myself to learn the answer from you.   Forgive me for being indiscreet enough to intrude on you unasked.—DORA LARIVIÈRE.' She is coming here !   What must I do ?   I shall have to see her, then.   There is no help for it, I suppose.   But as to swearing eternal friendship with her, that is quite another thing.   Oh, how simple existence would be if there were no other people in the world besides one's self—and one's husband, of course !   [*Door opens, servant announces.*

Serv.   Madame Larivière !

Al.   What, already ! she has lost no time.

Enter Dora.   Aline bows stiffly.

Dora.   I hope I am not being very indiscreet.

Al. (embarrassed).   Not at all ; I—I—am delighted ! Will you not sit down ?   [*Dora sits.*

Al.   It is very warm to-day, do you not think so ?

Dora.   Yes, very—at least, no—I find it, on the contrary, rather cold.

Al.   Ah, indeed—you have been driving, perhaps ?

Dora.   No, I walked here.   [*Pause.*

Dora.   I have the pleasure of knowing your uncle.

Al.   Yes. [*Pause.*] (Aside) What a wretch I am being —what is the use of being so ungracious ? (Aloud) He has spoken to me of you.

Dora.   Have you seen him since last night ?

Al.   Yes, he was here this morning.

Dora.   And he told you—that—that—he—that I——

Al.   That you had promised to be his wife—yes.

Dora.   And you—what did you say ?

Al.   I was a little taken by surprise, I must confess.

Dora.   A little taken by surprise—and also, probably, more than a little horrified ?   [*Al. is silent.*

Dora.   Why should it have been such a surprise, such

a blow to you ? did you not think your uncle would ever marry ?

Al. I really had not thought about it—it seemed to me so utterly unlikely to happen, that I never considered the subject.

Dora. Still, he is not at the age at which a man need necessarily remain a bachelor.

Al. Certainly not—in fact, I don't know that such an age is ever reached.

Dora. Do not you think that everyone is happier married ?

Al. It is very nice to be married, certainly.

Dora. Yes, you indeed are happy—you look as if you had never known what it was to be otherwise—is that not so ?

Al. Yes, I must admit that my life has been a singularly fortunate and happy one.

Dora. And in consequence, doubtless, you have a kind of feeling that when others are not so happy they deserve contempt for losing the chances life offers them ?

Al. No, indeed—I feel pity for them—pity—compassion.

Dora. Pity ! compassion ! yes, I know what that means ! the shadow cast by compassion is called—contempt !

Al. Nay—I assure you I should like everyone to be as happy as I am myself, if——

Dora (bitterly). Provided, you would say, that they do not come and disturb the quiet comfort of a well-organised home ! oh, I know how pitiless you happy and virtuous women can be to those whom you think not so good as yourselves ! You cannot realise that happiness is as happy to me at it is to you—that to me suffering is as keen—that for me to give up the joy and brightness of my life is as great a sacrifice as it would be to you—no, you know none of these things, for you have never even begun to try to learn them !

F

Al.   You wrong me, you do indeed.

Dora.   How do I wrong you ? Is it not true that when you heard your uncle had asked me to marry him, you instantly, without knowing me even, set your face against it ? Oh, if you knew how I longed as I came here to-day for some kindly woman's hand to be stretched out to take mine—to welcome me out of the storm into the harbour— why will you not do it ?

Al.   Indeed, indeed, you wrong me. I was unsympathetic, I know, at first—but I was coming to see you—my uncle asked me to do so—and I did not know you—I did not realise that——

Dora.   That I, as well as you, might be in love ? that I might be full of joy in my newly-found happiness, while you were calmly and judicially considering whether it ought to be left to me or not ?

Al.   Forgive me—I have been hard and unjust, I feel.

Dora.   If you knew the story of my life—how lonely I have been—how lonely I am—you would not be so hard on me.

Al.   Tell me—tell me something about yourself—I will sympathise with you—I will indeed.

Dora.   Oh, if you knew what your sympathy would be to me, in my loneliness ! I will tell you my story. My mother, a Russian, died when I was a child—my sister, a year older than I, and upon whom I leant entirely, died after a short illness, when she was but eighteen. I felt the whole world had changed for me. My father, an enthusiastic lover of sports and hunting, was oppressed at having the charge of a girl of my age, and encouraged me to marry the first suitor who presented himself—Armand Larivière. We came to Paris—I, a raw girl, was plunged into Paris society—my husband, I found, had made, and still continued to make, his fortune in speculations which were no better than gambling—I was giddy and thoughtless, and, as may be imagined, could not guide or steady him. At last reverses came, and dishonour—he—he—put an end to his life, leaving me to face the world, as best I might, alone.   I went back to Russia—my father was dead--I returned here, everywhere overshadowed by my husband's name and history.   I met your uncle—made friends with him—he entreated me to marry him—can you wonder that I should now be willing to assume the name offered to me by a good and honourable man ?

Al.   No, no, indeed—and now you have broken with your past, you will begin your life anew with him—you will make him happy, will you not ?—for he is the noblest and the best of men.

Dora.   I know it—I am sure of it.

Al.   He has been to us like a father—you cannot wonder that when we see him about to take such a momentous step, we should be anxious lest he should not be as happy as he deserves.

Dora.   Yes, yes—I feel it—of course——

Al. (taking her hand).   But, after what you have just said, I am sure you have a feeling heart—that you will know how to appreciate his fine and noble nature.   He is the very soul of honour—a man who would be morbidly sensitive to the faintest shadow on his good name—oh, keep it bright and unstained for him—value his upright and noble character as we do !

Dora (Aside).   Oh, what shall I do ?   I can endure it no longer !   (Aloud) Madame Darcy—but you must promise to keep my confidence sacred—swear that you will not repeat what I am going to say to you.

Al.   But I may tell my husband, of course ?   I always tell him everything——

Dora.   No, no—indeed—your husband least of all !

Al.   Very well, if you wish it—but it will seem very strange——

Dora. Listen—you have heard of the so-called crime, the mysterious crime that was committed at the Opera?

Al. Heard of it—indeed I have—my husband and my uncle talk of nothing else.

Dora. Do you know how much they have discovered yet?

Al. (hesitates). Not very much—but I don't think I ought to tell you—or anyone.

Dora. No, you are right, quite right—but I will tell you what I know—for I know more than they do!

Al. (starts back). You! . . .

Dora. Yes, I! . . listen—don't turn from me till you have heard my story. Fanny Duval, the wretched woman—who—who—died, had come into possession of a number of letters, written by other people in former days to a man who is now a friend of hers. Among them were some of mine.

Al. Of yours! . . .

Dora. Yes, of mine—girlish, foolish letters, with absolutely no harm in them, except that they were addressed to one whose admiration had flattered my youthful vanity, and to whom I had heedlessly written, without a thought of the possible consequences. The letters came into the possession of Madame Duval.

Al. Oh, that you should have had anything to do with that woman!

Dora. You shall hear. She came into possession of the letters, and, in order to extort money, wrote to me that she would restore them to me if I would go myself to fetch them at the Opera, where she was to be that night. I thought only of my anxiety to get them back—I felt that, before I married your uncle, I must break with the whole of my wretched past—I went. She gave me the letters—gave them to me with taunting and insulting words. In my agitation I made a hasty step forward—she started back, caught her foot and fell—I saw a shining thing in her hand—it was a little dagger that hung at her side in a sheath, and with which she had been playing as she talked. I left her—I was thickly veiled, so no one had recognised me. The next morning all Paris was ringing with the crime that had been committed at the Opera the night before, but which was no crime—the mysterious event of which I only knew the secret—and of which, before God, I have told you the true story now !

Al. (covering her face with her hands).   Oh, this is too horrible !

Dora.   What, can it be that you do not believe me ? that you can think me guilty of—of——

Al.   No, no—I believe you to be innocent of *that*—but the whole thing is so dreadful—that you should have been there—that you should have gone to that woman !

Dora: Yes, I know, I feel it all—but oh, I have suffered enough to expiate far more than a mere girlish imprudence.

Al. (starting).   Suppose my uncle were to find out you had been at the Opera that evening ?   oh, what would happen ?   [*Dora shudders.*

Al.   I verily believe it would be a death blow to him.

Dora.   But he never will know—he never need.   Oh, keep my secret !   I told it you because the burden was too great for me to bear alone—I am very, very unhappy !

[*Sinks down by table, with her face in her hands, and bursts into tears.*

Al.   I am so sorry for you—but I can do nothing for you, I feel—nothing——

Dora.   Yes, you can indeed, if you will only believe in me—your sympathy, your womanly support will be everything—you make me feel that my life is still worth enduring!

Philip (outside).   Your mistress is not gone out yet, I suppose ?

Al.   There is my husband !

Dora.   Oh, what shall I do ?

Al.   Come to my room, and bathe your face—I will tell him presently that you are here—that you are not well.

[*Exeunt together.*

Enter Philip, hurried'y.

Ph.   Aline ! Aline ! where are you ?   Aline !

Enter Aline.

Ph.   Aline, I have a piece of such good news for you -
I am on the track !   [*Al. starts.*]   Imagine my joy ! don't you understand ?   I have made a discovery—I am actually on the track of the mystery that has been baffling my sage uncle, and the whole of Paris, for the last month !   Are you not delighted ?

Al. (nervously).   Yes, dear Philip, yes—indeed—I am.

Ph.   You don't look it, I must say !   What is the matter ? you don't look like yourself— don't you feel well ?

Al.   Yes—that is I have a headache—a severe headache.

Ph.   It must have come on very suddenly.

Al.   Yes, it did—since you left me.

Ph.   Poor darling !   I am so sorry—but this news will do you good, I am sure.   I rushed off here at once, knowing how you would sympathise in my joy.

Al.   Of course, of course, dear Philip—you know I do.

[*Looking at door.*

Ph.   I will tell you how it was.   I went to the place where the *pièces de conviction* are—old Wartel is a great friend of mine, and let me in under seal of secrecy—I don't know what my uncle would have said if he had known ! Well, and one of these things was a splendid cloak with a fur lining.   I thought how I should like to have one like it for you !

Al.   Oh, don't, Philip——

Ph.   Why, what is the matter with you ?

Al.   You know how nervous it always makes me to hear about these things.

Ph. (vexed).   I should have thought that when it is something which affects me so nearly you could for once have put your nervousness aside—you cannot have realised how immensely important it would be to me and my whole future career if I, and no one else, had first got on the track of the discovery.

Al.   Yes, yes—I quite understand it ! forgive me, dear Philip—tell me the rest.

Ph.   Well, I was turning over this fur cloak, running my hand mechanically over the soft warm lining, when my hand slipped inside a slit in the fur, and there I found a crumpled-up letter, that had evidently slid into a hole in the lining by mistake, instead of the pocket.

Al.   A letter ! then was there anything to show who did—the murder ?

Ph.   My dear wife! certainly women were not cut out for judicial inquiries.   You don't suppose that the assassin wrote his victim a polite note, requesting the pleasure of her company at the Opera on such a night, to be murdered ? Ha ! ha ! no, that is not how those things are done, I fancy.

Al. (shuddering).   Don't, Philip, don't—you should not laugh at those horrible things.

Ph.   My dear girl, I am quite willing to admit that the whole thing is very shocking and so on—still I believe that everyone agrees that the poor creature who died is no great loss to society, and probably it will be found that she who did the deed—for I mean to find her, I can tell you—was not much better.

Al. (with emotion).   Ah, how can you know—how can you tell the history of the woman who has such a horrible misfortune on her conscience ?

Ph. Misfortune ! well, that is a polite way of putting it, certainly—it was a *contretemps* which I fancy might have been avoided.

Al. But how do you know that the woman who did it, or rather who is supposed to have done it, did it intention-ally ?

Ph. (stares at her). My dear little wife, you have encouraged yourself in these nervous apprehensions about crimes, and so on, till you are ready to work yourself into all kinds of imaginations about them. A murder is not a thing that one can commonly do from an oversight—people don't generally drop a corpse in an opera box with-out noticing it, as they would a pocket-handkerchief. No, no, depend on it, criminals are not such an ill-used class as you seem to think—and I am sure that when all this affair is brought to the light of day, as I mean it to be, even your sympathies will not be with the culprit.

Al. (with an effort). Does your uncle know ?

Ph. Of what I have found, do you mean ? no, he does not yet—but I have sent him an urgent note, asking him if he can come here in the midday interval, as I have some-thing important to communicate to him. I did not like to take it to him to the palace, after what he said this morn-ing, as he does not want the fact of his nephew's investiga-tions to be made public. And I did not like to meet him out of doors anywhere, as I feel this is so tremendous it ought only to be discussed within four walls !

> [*Takes a paper from his pocket. Aline looks at it,
> and gives a cry.*

Ph. Aline, what is the meaning of all this ?

Al. It is only that—that—I was agitated at seeing the letter found in such a place.

Ph. Upon my word ! I should have thought you were above these typical absurdities of women !

> [*Al. draws her handkerchief out to put it to her eyes—*

*the letter from Dora drops to the ground—she
snatches at it—Ph. picks it up without looking at
it, and holds it playfully behind him.*

Ph. Now, what will you give me, if I give you back
your dear *billet doux*? Only see what a model husband I
am! I don't even look to see whose writing it is! There is
this to be said, that you generally insist on my reading all
the effusions you receive from your dear friends, which has
given me rather a distaste for them—like the girls in the
confectioners' shops, who are allowed to eat bonbons till
they won't look at another. Come, give me a kiss, and you
shall have it.

Al. Very well. [*Kisses him hurriedly.*] Don't tease
me, Philip.

Ph. Good girl—here it is then! Why, you silly child!
your hands are trembling! let me put it into your pocket
for you [*As he puts it in he sees the writing on the envelope
and starts*]—why—stay!—where have I seen that writing
before? Why—good heavens!—Aline—from whom is this
letter?

Al. You said just now you did not want to know—
give it to me—give me my letter.

Ph. Aline, what does this mean? I am not violating
your confidence, as you may see—I have seen but the
envelope, not the contents of your letter—but this is too
important a coincidence not to be explained. Look at
those two letters—look at them!

Al. (faintly). I don't want to see them—you know I
told you I can't bear to see that kind of thing.

Ph. Nay, this is too serious to put me off with a whim
—you must look at those two letters side by side—one that
was found in the murdered woman's cloak, and one that has
just fallen out of your own pocket—look at them, and explain to me how it is that the handwriting is the same on
both!

Al.   I cannot—I cannot.

Ph.   You cannot? Great God! am I mad? Aline—Aline—what can you, my wife, have to do with this horrible business? what can you possibly have to do with it?   [*Al. is silent.*

Ph.   This, then, was the reason of your agitation when I came in and told you of my discovery—when you saw the writing on the letter! What does it all mean? Aline, my wife, tell me—I insist upon knowing—who wrote that letter in your hand?

            [*Dora has entered during the last sentence.*

Dora.   I did.

Ph.   Madame Larivière!! . . . I did not know you were here—still less could I have imagined that my wife knew of your presence at our interview, without telling me.

Al. (imploringly).   Philip!

Ph. (sternly).   Aline, perhaps you will be good enough to explain the mysteries and conspiracies you have suddenly taken to indulging in, and by which, I must confess, I am a good deal bewildered.

Dora.   It is not your wife's fault, Monsieur Darcy, that she has been led into a mystery—it is mine.

Ph.   Then it is you apparently, Madame Larivière, that I must ask for an explanation of what certainly needs most urgently to be explained—this letter to my wife, you say, is in your handwriting?

Dora.   It is.

Ph.   And this other one, then, which appears to be exactly like it—is that yours also?

Dora.   The other? . . [*Approaches, looks at it, and start*]—yes—yes, it is—where did you find that letter? it is mine—oh, give it me back!   .

Ph.   Nay, I am afraid I cannot do that, considering the circumstances under which it was found.

Dora.   Where was it found?

Ph. Inside the lining of a cloak, where it had slipped by mistake—a cloak belonging to Madame Duval, who was murdered at the Opera on March 20.

Dora. Good heavens ! I am lost, then !

[*Covers her face with her hands.*

Ph. Lost ! . . . what does this mean ?

Al. Oh, Philip, do not be cruel !

Ph. Cruel ! . . I am not cruel that I know of—but this has gone too far now to go back—I must have this explained.

Al. Oh, Philip—it was not her fault—it was not indeed !

Ph. What was not her fault ? Madame Larivière, I must ask you most solemnly and earnestly to explain how it was that a letter in your handwriting came to be found in such a place ?

Dora. I will tell you all there is to tell—you shall know everything.

Ph. I shall be much obliged.

Dora. Your wife knows already——

Al. Oh, yes, Philip, she has told me—and I quite understand how it was.

Ph. Dear Aline, let Madame Larivière tell her own story.

Dora (with an effort). I will. The letter of which that is a fragment is one of several which I wrote years ago, to one of my male acquaintance. They were such letters as a young married woman might write, without a thought of harm.

Al. Yes, indeed—oh, Philip, you will see——

Dora. We were on terms of easy *camaraderie*—he called me by my name and I him by his, in a way which to me then seemed natural enough, but which I know now would be disapproved of in more decorous society. Enough —I lost sight of him and of all the people I had known—for my husband died—I left Paris, and was thrown on the world alone.

Al.   Oh, Philip, think if I were thrown on the world alone, without you !   [*Ph. is silent.*

Dora.   I have told your wife all this story already.

Ph.   All the same, I must ask you to repeat it to me— it is absolutely essential that I should know it.

Dora.   I came back at length to Paris. I made friends with—with—your uncle, the best and most honourable of men—for his sake, I regretted the associations of my youth, the adventurers among whom my lot had been cast. Sheltered by his love, I looked forward to beginning my life again, to enjoying tranquillity and peace where I had only known a precarious and adventurous existence. I had known Fanny Duval years ago, when I first came to Paris, but I had never liked her. The other day I at last met her again, when I was with your uncle. She advanced, smiling, to claim my acquaintance—I was foolish enough to receive her with marked coldness—foolish, inasmuch as I did not realise that I might be making a deadly enemy of her. She took her revenge ! she wrote to me that evening, saying that she had found some letters of mine among the papers of a man we both knew, and that she would enclose them the next day to your uncle, Monsieur Darcy, unless I would go that same evening to the Opera, to beg them humbly from her myself. I went, in order that no trace of my past might remain to cast its shadow on my future—if I had had time to think, I should have gone straight to your uncle instead, and told him the whole story.   I humbled myself by asking her for the letters—she drew the packet from her cloak, and gave them to me with words of mocking con- gratulation—I started forward angrily—she drew back— as she did so she fell, I thought fainting—and I left her.

Al.   There now, you see, Philip—everything is ex- plained.

Ph. Hardly, it seems to me. Do you mean to say that you left her lying there alone, without an attempt to summon help ?

Dora. I thought she was only fainting, or even pretending to faint—and that in a moment she would recover—my one idea was to get away without being seen—and I succeeded in doing so, as the play was going on, and the passages were empty. I then made up my mind that the next morning I would tell your uncle the whole story. When the morning came it was too late—I learnt, to my horror, from the papers that the unhappy woman had been found dead where I left her.

Al. Now you understand it all, Philip—don't you ?

[*Anxiously.*

Ph. (pointedly). No, I cannot say that I do as yet—I heard [*to Dora*] that she had died of a wound in her chest, supposed to have been inflicted by some sharp instrument, which was afterwards found on the ground near her—how do you account for that ?

Dora. She must have fallen on the edge of a beautiful little jewelled dagger she always wore, which hung at her side, and with which she had been mechanically playing, pulling it up and down as she talked.

[*A moment's silence.*

Ph. Madame Larivière, you must see that it is impossible for me to keep the story you have just told me, to myself—it is of the gravest importance that my uncle should know it at once.

Dora. Your uncle ! . . . Oh, no—no !

Al. Oh, Philip !

Ph. That he should hear it, just as you have told it to me !

Dora. Oh, think what that means to me—think what a sentence of banishment—of death—you are pronouncing on my life !

[*Ph. is silent.*

Dora. Think of my marriage—of the happy life, the peace and shelter opening before me—of *his* happiness too, which you will destroy !

Ph. Yes, I think of it all—and your words make my duty doubly hard for me.

Dora. Duty ! and to that grim, pitiless abstraction you would sacrifice your uncle's whole life, as well as mine !

Ph. Nay, as for my uncle, remember that you are ready to sacrifice him also—for you would darken his existence with the shadow of your own disgrace.

[*Darcy has opened the door unperceived by the others, and overhears the last sentence.*

Darcy. Philip ! is it possible that you are addressing those words to Madame Larivière ? What does this mean ?

Ph. (gravely). Ask Madame Larivière herself what it means.

Darcy (with respectful tenderness, looking at Dora, who is leaning against the table, struggling with her emotion). No, I am not going to ask Madame Larivière for the explanation of the insults which I have heard.

Dora (with emotion). Ah, you are the most generous of men !

Ph. Uncle, I do not deserve your reproaches——

Darcy (coldly). Let us pass to the matter in hand. You have sent for me, I understood, on urgent business.

Ph. (with an effort). Yes, I had made an important discovery concerning the crime committed at the Opera— but since . . .   [*He hesitates.*

Darcy (coldly). Since, you have found that the important discovery comes to nothing ? that does not surprise me—I never had much faith in your investigations.

Ph. (slowly). No—it is that—that the discovery is yet more important than I thought.

Darcy (bewildered).   More important ?

[*He looks from one to the other. Philip's eyes are cast down, Dora hides her face in her hands.*

Darcy (speaks with increasing emotion). Philip, Dora—what is this mystery ? Your manner leads me to suppose that—that—no, it cannot be ! the thought is too horrible Dora—oh, speak : the discovery cannot be connected with—with you ?

Dora.   It is.

Darcy.   Good God !

Ph.   This paper was found inside the murdered woman' cloak.

Darcy (looks at it).   Ah ! !

[*He sinks into a chair by the table, utterly overcome, his head on his folded arms.*

Dora goes sadly out. As she reaches the door she says softly Good-bye—for ever !

Curtain.

A WOMAN OF CULTURE

COMEDIETTA IN ONE ACT.

CHARACTERS.

MRS. CHESTER, a young widow—a woman of culture.
EVELYN BARRINGTON, her ward.
MRS. SYMONDS.
MAJOR SYMONDS, one of Evelyn's guardians.
HERBERT SANDFORD, a rising barrister.

TIME.—July 1885.

SCENE.—*Mrs. Chester's drawing-room in Brook Street, well furnished. A great many books and papers about. Door at back, R.C. Writing-table at back, L.C., covered with papers—the table stands at right angles to the wall, and in such a way that the face of the person writing is turned from the door. Chairs R. and L. of writing-table. Sofa in front, R., parallel to side wall. Table R.C. Chair L. of table. Table L. against wall, with bookstand on it. Chair or divan L.C., &c. &c.*

Enter Major Symonds and Evelyn, from a walk.

Maj. S. (looking round). No one here !

Evel. Aunt Diana is out, I suppose ?

Maj. S. She is probably addressing the electors somewhere.

Evel. (laughing). Now, Uncle John, for shame ! you know you mustn't say that kind of thing here.

Maj. S. What, do people never talk nonsense in Mrs. Chester's house ?

Evel. (laughing). Never !

Maj. S. Ahem !—how do *you* get on then ? what about all the jokes we've been having during our walk, eh ? we must take care not to repeat any of them here ! We have had a very pleasant afternoon together, my dear— and I'm very much obliged to you for taking me out, though you *have* nearly given me brain fever by dragging me through the Inventions Exhibition !

Evel. Dear, dear uncle ! how I wish I were going back to Lowndes Square with you, instead of staying here !

Maj. S. Why, what nonsense, my little girl ! you don't seem to value your privileges in having such a clever woman as your aunt, Mrs. Chester, for your guardian— you will be much better off staying here with her than you would be with humdrum folks like us.

Evel. Oh, no, Uncle John, indeed I shan't. Aunt Diana is very kind, of course—and I'm sure she wants to do me all the good in the world——

Maj. S. That must be rather trying.

Evel. But oh, she is so clever, and so serious, and so terribly in earnest about everything, and so are her friends ! They none of them will talk to me, you know, because I am so stupid and ignorant.

Maj. S. That is their loss, then, my darling, I'm sure, not yours. Conversation with these argumentative people is like trying to walk along a road, and being pulled up at every dozen yards by a prickly hedge—you get through it and over it, somehow—but you are very much scratched before you get to your journey's end.

Evel. Except—except Mr. Sandford—he is very nice, and—and—I think he likes talking to me—but Aunt. Diana won't let him.

Maj. S. Why not ?

G

Evel. Because she doesn't like him to waste his time ! So she sends me away, and then she talks to him about art, and religion, and evolution, and ever so many other elevated subjects !

Maj. S. Why don't you learn to talk about them too, then ?

Evel. Oh, because I couldn't ! I don't know anything about Art—Ambulance classes make me feel sick, and so does Vivisection—and I don't understand Redistribution or Women's Suffrage—and Sanitary Dustbins, and Overcrowding, are dirty and horrid. And as for the last thing my Aunt has taken up, the Pyc—Phys—Pish—Psychical Society, it frightens me nearly to death only to think of it ! Would you believe that she is busy collecting one thousand well-authenticated ghost stories !

Maj. S. Ha, ha, ha ! then that is why she asked me so anxiously yesterday if I had ever seen an apparition—and was quite disappointed when I said I had never had the slightest symptom of one ! It is too absurd that she and all the other members of the society should go about saying to people, 'Put out your tongue and let's see if there's a ghost on it ! '

Evel. (in fits of laughter). Oh, Uncle John, if Aunt Diana heard you, what would she say ?

Maj. S. The fact is, Mrs. Chester wants some one to look after her—she was a very delightful woman before her husband died, when she had a sensible male mind to prevent her from taking up all these follies.

Evel. They are rather trying, certainly, at times. Uncle—I'll tell you a great secret—I wish she were not my guardian at all !

Maj. S. (pretending to be shocked). Evelyn ! you horrify me !

Evel. I don't care—I want to have only you for my guardian, you dear old uncle, nobody else !

Maj. S. Very well, then, I'll tell *you* a great secret—Mrs. Chester does not want to be your guardian either—she told me so the other day!

Evel. Oh, how horrid of her!

Maj. S. Well, upon my word, I don't see that. It isn't nearly as horrid of her as it is of you, you heartless, perverse, ungrateful little girl!

Evel. Oh, uncle, do tell me about it! am I not going to live here then, but to live with you always? how nice! and we'll ride in the Park, and read novels, and go to the theatre, and waste our time the whole day long! what fun we shall have!

Maj. S. My dear, you must have a little mercy on me! Pity the pleasures of a poor old man! Besides, what would your Aunt Diana say to such a programme?

Evel. (joyfully). She won't have anything to do with it!   [*Claps her hands and dances for joy, then stops abruptly as door opens.*

Enter Mrs. Chester, with papers in her hand.

Evel. (embarrassed). Oh, Aunt Diana—you are not out? you are at home, then?

Mrs. C. Yes, I am at home, as you may see—that seems an obvious and somewhat unnecessary remark of yours. I was receiving a deputation in the library, whence I heard—and *they* heard—[*severely*]—your shrieks of laughter just now.

Evel. I am so sorry, aunt.

Maj. S. Did we disturb the deputation? was it a nervous one?

Mrs. C. No, as it happens, you did not disturb them, as fortunately they were just taking leave of me. Otherwise, sounds of shrill mirth, not to say giggling, are not favourable to the consideration of serious questions.

    [*Goes to writing-table, to put down papers.*

Maj. S. (aside to Evelyn). I feel crushed—I'm going !

Evel. (aside to Maj. S). No, no—pray don't !

Mrs. C. (turning over papers). Major Symonds, before you go, I just wanted to ask you about a case I am interested in. (*Searching*) I wonder where those papers on the Welfare of the Blind have been put ? Dear me, here they are with the Bluebooks on Egypt—how very stupid of the maids ! [*Comes forward to Maj. S.*] I suppose you don't happen to want a servant ?

Maj. S. What sort of one ?

Mrs. C. Well—this man is blind—but it is really his only drawback.

Maj. S. Oh, indeed ! thank you, no—not just at this moment. I have as many blind servants as I want already, thank you—at least they have all the ordinary symptoms of blindness, as they never see anything they look for, or discover when a button is missing, or when my white ties are not ironed straight !

[*Evel. laughs—Mrs. C. looks at her severely.*

Mrs. C. This man is very clever with his hands, I assure you, in spite of his blindness—he was once a brushmaker and weaver, but now he wants to go into domestic service.

Maj. S. Well, it is very good of you to have thought of me, but I generally find that when people recommend their *protégés* to me, it is more from a consideration of their wants than of mine. I remember one *protégé* of yours that I took in, who was supposed to be in delicate health, and only to require rest and a comfortable home. He recovered so quickly under my care, that the night after he came he was able to sit up and see a few friends—with whom, and some of my forks, he departed in a state of inebriation, at two o'clock in the morning.

Mrs. C. Ah, I remember. Yes, I happened to be mistaken in that man, certainly—but of course everyone is liable to be mistaken at times, though I must admit it does not very often happen to me.

Maj. S. Besides, I would rather not have my brushes made by a blind man, thank you. He'd be putting the bristles into the wrong place, the handle or somewhere, I know !   [*Winks at Evelyn.*

Evel. (giggling). Oh, uncle, how can you ?

Mrs. C. (impatiently). Hadn't you better go and take off your things, Evelyn, and then get something to do ? There is no greater waste of time than to dawdle about with your bonnet on. It is quite impossible to settle to any serious occupation in a bonnet.

Evel. Very well, Aunt Diana. (Aside to Maj. S. as she passes) Try to find out about our secret, mind—don't forget.   [*Exit Evelyn.*

Maj. S. (looking after her with a smile). I must say, I can't fancy my little Evelyn sitting down to any very serious occupation, either with a bonnet or without one.

Mrs. C. No, it is what is inside her head, not outside, that is the obstacle. I fear she is deplorably shallow and frivolous.

Maj. S. Do you think so ? She seems to me to be one of the most charming girls I have ever met.

Mrs. C. Indeed ? I am afraid then that you have been unfortunate in your female acquaintance. She seems to *me*, on the contrary, just like a hundred other girls you may meet with on a summer's day.

Maj. S. That is the kind of summer's day I should enjoy—I should like to meet a hundred girls like her, very much.

Mrs. C. Because you are the sort of man who thinks any woman charming if only she smiles and simpers sweetly when she is spoken to, and agrees with everything that is said to her.

Maj. S. I quite admit it. I don't like those set-you-

down, advise-you-what-to-do young women, of which there
are so many in the world nowadays. I'm sure I don't
know where they all come from. Such things were never
heard of when I was young.   It is like one of these newly-
discovered diseases, unknown to our forefathers—an
epidemic of universal wisdom, to which the young are
especially liable ! ha, ha !   [*Mrs. C. remains grave.*

Mrs. C.   I wonder that Evelyn's parents, who in some
things were sensible enough, should have chosen for the
joint guardians of their child two people of such entirely
opposite views as you and myself, just because you happened
to be her mother's brother, and I her father's sister—especially with the absurd proviso, that for any decisive act in
her life she should require the consent of both of us.

Maj. S.   Yes, it is unfortunate—that might prove an
awkward condition, certainly.   (Aside) Especially with
regard to Sandford !

Mrs. C.   But, after all, I dare say it will not matter
much—for if the occasion were to arise, I suppose I should
be able to convert you to my opinion.

Maj. S.   Or perhaps I to bring you over to mine !

Mrs. C.   No, I hardly think that is likely, as mine
would probably be the right one.

Maj. S. (aside).   There is nothing like a modest self-con-
fidence to help one on in the world !   (Aloud) By the way,
Mrs. Chester, did you not ask me the other day whether,
after having assumed the office of guardian, it would be
possible to give it up ?

Mrs. C. (indifferently).   Did I ?   Yes, I remember now
that I did.   What about it ?

Maj. S. (with assumed unconcern).   Oh, only that as I
happened to be calling on Mr. Deeds, in Lincoln's Inn, the
other day, I asked him about the matter—and he said there
would not be the slightest difficulty.   So I begged him to

draw up the document, which now only needs your signature, and I brought it with me to-day to show you.

Mrs. C. Ah, indeed, thank you—but I almost think we had better leave things as they are. I don't think for Evelyn's sake that I ought to give it up, though I must say I despair of ever making anything of her.

Maj. S. Just as you think best, of course. (Aside) I must not show her how anxious I am, or she will not do it! (Aloud) But I should have thought that with your manifold occupations . . .

Mrs. C. Yes, it is very inconvenient. The fact is, that it was quite absurd making me her guardian at all, when one thinks of the numbers of idle women there are in the world, without an idea beyond matchmaking, who would have been too delighted to have taken charge of a commonplace girl like Evelyn.

Maj. S. (aside). Upon my word! (Aloud) Well, my wife and I fulfil those conditions. We are idle—we have no ideas, to speak of—we are commonplace—and we shall be delighted to take charge of Evelyn! Eh? ha, ha!

Mrs. C. (calmly). Yes, I know all that.

Maj. S. (nettled). Oh, you do, do you?

Mrs. C. But I doubt if I could reconcile it to my conscience to leave Evelyn entirely to your care.

Maj. S. (aside). Whew? . . . That's rather a heavy line to take! (Aloud) May I ask why?

Mrs. C. Because I fear that—you must pardon me for saying so—you have no lofty ideals, no progressive views, no ardent convictions, no desire to convert and improve the world, no comprehensive scheme of existence——

Maj. S. I beg your pardon—I have a very definite scheme of existence indeed, as far as Evelyn is concerned. I hope she will marry some nice young fellow, upright and honourable, with money enough to make her comfortable and give her as many new clothes as she wants—who will adore her, and make her as happy as she deserves to be.

Mrs. C.   Well—(*with a sigh*)—I suppose after all she is fit for nothing higher.

Maj. S.   Here is the deed I was speaking of, if you like to look at it.

Mrs. C.   Thank you.   [*Puts it carelessly on table.*]   I will look at it next week if I have time.   (*Then reflecting*) And yet, after all, Evelyn is the kind of girl whose only object it will probably be to marry and be established in life . . . she might perhaps be more likely to do so in a satisfactory way under your care than under mine, for of course none of the people she meets here are likely to be attracted by her—she is not intellectual enough.

Maj. S. (aside).   So much the worse for them, then, that's all I can say.   (Aloud) Ah, really.   I thought Mr. Sandford seemed to be attracted by her—but perhaps I was mistaken.

Mrs. C.   Mr. Sandford! what an utterly absurd idea! He sometimes, it is true, out of regard for me, is willing to descend to her level, and talk with her for a time, while I am busy—but it is out of pure kindness of heart, nothing else.

Maj. S.   What a very kind young gentleman he must be!

Mrs. C.   I can't imagine two people more dissimilar, less suited to one another, than Mr. Sandford and Evelyn.

Maj. S.   In what way?

Mrs. C.   In every way.   He is clever and ambitious— she is——

Maj. S.   Simple and domestic.

Mrs. C.   Well—I was going to say, humdrum and ignorant.   He is an ardent politician, of the advanced party— she does not know a Liberal from a Tory.

Maj. S.   Well, a good many people don't, nowadays.

Enter Evelyn.

Evel. What, Uncle John, still here?

Maj. S. Yes, you may well be surprised—you remind me that I have been here an unconscionably long time. My wife told me to wait here for her, but I don't suppose she will come now.

Mrs. C. (aside). Thank Heaven!

Maj. S. Good-bye, Mrs. Chester. (Carelessly) By the way, then, what about that paper? will you sign it now, and I will take it away with me, to save you any further trouble about it?

Mrs. C. What paper? Oh, yes—I remember. No, leave it there—I don't suppose I shall make any use of it after all.

Maj. S. (disappointed). Very well. Good-bye again, then. Good-bye, my little girl.

Evel. (aside). Well, uncle, well? what about it?—the secret?

> [*Maj. S. shakes his head, then points secretly to paper on writing-table. Evelyn looks about, bewildered—exit Maj. S.*

Mrs. C. (sitting at writing-table). What is it, Evelyn? what are you looking for?

Evel. (embarrassed). Nothing, aunt, nothing—I was just looking for—my book. Oh, there it is!

> [*Darts to other table and takes book.*

Mrs. C. I am glad to see you sitting down to read, Evelyn, instead of hanging about in that purposeless way of yours. What is your book?

Evel. 'Called Back.' Uncle John got it for me just now at the Underground station, and, oh! it does look so interesting!

Mrs. C. 'Called Back!' Nonsense! How can you waste your time over such things? [*Takes book from Evelyn,*

and throws it back on to table.] You had far better go and
get that Report of the Chamber of Agriculture I told you
to read, which is on the table in my bedroom.

Evel. Very well, aunt. (Aside) Just when I was so
comfortable !   [*Going.*

Mrs. C. (aside). What am I to do with this girl?
(Aloud) Here, Evelyn, wait a moment—I have been so busy
during the last week, ever since you came, that I really have
not had time to speak to you as seriously as I should wish
to do about the way you spend your time. [*Evelyn heaves a
sigh.*] If I were you I should map out each day according
to some settled plan. If you like, I will help you to draw
it up.

Evel. Oh, thank you, aunt, that is very kind of you—
but—but—I have an engagement book already, I suppose
that comes to the same thing.

Mrs. C. Where is it?

Evel. (unwillingly). Here.

Mrs. C. Let me see it. (*Reads*) 'Tuesday, 1st July'—
that is to-morrow—'nothing. Wednesday, Park at twelve
—Evening, Ver—Verbeck.' What is that?

Evel. (confused). Oh, that is the conjuror at Prince's
Hall, Piccadilly—Uncle John said he would take me.

Mrs. C. (grimly). So I should have expected. 'Thursday, Park at twelve—Exhibition at four with Loly Smith
—Friday, Whiteley's with Milly '—what on earth does that
mean?

Evel. Whiteley's is that big place in Westbourne Grove,
the shop, you know.

Mrs. C. And may I ask what you are going to do
there?

Evel. I only thought it would be amusing to go with
Milly Scott to see what it is like—she very often goes.

Mrs. C. I don't think that will be a very edifying
afternoon, I must say—to go across London with another

empty-headed girl, in order to gaze in at a shop window whose only merit is that it is a quarter of a mile long, to buy a dozen things you don't want, because they are a penny cheaper than anywhere else, and then pay two shillings for a hansom to bring them home in !

Evel. (timidly).   Of course, aunt, if you would rather I didn't . . .

Mrs. C. ' Rather you didn't ! '   I would rather you did not do anything that you do !   The way you fritter your days away is simply deplorable, nothing else !   Why don't you have some settled purpose, some definite scheme of life ? Everyone ought to have a definite purpose in life.

Evel. (ingeniously).   Oh, I think I should dislike that very much indeed !

Mrs. C.   Is there absolutely nothing you care about ?

Evel.   Oh, yes—heaps of things.

Mrs. C.   Nothing, I mean, that has any sense in it ? Are you fond of music ?

Evel.   Yes, passionately !

Mrs. C.   Yes, I know that is the consecrated phrase : everybody says they are passionately fond of music, even if they only go to a concert once a year, for which they are given a ticket !   Do you play at all ?

Evel.   A little.

Mrs. C.   And sing ?

Evel. (modestly).   A little—just enough to sing at parties, you know, while people are talking.

Mrs. C.   What sort of music do you prefer ?

Evel.   Oh, sheet music, certainly, that isn't bound —I hate having to take out a large fat book to dinner with me, for the sake of one song I may have to sing in the evening.

Mrs. C.   No—I mean the music of which particular school do you like best ?

Evel.   I liked the music at Miss Perkins's school best,

where they had none of those horrid concerts the girls have to play at, whether they like it or not, as they did at the one where poor Loly Smith was.

Mrs. C. (aside).   This is really hopeless ! (Aloud) You misapprehend my meaning—what I am trying to find out is, whether you prefer the music of one composer, or period, to another ?

Evel.   Oh, no, certainly not ! I don't care what it is. I like whatever takes my fancy, no matter where I find it, provided it is pretty.

Mrs. C. 'Pretty !' what an epithet to apply to music nowadays! You are quite mistaken—you should find out what you ought to admire, and like nothing else.

Evel. (impressed).   Really ? but wouldn't that be very difficult ? is that what you do ?

Mrs. C.   *I* am somewhat different—I, unfortunately perhaps for myself, have such keen, critical perceptions, such a sensitive impressionable nature, so fastidious a taste, that it is only what I know beforehand to be the very best of everything that in the least satisfies me.

Evel. (innocently).   Dear me ! how uncomfortable that must be !   Doesn't it make you feel very discontented ?

Mrs. C. (sententiously).   Discontent is the first step towards improvement.

Evel.   But one can't always be thinking of improvement.

Mrs. C.   I always am—if not of my own, of other people's.

Evel.   But do other people like being improved ?

Mrs. C.   They ought to, if they don't. And when I see they are going the wrong way about a thing, I tell them which is the right one.

Evel.   But suppose they do not consider it the right one ?

Mrs. C.   Then, they are mistaken. (Aside) Tiresome girl ! there is no making her understand anything !

Evel. I see !

Mrs. C. You have many opportunities of improving yourself here, where you associate with me and my friends. You should make the most of it, and endeavour, by intercourse with people of superior intellectual power, to get some ideas and information into your head.

Evel. Oh, aunt—it really is not my fault—but I never can find anything to say to your friends !

Mrs. C. And yet I saw you yesterday in conversation with Mr. Sandford. What were you talking about then ?

Evel. (smiling). Oh, Mr. Sandford, yes—*he* is very easy to talk to. Let me see—we were wondering how many lanterns are lighted every evening at the Inventions Exhibition—and then I asked him if we ought to say *Inven*tories or *In*ventories.

Mrs. C. I really believe you've got that Exhibition on your brain ! No wonder there is no room for anything else there. Could you have found no topic more likely to interest Mr. Sandford than such a very commonplace one?

Evel. What, for instance ?

Mrs. C. Let me see—the Channel Tunnel—I know he is interested in boring by compressed air—or the reorganising of the Household Suffrage. I think if you spoke to him on such subjects as these you would soon see a very marked alteration in his manner.

Evel. (aside). Yes, I think I probably should.

Mrs. C. Now do try to remember all I have been saying to you, like a good girl——

Evel. Yes, aunt, I will—and I will go now and get the Report on Agriculture to read.

Mrs. C. That's right. In the meantime just give me the 'Times' as you pass, off that table.

Evel. (looking at paper as she brings it). Why, here is Mr. Sandford's name ! Look !

Mrs. C. (eagerly). What about him ? [*Takes paper.*]

Good heavens ! the Member for Blackney is dead ! Mr.
Sandford has been asked to stand ! Dear me, how very
important ! we must take steps at once—not a moment
must be lost about the canvassing.   I will write directly to
Mr. Birmingham and Sir Charles Drake to ask them to
dinner to meet him.

Enter Maid.

Maid (announces).   Mr. Sandford.

Enter Sandford.   Exit Maid.

Mrs. C.   Mr. Sandford ! I am very glad to see you, as
indeed I always am, but more especially to-day, as we have
just seen the exciting news about Blackney in the paper.

Sandf.   Yes, it is exciting, isn't it ?   Were you excited
too, Miss Barrington ?

Evel. (shyly).   Yes, I was.

Mrs. C.   I am afraid Evelyn hardly cares enough about
politics yet to have been much interested.

Evel. (to Sandf.)   I was, though, all the same ! (Aside)
What a shame, when it was I saw it in the paper first !

Mrs. C. (to Sandf.)   And now, what are you going to do ?
I am frightfully and overwhelmingly busy to-day, but still I
must really hear all about your plans.   Evelyn, you will
hardly be interested in a dry political discussion, I imagine
—you need not stay if you do not feel inclined.   You will
find the pamphlet I told you of, in my room.

Evel.   Very well, I will get it.   [*Goes, slowly.*

Sandf. (opening door for her).   But why should you go
away, Miss Barrington ?

Mrs. C.   She will be much happier away !

Evel. (aside to Sandf.)   I shall come back again.

[*Exit Evelyn.*

Mrs. C.   It is much better that she should go—for it
would be very hard on you, when you have come intending,

I suppose, to have some sensible talk, that you should be put off with the meaningless chatter which girls of Evelyn's age consider conversation.

Sandf. Oh, not at all, I assure you—it is quite amusing hearing what they think !

Mrs. C. Yes, I know how good-natured you always are in that way. But now let us talk of something more interesting—about yourself, your views, and what you propose to do. Remember that you once promised not to take any important step without consulting me. (*Smiling.*)

Sandf. Indeed, I do remember—and it is for that I have come here to-day. I want to ask your advice.

Mrs. C. You know how delighted I always am to help you.

Sandf. You are the kindest and best of friends !

Mrs. C. Besides, I feel it is almost a duty with me not to keep my opinions to myself—I can't help realising that they are worth having, on most subjects, and that I *do* generally know better than other people.

Sandf. You do, certainly—and that is why I have come to appeal to your friendship, at a momentous crisis of my life.

Mrs. C. I have not the slightest hesitation about it— there is not a doubt in my mind as to what you should do.

Sandf. (surprised). Not a doubt ? . . .

Mrs. C. None whatever. You must organise your committee, make friends with the leading men on both sides, and begin canvassing at once, as energetically as possible. In the meantime I will ask Mr. Birmingham and Sir Charles Drake, and one or two other influential men, to meet you here at dinner, and then we can arrange the campaign.

Sandf. Oh ! . . . You were thinking of Blackney ?

Mrs. C. Of course ! Is it possible to think of anything else, while this immeasurably important question still remains unsettled ?

Sandf. Of course—what am I thinking of ?—certainly, some steps ought to be taken at once.   [*Preoccupied.*

Mrs. C. Who is your right-hand man—your chief supporter ? who is the Liberal agent for Blackney ? you were telling me his name the other day.

Sandf. Was I ? I don't remember. Oh, yes, to be sure I was.   It is Smith, I think—if it is not Smith it is Jenkins. . . .

Mrs. C. You are strangely absent to-day, and unlike yourself. Is there anything on your mind ? or is it the suddenness and agitation of all this that has upset you ?

Sandf. (hesitating). No, it is not that. . . (Resolutely) The fact is that it was not about Blackney at all that I came to ask your advice to-day.

Mrs. C. (eagerly and rapidly). Not about Blackney ? then what other place have you been asked to stand for ? you don't mean to say they've offered you Sleaford ? What a triumph it would be if you were returned *there*, in that nest of red-hot Tories.   Is it Sleaford ?

Sandf. No, it isn't.

Mrs. C. Then is it——

Sandf. It isn't any place at all.

Mrs. C. What, you don't mean to say it is a county ? Oh, how glorious ! only you must remember that a county is always much more expensive, as the voters who live in remote parts won't come to the poll unless you send cabs for them.

Sandf. (desperately). No, no, no ! Mrs. Chester, you have misunderstood me—it was not about Parliament at all that I came to speak to you.

Mrs. C. (disappointed). Not about Parliament ? then it can't be anything that matters much.   I shall be delighted to help and advise you all the same, of course, in any way I can—but still I feel that nothing else is of much importance just now.

Sandf. I wish I thought so too !

Mrs. C. (amazed). Why, what extraordinary change has come over you ?

Sandf. The fact is, that I am—I am—in love !

Mrs. C. In love !!

Sandf. In love. I must admit it !

Mrs. C. Oh, what a very unfortunate moment to have chosen !

Sandf. Yes, after all the discussions we have had on the subject, all the derision we have heaped upon it, all my firm resolutions not to succumb for at least ten years longer, I am as utterly, as ridiculously in love as it is possible for a man to be ! Now, do you despise me ?

Mrs. C. N—no—I don't despise you exactly—but I am a little surprised, I must confess.

Sandf. Yes, that comes to much the same thing—I know what people mean when they say they are surprised at you !

Mrs. C. I can't help regretting it should have happened just at this juncture, as I am terribly afraid it will stand in the way of your election.

Sandf. Don't say that you disapprove of me, just when I have come to ask your advice——

Mrs. C. And to disregard it, I suppose, as people always do on these occasions !

Sandf. I hope not.

Mrs. C. You must remember that I am still quite in the dark as to whether the object of your love is worthy or not.

Sandf. You ought to know that, of all people in the world—you who must best know her real character——

Mrs. C. I ? . . .

Sandf. Yes, you—you who have helped me for the last two years by your untiring sympathy and friendship—who

H

have been my guide and counsellor—the confidente of every hope, every ambition of mine as it arose——

Mrs. C. Mr. Sandford—you bewilder me——

Sandf. Listen to me again now! . . . in your hands the decision principally rests—the decision I await in trembling suspense, yet hardly dare to ask for.

Mrs. C. I am so taken by surprise that I hardly know what to say——

Sandf. Taken by surprise? Do you mean to say you had no suspicion of my attachment?

Mrs. C. Well, I have sometimes thought——But then, you know, people are so liable to be mistaken in these matters—one is so apt to believe the thing one wishes to believe!

Sandf. One wishes to believe! How good of you to say so! You will be on my side, then? your own kind heart will plead my cause with her whom I love.

Enter Major and Mrs. Symonds.

Mrs. C. (bored, aside). What, again?

Mrs. S. (effusively). Well, dear Diana, and how are you? It seems to me positively an age since we met!

[*Kisses her. Mrs. C. cold.*

Mrs. C. Does it? It has not seemed to me so very long.

Mrs. S. I said to John this morning, 'Now mind, whatever happens, I must go and see Diana this afternoon.'

Mrs. C. Too kind of you.

Mrs. S. Not at all, my dear—besides I knew you would never forgive me if I didn't come near you for so long. But John, great stupid creature that he is, instead of waiting for me here as I asked him, must needs leave before I got here [*smiling at her husband*]. However, fortunately I met him in Piccadilly on the way, so I brought him back again.

Mrs. C. I see. (Aside).

Maj. S. Behold the melancholy result of having a wife Mr. Sandford! Take a warning by me—I am not even allowed to walk down Piccadilly in which direction I like

Mrs. S. Now, John, you are really too bad ! [*Mrs. C bored.*] Very hot to-day, isn't it ?

Sandf. Very—one of the hottest days we have had.

Maj. S. But not quite so oppressive as last night—do you think so, Mrs. Chester ?

Mrs. C. I never discuss the weather.

Maj. S. Oh ! . . . I really beg your pardon.

Mrs. S. And what were you talking about, then, when we came in ? Something very clever, I am sure !

Mrs. C. (embarrassed). We were having a discussion on—on—politics.

Maj. S. On politics—indeed. Politics is a most absorbing subject, don't you find it so ?

Mrs. C. It is, indeed—the most absorbing of all.

Maj. S. Well, I don't know that I would go quite so far as that. And where is Evelyn ? she was not included in the political discussion, I presume ?

Mrs. C. No, she does not care about these things, I am sorry to say—she preferred to go to her room.

Maj. S. (aside). I dare say—yes !

Mrs. S. And so, Mr. Sandford, I hear you have decided to make the fatal plunge—that you are, in fact, in the position of a man who is going to propose, and does not know whether he will be accepted.

[*Mrs. C. and Sandf. startled.*

Sandf. Why, who told you . . . . ?

Mrs. S. (surprised). Who told me ? It was in the paper this morning—about your standing for Blackney John read it out to me at breakfast, didn't you, John ?

Sandf. (relieved). Oh, yes—yes! it is quite true, I am going to try my chance at Blackney.

Maj. S. Well, I wish you luck—though you are on the wrong side, mind!

Sandf. Thank you.

Mrs. S. I was *so* interested when I heard of it! I didn't read it myself till this afternoon, as John of course takes possession of the paper at breakfast, as every husband does, and I don't get it for ever so long afterwards.

Maj. S. (laughing). Of course. It is an Englishman's prerogative. What do women want with a newspaper at breakfast? they read nothing but the advertisement sheet, and the letters from British Matrons about the Royal Academy, and that sort of thing.

Mrs. S. (laughing). What a shame, John! That's the way he always goes on, Mr. Sandford—you wouldn't believe the things he says sometimes—it is too bad of him, it is really! Never mind, Diana, we know that we women are not quite so frivolous as he tries to make out, are we?

Mrs. C. (stiffly). Thank you, I am quite aware that *I*, at any rate, am not in the least frivolous—I do not feel the slightest anxiety on that score.

Maj. S. No, I must say I think you may feel quite comfortable about it, ha, ha!

Mrs. C. (coldly, looking among papers on writing-table). I am afraid that jokes are lost upon me—as I have often told you, I have no sense of humour.

Maj. S. (laughs aside). Why, what a formidable array of papers, Mrs. Chester! I don't wonder you can't lay your hand on the one you want. Is it the one I left with you this morning that you are looking for? that is it, I believe.

> [*Taking up deed. During the following, Mrs. C.
> and Maj. S. at back, R. and L. of writing-table
> Mrs. S. and Sandf. talking, R. at sofa.*

Mrs. C. No, that is not the one I was looking for. It was the draft of a scheme for a Mutual Improvement Society.

Maj. S. I see you have not signed this one yet—after all, as you say perhaps it is better left alone. I think I would rather you continued to share my responsibility—[*with intention*]—being a guardian takes up a great deal of time, and means a lot of worry and trouble to fulfil the duties properly.

Mrs. C. (with a sigh). It does, indeed! (Aside) Besides, how can I fulfil them now, after what has passed, and the new obligations I have undertaken? how can I now give up my time, to Evelyn or anyone else but—— [*Looks fondly at Sandf. Maj. S. putting deed ostentatiously into his pocket—Mrs. C. holds out her hand for it.*] Stay, give it to me—I have changed my mind—I will sign it. [*Maj. S. affects indifference to conceal his delight—Mrs. C. sits down to writing-table, holding her pen ready as she speaks—Maj. S. watches her.*] I feel I should never be able to fulfil the duties properly—I should have liked to have raised Evelyn nearer to my own level, but I am really too busy to attempt it—and now this election puts the finishing stroke, by overwhelming me with work for the next fortnight.

> [*Dips pen into ink. Just as she is going to sign, enter Maid.*

Maid. Please, ma'am [*Mrs. C. turns round and puts down her pen—Maj. S. makes a gesture of disappointment*]—the Committee of the Improvement Society is downstairs.

Mrs. C. Dear me, yes—I forgot they were coming so early, and I have not yet found that paper—how unfortunate! How many are there?

Maid. Seven ladies, ma'am, and one gentleman.

Mrs. C. I will go and speak to them. [*Goes to door—

turns bac'.] No—ask if they will have the goodness to wait a few minutes, while I get their papers ready.

Maid.   Yes, ma'am.   [*Exit Maid.*

Mrs. C.   I do wonder what I have done with that prospectus !   [*Turns over papers.*

Maj. S. (indifferently).   What about this, then ? will you sign it now ?

Mrs. C.   I really don't think I have time to-day.

Maj. S. (carelessly).   Just as you like, of course—but it would not take you long just to write your name, and I really don't see how you can possibly have time to look after Evelyn, with committees, and elections, and all that you have to do.

Mrs. C.   No—that is true—I suppose I must give it up.
    [*Hesitates a moment, then signs paper and gives it to Maj. S.*

Maj. S.   Thank you. (Aside) Victory ! my little Evelyn will thank me for this morning's work ! *now* we shall see !   [*Puts paper in his pocket—comes forward, L.*

Mr. C.   Ah, here is the prospectus, at last.
    [*Comes forward with paper.*

Mrs. S.   What is it about ?

Mrs. C.   It is the draft scheme of the society (To Sandford) we were speaking of the other day.

Mrs. S.   But may *we* not hear about it too ? I am very much interested in schemes, I assure you, though I don't understand anything about inventing them, ha, ha !

Mrs. C.   I don't suppose that this will interest you in the very least. It occurred to me as desirable that a small number of suitable people should form themselves into a Society, to be called the Society of Mutual Improvement, each member of which should make it his or her duty to improve all the other members.

Maj. S.   It will be rather a dangerous experiment, I should imagine.

Mrs. C. I don't see why.

Mrs. S. If I were to try to improve other people, I should be so afraid that they might know better than myself after all !

Mrs. C. (pointedly). Of course, that is more likely to happen in some cases than in others—besides, people with any misgivings of that kind are not fit and proper persons to join the Society.

Sandf. Have you drawn up the rules of the Society yet ?

Mrs. S. Yes, pray do let us hear how they are to set about improving each other.

Maj. S. First rule—'No member to improve more than two other members at the same time !'

[*Mrs. S. and Sandf. laugh—Mrs. C. looks severe.*

Mrs. C. (reads from prospectus). 'By pointing out the weak places in each person's pet theory—by contradicting and correcting them whenever they make a statement of fact—by questioning any authority they may bring to bear on the subject, and by generally setting them right on any political, social, or general topic they may happen to discuss.'

Mrs. S. Dear me, I am afraid it won't be a society for improving people's tempers, then ! [*Sandf. laughs.*

Mrs. C. (vexed). This is not the proper spirit in which to discuss so serious a scheme. (To Sandf.) I should hardly have thought that *you* would have joined in throwing ridicule on it, especially as I have drawn it up.

Sandf. (becoming serious). You know how deeply in terested I always am in everything you do.

Maj. S. (looking at them, aside). I wonder where Evelyn is all this time ?

Sandf. I am more than ready to help you to set it afloat.

Mrs. C. (tenderly). Thank you, dear friend—I know I can always rely on your support.

Sandf. In the meantime, can't I interview this committee downstairs for you, and get rid of them for the
moment ?

Mrs. C. Thank you so much—if you will really be so
good, (aside) as these two tiresome people show no signs
of going away ! (Aloud) Here is the prospectus—will you
give it to them, and tell them they shall hear from me
within the next fortnight ?   [*Exit Sandf.*

Mrs. C. It is absurd to think of attempting to organise
the society, or to attend to anything else, in fact, till the
election is over.

Mrs. S. But why should the election prevent *you* from
doing anything else, Diana ? you are not going to stand,
are you ?

Mrs. C. Not on this occasion, though I claim an entire
right to do so whenever I please—I was thinking only of
Mr. Sandford's election. There will be a great deal of
canvassing to be done, which ought to be begun as soon as
possible. Not a stone must be left unturned to secure his
return—we can't afford in these times to lose a good
Liberal in the House.

Mrs. S. Well, I'm glad I am not so fond of politics—
it must be very trying work, getting people elected in this
hot weather !

Maj. S. What will become of Evelyn, then, while you
are canvassing ? she will not be canvassing too, I imagine ?

Mrs. C. I imagine not.

Mrs. S. Then I hope we shall see a little more of her,
as you will be busy. She is the very dearest girl, to be
sure ! I quite envy you, having had her to stay with you
for a fortnight.

Mrs. C. (coldly). She is quiet and unobtrusive, certainly—and not more disturbing to have in the house than
an idle visitor must necessarily be.

Maj. S. She is so full of fun and animation—so much

to say for herself ! she quite kept the place alive when she was with us.

Mrs. C. She has plenty to say about the Inventions Exhibition, I dare say.

Maj. S. Well, it certainly offers a large field for conversation.

Enter Evelyn, with a large blue paper book open in her hand.

Evel. Aunt Diana, I just wanted to know—[*Looks round for Sandf.*] Oh, dear Aunt Lucy ! I didn't know you were here—why, Uncle John, you don't mean to say you have come back again ?

Maj. S. (laughing). Yes, I've come back to look after you, because I can't trust you out of my sight !

Mrs. S. There he is, at his jokes again as usual !

Evel. (aside to Maj. S.) Where is Mr. Sandford ? Is he gone ?

Maj. S. (points downwards mysteriously). Down there— that's where he is. [*Evel. looks bewildered.*] He is downstairs—to interview a committee—an improving committee !

Evel. (aside). Oh . . . . I see. (Aloud) Bother all these committees !

Maj. S. (aside). That's just my view. (Aloud) And what are you reading, Evelyn ? You see I was right to come and look after you, for the moment my back is turned you go and read a great fat blue book that I am sure you don't understand a word of !

Evel. First of all, it isn't a Bluebook.

Maj. S. Not a blue book ? What is it, then, pray ?

Evel. I mean it isn't what is called a Bluebook.

Maj. S. Oh, indeed ! then I must be getting blind, I suppose—I shall have to take to brush-making, or to domestic service, like Mrs. Chester's friend !

Evel. For shame, Uncle John ! [*Laughing.*] I know

what a Bluebook is, for Aunt Diana told me, and she is always right.

Maj. S. (aside). Except when she's wrong !

Evel. It is a kind of book they have in Parliament, with all the despatches from everywhere about everything printed in it, and it is always brought and read whenever there is a fuss.

Maj. S. I see ! you will become a very learned young woman in time, if you stay here long enough ! And what is this, then, may I ask ? 'Report of the 5th Session of Agriculture.' Good Lord ! do you understand any of it ?

Evel. Not much—in fact, I brought it down to ask Aunt Diana something. I want to know what 'unearned increment' means ? Do you know, Aunt Lucy ?

Mrs. S. My dear ! of course I don't ! Diana !

Mrs. C. Yes—what is it ?

Evel. I only wanted to know, aunt, what 'unearned increment' means ?

Mrs. C. Dear me, child, do you mean to say you don't know that ? Why, it is elementary ! 'unearned increment' means—but I really have not time to explain it to you now.

Enter Sandford.

Maj. S. Ah, there is Mr. Sandford ! he can tell us, I dare say, what it is all about.

Sandf. What is it ? Can I help you, Miss Barrington ?

[*Takes book.*

Evel. I thought you were gone !

Sandf. As if I should have gone without seeing you again !   [*Mrs. C. comes forward between them.*

Evel. (aloud). Here it is, you see—the 'unearned increment.'

Mrs. C. No, no—don't explain it to her, Mr. Sandford—one learns so much better by investigating things for oneself. Evelyn, if you will go into my room, and look on the bookcase to the right of my fireplace, you will see a thick brown book in four volumes, called ' Boodles on the Land Laws,' which will tell you everything you want to know.

Evel. Thank you very much, aunt—I will go presently.

Mrs. C. You had far better go now, while the passage is fresh in your mind.

Mrs. S. (to Evel.) Wait one moment, dear—don't go and study Mr. Boodles till we have left—we shall be going directly.

Evel. Where to ?

Maj. S. (to Evel.) It is a great secret—to the Inventions Exhibition !

Mrs. S. Won't you come too, Evelyn ?

Evel. I think not this afternoon, thank you, dear Aunt Lucy.

Mrs. C. What is that ? Where are you going, Lucy ?

Mrs. S. (apologetically). Why, my dear, we thought we would just go round by the Exhibition and hear Strauss's band they all make such a fuss about—I was asking Evelyn if she would not come too.

Mrs. C. (cordially). Oh, yes, do, Evelyn—go by all means !

Evel. I was just saying I would not go to-day, Aunt Diana—I have been thinking of what you said to me, about the Exhibition taking up too much of my time and thoughts, and I have decided to remain at home this afternoon.

Mrs. C. (vexed). Just as you like, of course. (To Sandf.) Did you hear that ? What do you say to it ? what shall we do ?

Sandf. I say it is delightful. Nothing could suit me better—we will have a most blissful afternoon.

Mrs. C. But do you realise that we shall be three instead of two ?

Sandf. Since the three are you, Miss Barrington and myself, nothing could be better.

Mrs. C. Then what about the election, and the letters was to write ?

Sandf. If you will be so good as to write them, Miss Barrington and I will entertain each other.

Mrs. C. You good, kind creature ! if you are really sure you don't mind that arrangement ?

[*During the above Evel., Maj. S. and Mrs. S. talking.*

Sandf. Mind it ! . . .   [*Maj. and Mrs. S. going.*

Mrs. S. Good-bye, then, dear Diana—so glad to have had this peep of you. When shall we meet again ?

Mrs. C. I really cannot tell.

Mrs. S. Won't you come to luncheon with me some day ? Do—and then we can have a drive afterwards, and do our shopping.

Mrs. C. (stiffly). Thank you, I am afraid that would hardly suit me—I make a rule of never going out to luncheon, as it breaks into my morning—I have no time to drive—and I never shop.

Mrs. S. Then when do you buy the things you want ?

Mrs. C. I don't.

Maj. S. Now, Lucy, are you coming away, or are you not ? It is no good, my dear, your trying to understand Mrs. Chester's scheme of life—it is quite beyond both of us, I assure you, ha ! ha ! come along.

Mrs. S. (laughing). Now just listen to the way he goes on ! Did you ever hear anything like him ? Good-bye, then, my pet. (To Evel.) Sorry you won't come with us. I really think that if Strauss is as good as they say, I shall have to come back and carry you off after all.

[*Exeunt Maj. and Mrs. Symonds.*

Mrs. C. I wonder, Evelyn, that you can encourage your uncle in his ill-timed pleasantries by laughing at them as persistently as you do.

Evel. (trying not to laugh). I am so sorry, Aunt Diana

—but he certainly is very funny sometimes, don't you think so ?

Mrs. C. (gravely). Not in the least. [*Goes to table at back. Sandf. and Evel. looking at each other.*] Now, Mr. Sandford, what about writing to these people ?

Sandf. Writing to . . . ?

Mrs. C. To the people I am to have to dinner to meet you.

Sandf. (confused). Oh, yes, of course—it will be good of you to write to them.

Mrs. C. But to whom ?

Sandf. All the influential people you can think of—as many Cabinet ministers and grand old statesmen as your dining-room will hold.

Mrs. C. Very well, I will make a list. Evelyn, you must entertain Mr. Sandford while I write my letters.

Evel. (demurely). Yes, aunt, I will try.

Mrs. C. (to Evel.) Just give me the 'Court Guide' from that table, will you ?

[*Evel. gets it from bookstand on table, L.*

Mrs. C. (aside to Evel.) And remember what I told you about talking as intelligently as you can—I want my niece to make a favourable impression on him.

Evel. (delighted). Oh, aunt, how good you are ! (Aside) What a change ! What can be the meaning of it, I wonder ?

[*Sits on sofa. Sandf. L. of table—he drops afterwards into chair behind it—Mrs. C. sitting at writing-table with her back to the others.*

Sandf. (to Evel.) Was this very portentous-looking volume the one you were studying upstairs ?

Evel. (Nods silently).

Sandf. What on earth were you doing it for ?

Evel. Because I was told !

Sandf. 'Reports on Agriculture !' I shouldn't have thought that was much in your line.

Evel. It isn't.

Sandf. And so, in order to read this, you went and sat upstairs all the time I was here !

Evel. It was not my fault, I assure you.

Sandf. Are you going to Lady Danby's to-night ?

Evel. No, I'm afraid not—we are going to the Royal Institution, to hear Professor Hibbert's lecture on the Theory of Atoms.

Sandf. (contemptuously). Theory of Grandmothers !

Evel. No—that's Darwin !   [*Both laugh.*

Sandf. Atoms, indeed—as if it were worth while troubling oneself about things of that size !

                       [*Both in fits of laughter.*

Mrs. C. (looking round surprised). What is the matter ? what are you saying ?

Sandf. (gravely). We were discussing the Theory of Atoms.

Mrs. C. (looks dubious). Oh, indeed—most deeply interesting—we shall hear all about it at Hibbert's lecture this evening.

Sandf. (to Mrs. C.) Don't you think you ought to go to Lady Danby's instead ? All the politicians in London will be there—we shall hear what is said about Blackney.

Mrs. C. That is true, yes—perhaps I ought to go—I suppose I must give up the lecture.   [*Evel. looks delighted.*

Mrs. C. But that is no reason why you should give it up too, Evelyn—I will write to Miss Poole to call for you, and you can go with her.

Evel. Oh, thank you, aunt—but I really don't care about it.

Mrs. C. Nonsense—you would care still less about Lady Danby's, where people would talk of nothing but the political situation.

Sandf (aside to Evel.) I have an idea—I will go to the lecture too !

Evel. Oh, will you ? How delightful !

Enter Maid.

Maid. Please, ma'am, a deputation from the Society of Ancient Buddhists is downstairs.

Mrs. C. Dear me, I wonder if I must see them. Is it a large deputation ?

Maid. Six young gentlemen, ma'am, and one old lady.

Mrs. C. Very well, show them into the library.

[*Maid he·itates.*

Mrs. C. Well, what is it ?

Maid. If you please, ma'am, three members of the Society of New Believers of the East arrived at the same time, and, as they are not on speaking terms with the Ancient Buddhists, they are all quarrelling in the hall.

Mrs. C. Oh, how very shocking ! these feuds are most unedifying. I must go and see what is happening.

[*Exit Mrs. C. hurriedly, followed by Maid.*

Sandf. How kind of the Old Buddhists, and New Believers, or whatever they are called ! Do you know that I have not had an opportunity of speaking to you alone for more than a week ?

Evel. Yes, I know—just a week—not since the ball at Mrs. Vernon's, where we sat under the stairs.

Sandf. And there is so much I want to say to you !

Evel. But Aunt Diana told me you would like me much better if we talked about other things.

Sandf. Did she ? What were they ?

Evel. Oh, all kinds of learned subjects— Household Suffrage—the Channel Tunnel—boring by compressed air, especially.

Sandf. I should be bored by compressed conversation if you did, I can tell you !

[*As door opens, Sandf., who has been getting closer to Evel., moves quickly away.*

Enter Mrs. Chester.

Mrs. C. What were you two talking about ?

Sandf. We were talking about—boring by compressed air !

Mrs. C. (looking approvingly at Evel.) A most interesting subject ! (I believe she might be made something of after all, if she would follow my directions.)

[*Goes back to her writing.*

Evel. And what about the deputation ?

Mrs. C. Would you believe that they had every one of them gone when I got downstairs, because the two parties wouldn't wait under the same roof ! I have no patience with them.

Evel. (to Sandf.) Perhaps, like the Kilkenny cats, they've devoured each other.

Sandf. (to Evel.) Happy thought—Kilkenny Buddhists —nothing left of them but their pigtails !   [*Both laugh.*

Evel. Do Buddhists wear pigtails? are they Chinese? I am very vague about them.

Sandf. So am I.   [*Both laugh.*

Mrs. C. What is that you are saying ?

Evel. Do Buddhists wear pigtails, Aunt Diana ?

Mrs. C. (angrily). My dear girl ! what a very silly question ! Mr. Sandford, do enlighten her—I can't bear to hear her exposing her ignorance.

Sandf. (severely to Evel.) No, Miss Barrington, no— Buddhists do not wear pigtails—far from it ! do not think it for a moment !

Evel. (trying not to laugh). Then what do they wear ?

Sandf. They wear—they wear—why, that depends on the weather, I suppose, or the kind of party they are going to !   [*Both laugh.*

Mrs. C. (exasperated) (aside). Dear me, how bored the poor fellow must be at all this giggling ! (Aloud) Evelyn, tell Mr. Sandford about that blind man of whom I was speaking to your uncle—perhaps he can do something for him.

Evel. (to Sandf.) This is a very interesting case———

Sandf. (interrupts her). But I know a more interesting one, I assure you, of which I was going to tell you just now—may I count on your sympathy?

Evel. Yes—you may.

Sandf. Is it possible that you can be so blind—(aloud) so very blind———

Mrs. C. Ah, yes, indeed—quite stone blind—most distressing.

Sandf. As not to see that I am in a far more hopeless state than any *protégé* of yours that you can mention?

Evel. (aloud). He is not a *protégé* of mine, exactly.

Mrs. C. We are all much interested in him.

Sandf. (to Evel.) My malady is desperate—incurable. (Aloud) Quite incurable!

Mrs. C. Incurable, I fear so. Still, one hears of such wonderful recoveries nowadays with this new treatment———

Enter Maid.

Maid. Please, ma'am, the Secretary of the United Ghosts' Club is downstairs, and wants particularly to see you for a minute. [*Gives card.*

Mrs. C. (reads). 'I have three absolutely authentic cases of apparition to communicate to you. Can you spare me a few moments?' Oh, how wonderful!—that makes 937! I must go and hear them—I will be back directly.
[*Exit Mrs. C.*

Sandf. Most delightful United Ghosts! Evelyn! my darling———

Evel. Oh, Mr. Sandford, take care—oh, pray take care! suppose Aunt Diana were to come in again!

Sandf. Not she—you forget that she has to listen to

I

three ghost stories ! she won't be back for ever so long.
We are alone, at last ! Evelyn, you know what I have
to say to you, don't you ?

Evel. (shyly). Yes, I think I do.

Sandf. You must have seen that I cared for you, have
you not ? ever since that night we first met.

Evel. I have thought sometimes that you cared—but
then I remembered how clever you are—and how stupid I
am—what nonsense I talk compared to you—and so I
thought it was impossible.

Sandf. Now you are talking nonsense, certainly, but it
is the first time I have ever heard you do so ! You know
quite well that the only impossible thing is that I shouldn't
care for you—so make up your mind to that ! Evelyn—do
you care for me at all ?

Evel. Yes.

Sandf. How much ? a little ?

Evel. Yes—a little.

Sandf. More than a little ?

Evel. More than a little.

Sandf. A great deal ?

Evel. A great deal.

Sandf. More than a great deal ?

Evel. More than a great deal.

Sandf. My own ! . . How good it is of you to care
for me ! why do you, I wonder ?

Evel. I really don't know—I suppose because it never
occurred to me to do anything else ! why do you care for me ?

Sandf. Because you are sweeter, and nicer, and more
charming than anyone else in the world—and because I
want you for my wife !

Evel. Do you really think me nicer than anybody else ?
are you sure ?

Sandf. Of course I am—quite sure.

Evel. Oh, I'm so glad ! do you know, I was really

getting quite unhappy about myself, for Aunt Diana is always telling me how dull I am !

Sandf. Is she ?

Evel. Oh yes—she thinks me very tiresome indeed, I assure you.

Sandf. Darling, that must be because you won't talk to her on the subjects which interest her—you know how very keen she is about politics, for instance, and all public questions—she is a very superior woman, of a great deal of culture.

Evel.. (with a sigh). Yes, I suppose she is ! do you like women of culture ?

Sandf. I like Mrs. Chester, certainly.

Evel. But you don't like her better than you do me ?

Sandf. Better than you ? my own love, what folly ! I like her in quite a different way. She has been to me one of the best friends a man ever had—she has constantly helped me with her sympathy and advice—I admire and respect her—but of course I should never dream of being in love with her ! I would as soon think of falling in love with my sister, or my aunt !

Evel. (with a sudden thought). Why, only think !—if —if—I were to marry you, you know, as you suggested——

Sandf. 'If ?' there is no 'if' in the matter. Of course you are going to marry me !

Evel. Why then, Mrs. Chester would be your aunt, wouldn't she ? oh, how funny ! I wonder if she would like it ?

Sandf. (surprised). Why shouldn't she ?

Evel. Because—because—no—I ought not to say this ! do you mean to say you have never guessed it ?

Sandf. (bewildered). Guessed what ?

Evel. It is only an idea of mine, of course—and I dare say I am mistaken—but I used sometimes to think that— that—she cared a little for you herself !

Sandf. Mrs. Chester ! ha, ha ! what an absurd idea ! there never was a more mistaken notion, I assure you ! Nothing could be further from her thoughts !

Evel. I am glad of that—for, to tell you the truth, I am feeling rather anxious as to what she will say to us— she is my guardian, you know, and I can do nothing without her consent—think how dreadful it would be if she refused it !

Sandf. It would, indeed ! but I don't think you need be anxious on that score—I spoke to her before you came down this afternoon, and I think she will be favourable to us.

Evel. But how was it that you ventured to speak to anyone about me without having asked me first ? how did you know I should accept you ?

Sandf. I relied on the sweet, silent consent of your eyes, that have so often told their tale, though your tongue has been mute.   Besides, (*smiling*) I was rather bound to tell Mrs. Chester, as I once promised her I would never take any important step in my life without consulting her.

Evel. I don't think that was at all a good plan ! I don't like having people's advice asked about me. Suppose she had advised you not to propose to me, what should you have done then ?

Sandf. I should have done it all the same, of course ! I promised I would *ask* her advice—I did not say I would *take* it !

Evel. In that case, it is different—I forgive you.

Sandf. Show me how you forgive me.

Evel. No—Mr. Sandford——

Sandf. Don't you know what my name is ?

Evel. Yes.

Sandf. Then why don't you call me by it ?

Evel. (shyly).   I can't—I can't say it.

Sandf. What can't you say ?

Evel. I can't say—Herbert!

Sandf. There—you see how easy it is! now you have mastered that, you shall go on to the next exercise—say, 'Herbert, I love you!'

Evel. Oh, no—that's much too difficult! you forget how stupid I am—you mustn't expect me to get on as fast as that!

[*Door opens—Sandf. and Evel. fly apart—enter Maj. Symonds. Evel. stands L., Sandf. R., with their backs to door, not daring to look round.*

Maj. S. Ahem! . .

[*Evel. turns round, and flies into his arms.*

Evel. Oh, dear uncle, it is you! I am so glad! you are the very person we want!

Maj. S. Why, what is the matter now? what do you want me for, Evelyn! is the conversation getting too intellectual for you, eh? [*Evel. R., Maj. S. C., Sandf. L.*

Evel. No, so far I have understood it very well indeed.

Sandf. Yes, sir, I think that we have thoroughly mastered our subject.

Maj. S. Indeed? and pray what is the subject, may I ask? is it the Redistribution Bill, or the Mutual Improvement Society?

Sandf. It is a mutual improvement society, on a small scale—consisting of only two members! Major Symonds, I have asked your niece to be my wife.

Maj. S. (delighted). The deuce you have! and a most sensible thing to do! My dear sir, I congratulate you—I do, with all my heart! [*Gives him his hand.*

Sandf. Then may I hope that, as one of her guardians, you will give your consent?

Maj. S. Of course I will—as her sole guardian, my good friend, her sole guardian!

Evel. My sole guardian?

Sandf. Her sole guardian?

Evel. What, is not Aunt Diana my guardian any longer?

Sandf. Is not her consent necessary too?

[*Maj. S. standing between them, shaking his head and rubbing his hands.*

Maj. S. Mrs. Chester, overwhelmed by the cares of state, and unable to manage such a troublesome young woman as Evelyn, finally made up her mind this morning to resign her office, and signed a deed making over all her powers and responsibilities in the matter to me.

Evel. Oh, uncle, did she really? is it actually signed?

Maj. S. Not only signed, but in the possession of Mr. Deeds, the lawyer, to whom I posted it at once, and who has it in his safe keeping.

Evel. Oh, how delightful! to think of your being my sole guardian! then I need not obey anybody else ever again, as long as I live.

Maj. S. Hey-day! then what about my young friend here? are you never going to obey him?

Evel. Of course not! what an absurd idea!

Maj. S. That's a pleasant look-out for you, Sandford, I must say!

Sandf. (smiling). I am not at all afraid of the prospect, sir, thank you.

Maj. S. Well, I am bound to say my wife never obeyed me in her life—it is always I who am ordered about, and have to do as I am told! And bless me! that reminds me —she is waiting downstairs in the carriage all this time. I came here with a message, my dear (*To Evel.*), but you put it out of my head, with all this folly! your Aunt Lucy would insist on coming back here again, to fetch you to hear Strauss's band.

Evel. (laughing). I really don't think I can go and hear it this afternoon, uncle—I am very busy—very busy indeed.

Maj. S. (going). Very well, then, I will go down and tell your aunt you won't come—she will be wondering what has become of me.

Evel. No, no—you mustn't go away before Aunt Diana comes in—you must not, really.

Maj. S. Where is she ?

Sandf. She is downstairs with a ghost.

Maj. S. What ? . . .

Evel. With the United Ghosts' secretary, listening to three well-authenticated ghost stories ! oh dear, it makes me shudder to think of them. I've heard so many since I have been here, that every time the door opens it makes me jump !   [*Door opens suddenly, Evel. starts.*

Enter Mrs. Symonds.

Mrs. S. Well ! I came up to see what you were doing all this time. What have you been about, John ?

Maj. S. Ah, you may well ask—you don't know what dreadful things have been happening here !

[*Mrs. S. looks at Evel. and Sandf., who are standing together, looking conscious.*

Mrs. S. What, Evelyn, my little girl—and Mr. Sandford—it surely can't be——

Maj. S. Yes, it is though, I assure you ! Did you ever hear of two such foolish young people ? the very moment they are left alone, instead of talking about the election, or unearned increment, or something equally interesting, they must needs go and propose to one another !

Mrs. S. (delighted). Evelyn, my darling ! [*Kisses her.*

Evel. Don't say 'proposed to one another,' uncle, please ! it was only one of us who proposed.

Maj. S. But the other one agreed !—you are an accessory before the fact, there is no denying it !

Mrs. S.   And what does your Aunt Diana say to it ?

Maj. S.   She doesn't know yet !

[*Smiling aside at his wif*

Evel. (anxiously).   Here she comes, I think.

[*All wait in suspense.*

Enter Mrs. Chester.

Mrs. C.   I am afraid I have been a very long time.   Why,
Lucy—and John !   I did not know you were here.   (Aside)
For once I am glad to see them, as it must have relieved
the tedium of that incongruous *tête-à-tête* !

Mrs. S.   Yes, we came back again, to see if Evelyn
would come with us to hear the band.

Maj. S.   But we found she couldn't come—being
engaged ! !

Mrs. C.   Why, what is she going to do ?

Maj. S.   Can't you guess ? what do you suppose these
young people have been doing, while you were downstairs
listening to ghost stories ?

Mrs. C.   I have absolutely no idea.

[*Mrs. Symonds, R.—Maj. S., R. C.—Mrs. Chester,
C.—Evel., L. C.—Sandford, L.*

Maj. S.   Look at them—juvenile offenders appearing
before the Board of Guardians !   [*Mrs. C. starts.*

Sandf. (going to Mrs. C.) [*Mrs. S. crosses to speak to
Evelyn*] Dear Mrs. Chester, after what I told you to-day
of my love for your niece, you will know what we have to
tell you.

Mrs. C. (bewildered).   Mr. Sandford !—is it possible——

Sandf. (astonished).   Did you not tell me yourself that
we might count on your sympathy and support ? that you
wished to see us attached to each other ?

Mrs. C. (recovering herself).   I did—yes—only—only
—I am a little taken by surprise, as I did not know you

contemplated such a very immediate step—I must have a moment to reflect, before I can give my consent.

                   [*Goes, R.—Major S. follows her.*

Maj. S. (to Mrs. C.) But if you are too busy about the election, or the ghosts, to be able to give any time to this, it does not matter—there is no need for you to worry yourself about it—for you will remember that, since you signed that paper this morning [*With assumed carelessness*], the whole responsibility of Evelyn's vagaries now rests on my unfortunate shoulders, as I am her sole guardian.

Mrs. C. Ah, that is true !—where is that paper ?

Maj. S. (carelessly). It is at Mr. Deeds', in Lincoln's Inn—I sent it to him at once, as I never like carrying a legal document loose in my pocket, for fear it should explode !

        [*Goes back to the others, leaving Mrs. C. plunged in thought.*

Mrs. C. (aside). Yes, it is true—I am powerless to prevent it, even if I wished it—but I don't think I do ! a man who can consecrate his life to a girl of that type is not worth having. *How* I have been mistaken in him ! However, no one shall ever know, he least of all, that I misinterpreted his words to me—and after all these things are a great waste of time—I am well out of such follies !

Evel. (advancing, timidly). Dear Aunt Diana, you are not vexed with me ?

Mrs. C. (with extreme cordiality). Vexed, my dear child, how could you imagine such a thing ? on the contrary, I am delighted !—the only reason that I was a little taken aback was, that I did not expect it quite so soon—I should like you to have had a little more time for cultivation and improvement before becoming Mr. Sandford's wife—but you must do your best.

Evel. Indeed, dear aunt, I will—and you will help

me, won't you, and tell me what I must read, in order to become less ignorant ?

Sandf.   And I will sit by you with a dictionary, to explain the words you don't understand !

Mrs. S.   Why, Evelyn, in another year you will be so learned and clever, we shall hardly know you again !

Maj. S. (to Evel.)   Yes, my little girl ! by that time even *you* will be on the high road to becoming—a Woman of Culture !

Curtain.

IN A FIRST-CLASS WAITING-ROOM

COMEDIETTA IN ONE ACT.

CHARACTERS.

MISS SELINA TIMMERSOME.   MR. WALTER GRAHAM.
A RAILWAY PORTER.

SCENE.—*A Waiting-room at Barningham Station—benches, advertisements, &c. Fireplace left-hand corner. Door R.*

Enter Porter carrying luggage, followed by Miss Timmersome.

Porter. This way, mum, this way.

[*Putting down bundle.*

Miss Timmersome (looking round). Is this the first-class waiting-room ?

Porter. Well, mum—the fact is, that this is the only sort of waiting-room we have just now—a sort of general waiting-room, do you see ?—as the first-class ladies' is being papered, and the first-class gentlemen being whitewashed —and so everybody has to use this.

Miss Timmersome. Then do you mean to say that anyone who likes may come in here ? that I shall be exposed to the company of the ruffians who infest railway stations ?

Porter. Not many ruffians at this time of the year, mum—they're not in season yet—they generally come later on, for Barningham races.

Miss Timmersome. Good heavens ! I wonder if I am in safety here ?   [*Looks nervously round her.*

Porter. Oh, quite, mum, I assure you. This room has been cleaned and done up since the spring races, so there can't have been any ruffians left in the corners. [*Looking about, goes to door—turns round.*] If you want anything, mum, just step to the door and call me, will you ?

Miss Timmersome. Oh, thank you, I will. What is your name ?

Porter. My *name* is Alexander Magillicuddy, but I don't know that I should recognise it if I heard it unexpectedly—(*reflectively*) if it's anything very special you might call me by it and see—if not, then just call Porter —and if I'm not there, some one else will come——

Miss Timmersome. Oh, are you sure ? *sometimes,* when I've called Porter, nobody has come, and I remember the same thing once happened to one of my aunts.

Porter. You don't say so, mum ! I never heard of such a thing before ! Nothing of that kind happens here. I'll come to tell you when your train is coming, mum —you've half an hour yet. [*Going, then turns back.*] Oh, I forgot the fire.

[*Pokes the fire, gathers the fire-irons together and takes them away.*

Miss Timmersome. Why are you taking the fire-irons away ? I shall not be able to poke the fire, if I wish to !

Porter. No one but the servants of the Railway Company pokes the fire here, mum, with the permission of the Company, or with anything else either. Certainly not with a poker, which is *the* most mischievous instrument that was ever invented for making the fire burn up, and wasting the Company's fuel ! [*Bell rings.*] There's the express ! [*Going.*] I'll come and tell you, mum, when your train comes in. You've plenty of time yet.   [*Exit.*

Miss Timmersome. What a difficult and alarming thing

a journey is for a solitary woman ! If only I had a father —or a brother—or (*coyly*) even a husband—it would make me feel so much safer ! but I have no one. The one relation I have in the world is a cousin, in India, so I am quite unprotected. Dear Walter ! he writes me such nice letters every Christmas—I have not seen him since he was six years old. I wonder what he is like now? I sometimes think that when he comes home, we shall . . . . meet ! but goodness knows when that will be. [*Looks at watch.*] I wish I had something to read. Ah, here is a newspaper— that is something at any rate. And it is the interesting part too—the advertisement sheet. [*Sits down to read.*] 'Fifty pounds reward—A diamond brooch—Five shillings a bunch of keys—Two-pounds-ten a lap-dog.' I remember, when I was a child I used to think how delightful it would be to meet with the missing object and claim the reward—Not if it were a thief or a murderer though. '500*l*. reward—Missing from Pentington Prison, since the 21st instant, Henry Brownlow, aged 30. Medium height— dark complexion, saturnine cast of features, a deep scar on his right hand—hair closely cropped, face clean-shaven, or beard of few days' growth—last seen in the neighbourhood of Blackney.' Dreadful to think he is still at large ! but I am glad he is in the neighbourhood of Blackney, as that is a long way from here, but still, that means nothing—as seeing himself described as being at Blackney, he would probably go somewhere else, as far off as possible. Supposing he were to come here ! Oh dear, I feel very nervous—I don't know whether to wish that anyone should come in, or not . . .

Enter Graham carrying rugs, &c. Miss Timmersome shrinks into her corner with great timidity.

Graham (heartily). Very cold to-day !

     [*Miss Timmersome makes no answer.*

Graham (louder). Very cold indeed to-day !

Miss Timmersome (nervously). Very.

Graham (going to fire). They don't seem to keep up very good fires here, either. [*Looks about everywhere for the fire-irons. Miss Timmersome says nothing.*] I wonder where the fire-irons are kept ?

Miss Timmersome. The porter has taken away the fire-irons.

Graham. Taken away the fire-irons ! How very odd ! what for ?

Miss Timmersome. So that no one might poke the fire. He says it wastes the Company's fuel.

Graham. Then he must think that the people who wait in here must be people of very limited capacity indeed, not to poke the fire because the poker's gone ! what do chairs have legs for then ?

Miss Timmersome (starts. Aside). I believe he is of unsound mind ! . . . Chairs . . . . Legs? really . . . . (Aloud) I should say, to walk with—I mean to sit down with—at any rate, they have nothing to do with poking the fire.

Graham. If you had ever been a school-boy you wouldn't say so !

Miss Timmersome. I never was !

Graham. At the school I was brought up at, we used to inscribe a word on a door with the blackened leg of a chair, some weeks before the holidays, and rubbing out a letter every week. I will give the Directors of the Company an opportunity of recalling their past youth ! So here goes ! [*Seizes up chair and pokes the fire violently.*

Miss Timmersome. Oh, dear me, you'll break its leg !

Graham. And if I do, I believe that all the railway porters are made to attend ambulance classes nowadays, so that they will be able to bind it up again. Besides, I won't break it—only blacken it a little. [*Poking vigorously.*] I dare say it won't be the first blackleg that has appeared at this station. I only wish all the others could be as easily sat upon as this one! [*Looks up at Miss Timmersome and smiles. She is stony.*] (Aside) That joke wasn't very successful, I'm afraid. Never mind—*I* enjoyed it! [*Finishes poking and puts down chair with a bang.*] There now! the next Director who 'takes the chair' at a meeting had better take care that it isn't *that* one he takes, or the consequences would be surprising! [*Draws it up to the fire and sits down cautiously.*] It is a little rickety, certainly—it is more like a rocking-chair now, but there is no harm done. [*All this time Miss Timmersome pays no attention. Graham takes off his hat and puts on a travelling cap.*] I must apologise for keeping my head covered, but the fact is, that I have just had a fever, after which my hair was cut very short—so I am obliged to be very careful, especially when sitting in a room which is about as sheltered as a breezy common! [*Pulls coat collar up.*] There are as many draughts here as—as—on a draught-board! Ha! ha!

[*Miss Timmersome snatches tremulously at paper.*

Miss Timmersome (aside). Hair closely cropped! Oh, it must be only a coincidence.

Graham (reading off paper on wall, crosses and reads off time table). How very badly the connection of trains is managed in England! At this station, for instance, here are five trains get in from Dodgeborough during the day—and they one and all get here just after another train has left to go somewhere else—don't matter where—and then one has to wait ever so long. Has it been fine in this part of the world to-day?

Miss Timmersome. I really don't know—I only arrived here from Crosswell at two o'clock—there it was fine.

Graham. Oh, I asked because the showery weather has been very local. At Blackney, for instance, where I was yesterday——

Miss Timmersome.   Blackney ! . . . Ah ! . .

[*Shrieks, falls back in chair, rises and goes up stage.
Graham goes to her to see what is the matter—she
waves him back still more violently.*

Miss Timmersome.   Go away !   Go away !

[*Barricades herself.*

Graham (aside).   She must be a lunatic, I think—what
can be the matter ?   I wonder if she is mad—it's dangerous
to be shut up with her !

Miss Timmersome (agitated—taking up paper, reads
description aside).   'Henry Brownlow, aged 30—medium
height, dark complexion, saturnine cast of features—a deep
scar on his right hand, hair closely cropped, face cleanly
shaven, or beard of a few days' growth—last seen at
Blackney.'   Alas !   It is all *too* plain—there can be no
mistake.

Graham.   I'm sure she is insane—there can't be a
doubt of it !   I see it in the anxious glare of her eye when
she looks at me—these maniacs are always suspicious of
violence being done them.   [*Miss Timmersome has retreated
into the furthest corner of the room, and barricaded herself
with a chair.   Graham looks nervously at her.*]   I hope she
won't attempt any violence—I believe they possess super-
human strength at these times.   I wish I had sat on the
other side of the fire—if I go away she may spring at me as
I pass !   I had better humour her in all she says.   (*Aloud,
with exaggerated heartiness of manner*) Yes, very unfortunate weather for travelling, is it not ?   However, even
this drizzling mist, with the fresh country air blowing
through it, is acceptable to me after being imprisoned so
long in London.

Miss Timmersome (aside).   Imprisoned !—there is no
further concealment in the matter.   I don't want to arouse
his suspicions by going away—I must simply make the best
of it until I see a porter outside.

Graham. Ah, London is a very horrid place of deten-
tion for those who love the country. [*Miss Timmersome
doesn't answer.*] (Aside) I must rouse her out of herself.
It appears to be a melancholy madness. Don't you think
so, madam? London, I was saying [*Very loud*], is a most
tantalising place of confinement to the lover of the country.

Miss Timmersome (flurried). I dare say—I have no
experience of it.

Graham. Really? Have you never been to London?
You surprise me.

Miss Timmersome. Oh, yes—of course I've been to
London—but not in *that* way.

Graham. In that way? [*Bewildered.*] Do you mean not
by train? It is rather too far for a walk, is it not, from
most parts of England? (Aside) She won't feel so singular,
perhaps, if she hears me talking like a maniac too—it will
be company for her!

Miss Timmersome. I mean that when I have been in
London I have always been at large—at least—— (Aside)
I really don't know what to say—I am afraid of offending
him, and then he might spring upon me and murder me on
the spot!

Graham. At large? Have you, indeed? (Aside) I
wonder at that—I suppose the poor thing means she has
never been in an asylum there! (Aloud) It's a very pleasant
place to be at large in, I dare say, though my experience of
it is being always chained to the same spot. The people who
are at liberty to roam about the fields, and enjoy themselves at their own sweet will, don't appreciate their freedom —they don't know what it is to be a galley slave!

Miss Timmersome (starts. Aside). Is it possible that
there can be any further doubt about it—and yet——
(*Reads*) 'A scar on the right hand.' I have not seen that
yet—there may be a chance still. I wish I could make him
show it to me, somehow. [*Watches him. He mechanically*

K

puts his hand into his pocket.] It is evident he is hiding it.
I will try to make him show it. (Aloud) Don't you think
the fire wants poking a little ?

Graham. Do you think it does ? Perhaps you are
right.   [*Pokes it vigorously with his foot.*

Miss Timmersome (aside). What a savage, to use his
feet instead of his hands ! He *must* be a convict. But I
will make him take it out. (Aloud) Would you kindly
pass me that—that—volume lying on the chimney-piece ?

Graham (takes it up and looks at title without handing
it). Is this what you want, madam ? I don't think you
will find it very pleasant reading—it is the cover of an old
Railway Guide, with the bewildering inside torn out !
The only piece of information it contains is, on one side
Horniman's Pure Tea, and on the other Powell's Balsam of
Aniseed, with an interesting-looking lion just recovering
from a cold ! Is this what you want ?

Miss Timmersome. Yes, it is what I want—give it
me, I entreat you—you dare not refuse me !

Graham. Certainly, certainly—here it is [*Hands it
with his left hand*]—only I'm afraid it won't be very profit-
able reading. (Aside) I always wondered who the people
were who bought things from these advertisements—I see
all now—they are lunatics ! [*Miss Timmersome looks at it
for a minute, then tosses it down.*] Ah, it isn't equal even to
her intellect, I see. (Aloud) Find it pleasant reading ?
I don't think the plot is fully developed—there are not
enough incidents in it for my taste—a work which consists
of nothing but the frontispiece and one of the covers seems
to me rather incomplete, don't it to you ? Ha, ha ! I'll go
and see if I can get a newspaper, with rather more information in it.   [*Exit. Miss Timmersome comes forward.*

Miss Timmersome. He is talking quite at random—
quite wildly ! can he be insane ? I have heard sometimes
of the pressure of remorse, and the dread of discovery,

driving criminals out of their mind—what an appalling thing it would be to be shut up in here with a lunatic ! Yet it is so damp outside—and I might meet him on the platform, besides. I wonder where that remarkable porter has gone to. (*Puts her head out—and calls timidly*) Porter ! Porter ! [*No answer.*] What did he say his name was ? something beginning with *Mac*, I know—Macpherson ? (*Calls timidly*) MacIntyre ! Macdoodle ! Macfarlane ! Mackintosh ! Macnab ! Macwheeble ! Mackenzie ! Macbeth ! Mac—(*with an inspiration*) Mac-gillicuddy ! ! I believe the station is deserted. Here is some one coming.

> [*In an expectant attitude. Door opens, re-enter Graham with a newspaper. Miss Timmersome retreats into corner.*

Graham. Don't be alarmed—I'm not dangerous !

Miss Timmersome. Are you sure ?

Graham. Oh, quite ! Did I hear you calling as I came up ? You seemed to be expecting some Scotch friend—quite a gathering of the clans, it sounded like !

Miss Timmersome. Oh, no—I was just calling for a porter—and happening to know his name—or I should rather say happening to have forgotten his name——

Graham. You called him by it. I see ! Can't I do anything to help you ? Do you like your porter with a head ? as that kind doesn't seem to exist at Barningham Station.

Miss Timmersome. No—thank you—I didn't want anything particular—I was only calling him because I wanted him to—to—to poke the fire !

Graham. What, again ? Why you know I can do that beautifully—here goes ! [*Seizes the chair and batters the fire with it.*] There now, I flatter myself that a professional poker wouldn't have done better than the leg of that chair, which is after all only an amateur, and pokes for its amusement. There is always a want of finish about everything amateurs do, don't you think so ?

Miss Timmersome (stiffly). I think that if the chair is spoilt, the railway authorities will make you pay for it.

Graham. Perhaps they will. (*Considering the chairs with his head on one side*) I should think the market value of that chair was about ninepence! (Aside) Now that was a very sensible remark of hers—this must be one of her lucid intervals. I'll make the most of it. (Aloud) Here is the paper I brought you in—would you like to see if there is any news?

Miss Timmersome (taking it timidly). Thank you.

[*Looks through it eagerly and hastily—then puts it down with an air of disappointment—gives it back to Graham.*

Graham. No news?

Miss Timmersome. None, that I can see.

Graham (takes up paper and looks through it). What a very funny way women have of reading the paper! I don't know what on earth they expect to find in it. This seems to me to have plenty of news. China declared war to France—half London blown up by Fenians—three railway bridges collapsed. I wonder what her notion of something interesting is! Ah, this is the sort of thing, I suppose—(*To her*) ' Marvellous escape '—are you interested in escapes?

Miss Timmersome (starts). Oh, dear—who *has* escaped now? It is quite dreadful the number of escapes there are.

Graham. Dreadful? (Aside) What an extraordinary woman—it must be homicidal mania she has. (Aloud) *I* think it is a subject of rejoicing, that even an unknown fellow-creature should have escaped from drowning.

Miss Timmersome. From drowning?

Graham. Yes. An unfortunate youth who had never been in the sea in his life must needs go to Shrimptonville for the day, and bathe. Queer people these excursionists are! Those who can't swim always bathe—those who have never been on a horse invariably ride. Well, this youth naturally enough got out of his depth, and equally naturally there was no appliance of any kind that could be of the least use to him except the life-boat, which was about a mile and a quarter off—but another excursionist, who *could* swim and had therefore gone for a ride, came up, dashed into the water and saved him. You surely don't grudge him that escape !

Miss Timmersome (fervently). Oh, no. I thought you meant an escape of another kind.

Graham. Of what kind ?

Miss Timmersome (hesitating). Some—some—criminal, perhaps——

Graham (meaningly). Or some lunatic, more likely !

Miss Timmersome (terrified. Aside). Can he be mad too ?

Graham (aside). It is evident I have hit the right nail on the head !

Miss Timmersome (aside). He sees I know his secret— What if the fear of discovery render him desperate, and he turn upon me ?

Graham (aside). She sees I have guessed her secret— suppose she becomes violent and springs upon me ! (Aloud) Now, madam, you will forgive me if I say that I penetrated the cause of your emotion, when I spoke of an escape——

Miss Timmersome. Unfortunate man ! You did ! ! ·

Graham. I did. I can imagine what your feelings must be, and I am ready to offer you any help in my power—but I must say I do not consider the course you have adopted to be a wise one——

Miss Timmersome. What course ?

Graham. The one which—which has brought you here to-day.

Miss Timmersome. I haven't an idea what you mean.

Graham. Then, if you force me to speak plainly. I mean that of escaping from those under whose charge you were, and to whose care it will be my duty to help you to return.

Miss Timmersome (aside). Gracious Heavens ! there is no doubt of it—his crime has turned his brain ! Oh if some one only would come !

Enter Porter with two pieces of coal and the fire-irons.
Miss Timmersome rushes to him.

Porter. Bless me, mum, gently ! What's the matter ? you've made me drop one of my pieces of coal – and I only had two !

Miss Timmersome (wildly). Never mind the coal—the matter is, that there stands the escaped convict, Henry Brownlow !   [*Sinks into a chair.*

Porter. What, sir !

Graham. The meaning of it is, that the poor lady is evidently of unsound mind, and has escaped from some private lunatic asylum, *I* should say.

Miss Timmersome. What, *I* escaped ? *You* escaped ! !

Graham. I ?

Miss Timmersome. Yes. You !

Porter. Then where do you think that this gentleman's escaped from, mum ?

Miss Timmersome. From prison, of course. He's a convict !

Porter (to Graham). I thought she was rather flighty and excitable when I first brought her in here. But why do you think the gentleman's a convict, mum ?

Miss Timmersome. Because here's the description of him in the newspaper, accurate in every point—and he has himself admitted he has just been imprisoned in London !

Graham. Would you kindly let me look at the paper ? [*She puts it down near him and starts away.*] Oh, don't be afraid—I am not in a murderous fit just now ! this is not one of my working days ! [*Looks at paper, bursts out laughing.*] Why the date of this paper is six months ago ! I hope *this* individual's affairs have been settled before now !

Miss Timmersome. Is it ? . . . is it really ? . . dear me—so it is ! of course, it was a paper some parcel had been wrapped up in ! How can I apologise for my absurdity ?

Graham. Then do you mean to say that all this time you have been thinking *I* was the person referred to in that description ?

Miss Timmersome. Of course I have, and I don't wonder that you should have been thinking I was out of my mind !

Porter. The Cranbourne train is signalled, mum.

Graham. The Cranbourne train ! Are you going to Cranbourne ? that is the place I am bound for.

Miss Timmersome. Oh really ! how curious ! I live at Cranbourne—it is my home.

Graham. Indeed ! Then perhaps you know something of the person I am going there to see ? a relation of mine, the only relation I have in the world—in fact—I haven't seen her since I was six years old.

Miss Timmersome. Since you were six years old ! The only relation you have in the world ! May I ask what your name is ?

Graham. My name is Walter Graham.

Miss Timmersome. Walter. Graham ! My dear, dear cousin !

Graham. What—are you——

Miss Timmersome. Selina Timmersome ! Yes ! I am your cousin Selina !

Graham (shaking hands heartily). My dear cousin, how glad I am to meet you again ! though it must be confessed that our acquaintance has not been renewed under very happy auspices, since you took me for an escaped convict !

Miss Timmersome. And you took me for a lunatic !

Graham. It is all the pleasanter to wake up to the reality of what delightful people we both are !

Miss Timmersome. Oh, how kind of you to say so !

Enter Porter.

Porter. Cranbourne train due, sir. Why what has happened to the leg of that chair ? looks as if it had been burnt, don't it ?

Graham. Come, my man, make haste or we shall miss the train—you can come and look over the furniture when we are gone. (To Miss T.) If you will allow me, then, I will escort you to Cranbourne.

Miss Timmersome. That will be delightful. (Aside) Oh, how safe that makes me feel !

Graham. And I hope you will meet with no more escaped criminals on the way !

Miss Timmersome. I don't wonder at your laughing at me ! but the fact is, I am so nervous about travelling alone, that I am ready to fancy myself in danger every·where—even in a First-Class Waiting-Room !

[*Exeunt, preceded by Porter with luggage.*

Curtain.

A JOINT HOUSEHOLD

COMEDIETTA IN ONE ACT.

CHARACTERS.

MRS. STUBBS.   MRS. TALLETT.

SCENE.—*A gaudily furnished drawing-room in a lodging-house at Scarborough. Two unopened letters on table.*

Enter Mrs. Stubbs, in travelling costume, bag in hand— she puts down bag and hangs coloured woollen shawl over back of chair.

Mrs. S. (looking round). And so this is the drawing-room! Well, I don't think much of it. I might have known this would be the kind of place my husband would choose. It is extraordinary how little sense husbands have! For my part, I think the whole arrangement a mistake. It is absurd, that because my husband and Mr. Tallett are together in a bank in Leeds, Mrs. Tallett and I should take a house at Scarborough together for six weeks, that those two men may run down from Saturday to Monday. However, we shall see how it answers. If Mrs. Tallett is pleasant to live with, and lets me have my own way in the house, I dare say we shall get on well enough. I am glad that I changed my plans, and came on by the afternoon train instead of the evening one, as I shall have time to look round me and settle things a little before she comes. [*Looks round.*] That's not a bad armchair—I can have that of an evening, and my husband the rocking-chair. Then Mr. and Mrs. Tallett can sit on the sofa. Ah, the piano is open, I see ! [*Locks it and takes key.*] I can't be distracted by Mrs. Tallett's strumming all day, as I have no doubt she would like to do. I shall tell her plainly from the first what my likes and dislikes are, then we shall understand one another. What a glare ! [*Pulls down blind as she passes.*] Ah, there is a letter from dear George, and one for Mrs. Tallett from *her* husband, I suppose. [*Reads*] 'Dear Maria, I hope this will find you comfortably settled in your new quarters. I fancy you will find Mrs. Tallett easy enough to get on with. The landlady said something about the kitchen range being wrong—you had better ask about it. I shall be down on Saturday. Your affectionate husband, George Stubbs.' Dear fellow ! I do hope he will be comfortable here. Now I must go and see the bedrooms, as I should like to take the front one for myself. I can't sleep in a room that doesn't face south. If Mrs. Tallett is reasonable, she won't mind the back one. [*Exit Mrs. S.*

After a moment, enter Mrs. Tallett in travelling costume.

Mrs. T. And so this is the drawing-room ! Well, it isn't bad, but I would have chosen a better one, if it had been left to me. However, I dare say it will do well enough. On principle, I don't like sharing houses with other people—but my husband and Mr. Stubbs were both so bent on the plan, that there was nothing to do but for their unfortunate wives to submit. [*Smiling.*] I wonder what Mr. Stubbs is like now ? I haven't seen him since— let me see—ten years ago, when he did me the honour of proposing to me, at a tea picnic at Maidenhead. Oh, what quantities of tea he drank ! and how glad I am I didn't accept him ! I do dislike short, fat men with red hair. How different from my darling Edwin ! Ah, there is a letter from him ! [*Reads.*] 'Darling Popsey '—so like him,

that is ! ' I hope you are getting on all right. Mrs. Stubbs
is a rather alarming, managing person, I believe, but if you
give her head, you will get on capitally. There's a darling
dicky-bird ! Her own Doodles. P.S. Stubbs asks me to
enclose this note to you—it's about the kitchen range, I
believe.' [*Opens it.*] ' Dear Mrs. Tallett, I hope you will
find the house I have chosen to your liking. I have only
just discovered that you are the Miss Blanche Mervyn I
once knew. Perhaps for the present it might be well to
sink the past, until I have an opportunity of explaining to
Mrs. Stubbs that I have already had the pleasure of
making your acquaintance. Yours truly, GEORGE STUBBS.'
Ha, ha, poor terrified soul ! Well, I am quite ready to sink
the past, I am sure—I wouldn't resuscitate it for the world !
[*Looks round.*] And now I must look round me a little.
Ah, that isn't a bad chair—that will do for Edwin, and
I can have the rocking-chair, and the Stubbses will be quite
comfortable on the sofa. A piano, too, how nice ! Why,
it is locked. I must get hold of the key, as I mean to
practise vigorously while I am here. It will be a capital
opportunity. [*Pulls up blind.*] What a nice sunny room !
It is certainly very amusing, feeling one has come away for
a holiday, and may live anyhow. I wonder what the bedrooms are like ? I had better go and see. I do hope there
is a front one I can have, as I like a cheerful look-out. I
am glad I came early, so as to be settled here before Mrs.
Stubbs comes.

    [*As she goes towards door, Mrs. Stubbs comes in, in
       indoor costume.*

  Mrs. T. Oh, are you the landlady ?

  Mrs. S. (indignantly). The landlady ! No ! Are you ?

  Mrs. T. Certainly not. I am one of the lodgers, and
this is my drawing-room.

  Mrs. S. Your drawing-room ! and may I ask what
your name is ?

Mrs. T.   Mrs. Tallett.

Mrs. S. (stiffly).   Oh, indeed! I am glad to see you, Mrs. Tallett, and to welcome you to my house.   I am Mrs. Stubbs.

Mrs. T.   Mrs. Stubbs!   I beg your pardon.   I thought you were not coming till this evening.

Mrs. S.   No more I was, but I changed my plans.   I thought *you* were not coming till this evening.

Mrs. T.   I changed mine, too.

Mrs. S.   I see.   [*A pause.*

Mrs. T.   I was just going to see what the bedrooms were like.

Mrs. S.   Not bad.   I have chosen mine, the one over this.

Mrs. T.   Over this?   The one on the front?

Mrs. S. (firmly).   On the front.

Mrs. T. (aside).   Upon my word!

Mrs. S.   There is a nice room at the back that I thought you would like, as it is so quiet.

Mrs. T.   Thank you.   I should have liked to see the rooms before making a final decision.

Mrs. S.   Well, you see, now I have put my things into the front room—my bonnet is in the cupboard and my cloak hanging up.

Mrs. T.   Still, I suppose, if necessary, the bonnet and cloak could be moved.   They are not glued to the shelves, I imagine.

Mrs. S. (aside).   Rude woman!   (Aloud) No, they are not glued, but it is hardly worth while to move them again, especially as there will be a good deal to do before we are settled.

Mrs. T. (looking round).   Yes, and we shall have to begin by turning a good many unlovely things out of this room, I think.

Mrs. S.   Do you think so?   This room struck me as

being furnished with very good taste. I don't see that we need remove anything.

Mrs. T. (taking up Mrs. S.'s shawl). Surely you wouldn't keep this thing here! do let us put it away somewhere.

Mrs. S. (taking it, with dignity). It shall be put in the cupboard in the front room, Mrs. Tallett—that is my shawl.

Mrs. T. (confused). I *beg* your pardon! I thought it was one of the things that people hang over the back of chairs.

Mrs. S. So it is! but I will take care that it doesn't happen again.

Mrs. T. (aside). That was unfortunate! (Aloud) What a bright, sunny room this is!

Mrs. S. Yes, too sunny, in fact. There is quite a glare.

Mrs. T. Do you think so?

Mrs. S. Yes, I was just thinking I would put up some nice red curtains I have, as my husband, who will like that rocking-chair in the window, cannot endure a glare.

Mrs. T. Curtains! What a pity! A room cannot be too sunny for me. I was thinking how I should enjoy sitting on that chair with baby, and looking out at the sun shining on the water.

Mrs. S. Then do you mean to use this room as a sitting-room for the children?

Mrs. T. (apologetically). Well, you see, there are only two of them, and they are really very little trouble—Jacky is only two, and the baby not quite a year.

Mrs. S. Do you consider those are ages at which children give no trouble?

Mrs. T. I don't say that exactly. But still, it isn't like having two extra grown-up people in the room.

Mrs. S.   I quite agree with you, it is not like having grown-up people in the room. I should have thought it would have been much better for the children to be in the little room at the back, under the stairs.

Mrs. T.   Oh, I shouldn't like that for them at all. Besides, I want baby to be in the same room as the piano— I am quite sure she is going to be musical.

Mrs. S. (bored).   Indeed ?   How does she show it ?

Mrs. T.   Whenever I say, ' Baby, where's the piano ? ' she begins drumming with both fists on her nurse's face.

Mrs. S.   Then can't she do that in a room without a piano ?

Mrs. T.   She wouldn't enjoy it nearly so much—but we will see when Edwin comes. By the way, I see the piano is locked.   Have you asked for the key ?

Mrs. S.   No, I have not asked for it.

Mrs. T.   I must try to get hold of it presently.   It will make all the difference to me to have the piano going constantly.

Mrs. S. (aside).   It would make a greater difference to me to have it gone altogether.

Mrs. T.   Dear me, I am getting very hungry ! I wonder if there is anything in the house to eat ?

Mrs. S.   I was just going to draw up a list of the things we should need.

Mrs. T.   It will be rather amusing living from hand to mouth for a little—I feel quite as if we were come out for a picnic !

Mrs. S.   In what respect ?

Mrs. T.   Oh, I mean not knowing what one is going to eat, and so on.

Mrs. S.   I assure you that I always know very well indeed what I am going to eat.

Mrs. T.   I mean, feeling that it doesn't matter.

Mrs. S.   It always matters. [*Sits at table.*] I will make

a list of the joints we may require during the next week.
[*Pulls letter out of her pocket and writes on back*] A leg of
mutton, a loin of lamb——

Mrs. T. Edwin likes a shoulder.

Mrs. S. A most extravagant, wasteful joint. I never
order a shoulder. A neck, to cut into cutlets——

Mrs. T. The cutlets off the neck are so scraggy. Edwin
doesn't like them scraggy.

Mrs. S. Not if they are properly cooked, which mine
always are.

Mrs. T. I shouldn't have thought we needed all these
things, while we two women are alone here. I suppose we
shall not dine late, shall we, till our husbands come?

Mrs. S. Not dine late? Why not?

Mrs. T. It is so much nicer to have supper.

Mrs. S. I don't agree with you at all. That seems to
me a most slovenly habit.   [*Walks to window. Pause.*

Mrs. T. How are we going to arrange about the housekeeping?

Mrs. S. What about it?

Mrs. T. I mean, who is going to undertake it?

Mrs. S. I am, I suppose.

Mrs. T. Altogether?

Mrs. S. I am very particular about housekeeping. I
don't think I could endure to live with anyone who did not
conform to my ideas on the subject.

Mrs. T. But I think I ought to have a little say on the
subject sometimes.

Mrs. S. Oh yes, of course you can have a say in the
matter.

Mrs. T. (aside). Not much good having a say if I
mayn't have a do as well!

Mrs. S. We can discuss the various points as we go
on. Now, about breakfast. You put down your items on
your list, and I on mine.

[*Mrs. T. pulls Mr. S.'s letter out of her pocket, smiling
aside as she does so, tears off the half-sheet on which
the P.S. is written and begins making list on it.
Mrs. S. and Mrs. T. with lists at different sides of
table.*

Mrs. T.   I was thinking that perhaps I might pour out
the tea at breakfast, and you might carve at luncheon.

Mrs. S.   Yes, I think I had better carve at luncheon,
certainly, but I am not sure about your plan for breakfast
—so few people know how to manage a teapot.

Mrs. T.   Oh, I think I can manage a teapot, if it is not
too headstrong ! what is the difficulty ?

Mrs. S.   The way you speak of it shows you don't
realise the importance of it.   George is most particular
about his tea.

Mrs. T. (smiling, aside).   Yes indeed !   (Aloud) I
know what I can look after for breakfast !   the toast !
Edwin always says no one can make such good toast as
I do.

Mrs. S.   Is Mr. Tallett very particular ?

Mrs. T.   I really don't know—he generally likes what
I give him.

Mrs. S.   George is extremely particular.

Mrs. T. (aside).   Oh, what an escape I had

Mrs. S.   Especially about his bacon in the morning.

Mrs. T. (aside).   Little wretch !

Mrs. S.   What kind of bacon do you get ?

Mrs. T.   Oh, I don't know.   Fat, streaky bacon.

Mrs. S.   Is it Cumberland, Wiltshire, smoked, or
American ?

Mrs. T.   I really don't know.

Mrs. S. (after a moment).   Then perhaps you had better
let me see about the bacon.

Mrs. T.   Perhaps I had.   [*Mrs. S. puts it down.*

Mrs. S.   Now, about the marmalade.

Mrs. T. Oh, that I can choose, I'm sure! I'm devoted to marmalade.

Mrs. S. What is your recipe?

Mrs. T. My what?

Mrs. S. Your recipe!

Mrs. T. My recipe for what?

Mrs. S. (aside). The woman is an idiot, I do believe! (Aloud) For making marmalade, of course.

Mrs. T. Oh! I haven't any, I buy it.

Mrs. S. You buy it! Gracious heavens! I should never think of eating marmalade bought in shops!

Mrs. T. Where should one buy it, if not in shops?

Mrs. S. One should never buy marmalade! one should always, always make it at home. My mother had a better recipe than anyone else for making it, and I do it in the same way.

Mrs. T. My mother used to make it too, I remember.

Mrs. S. Did she? But I don't suppose her recipe was as good as mine. My mother never put any water into her marmalade. Did your mother put any into hers? If she did, you may be sure it spoilt before the year was out.

Mrs. T. I really don't know whether she did or not. Her marmalade never had a chance of spoiling, for it was so good it was eaten long before the year was over.

Mrs. S. Oh, then she did not make enough. That is what so often happens to unskilful housekeepers.

Mrs. T. My mother was an excellent housekeeper. I only wish I had benefited more by her instructions!

Mrs. S. It would have been better, certainly, especially if you are keeping house with some one else.

Mrs. T. (aside). I wonder why I ever said I would do it!

Mrs. S. Then shall I see about the marmalade? I had better, I think. [*Puts it down.*

Mrs. T. Yes, please, if you will. And after all, if

L

there is good butter, I don't care so much about the marmalade.

Mrs. S.   Ah, yes, about the butter, this is very important.   I allow half a pound per head at home, not a scrap more.   Let me see, how many shall we be ?   Yourself, and myself, and George——

Mrs. T.   And dear Edwin——

Mrs. S.   Four—that makes two pounds.

Mrs. T.   Then there is Nurse—she seems to eat a great deal of butter.   I should almost think she might want more than half a pound.

Mrs. S.   I hope you don't pamper your nurse, Mrs. Tallett—it's a great mistake.

Mrs. T.   Oh, I dare say she is a little indulged, of course.   She is such a nice woman !   She came when Jacky was born, two years ago, and she has been the greatest treasure ever since.

Mrs. S.   I don't see why, because a woman has been with you two years, she should eat more butter than anyone else in the house.

Mrs. T.   It is only the idea, of course . . .

Mrs. S.   It's an idea I wouldn't let her put into practice, if I were you.

Mrs. T.   Well, we will see about it when Edwin comes.

Mrs. S.   Very well.   Then perhaps I had better see about the butter.   [*She puts it down.*

Mrs. T. (aside).   It doesn't seem to me as if I were going to see about anything !

Mrs. S.   And now we come to something very important—the hours of our meals.   What time shall we breakfast ?

Mrs. T.   Oh, not too early, pray !

Mrs. S.   No, I think, as we are in holidays, we may quite well say a quarter-past eight.

Mrs. T. A quarter-past eight ! I was going to say a quarter-past nine !

Mrs. S. I should think it extremely wrong to breakfast at a quarter-past nine.

Mrs. T. Wrong ? Why ?

Mrs. S. Because it is lazy and self-indulgent. I'm sure George wouldn't think of it for a moment.

Mrs. T. And I'm sure Edwin will never come down earlier.

Mrs. S. I must say, I think George's tastes should be deferred to.

Mrs. T. And I think Edwin's should be consulted.

Mrs. S. Well, we'll ask them when they come.

Mrs. T. Very well.

Mrs. S. And in the meantime I will order it at a quarter-past eight.

Mrs. T. Then where are the children to breakfast ?

Mrs. S. Dear me, I forgot about the children ! Really, in many ways, it will be extremely inconvenient having the children here.

Mrs. T. Inconvenient ! Why, that was the very reason Edwin and I were so anxious to come !

Mrs. S. But I think that you must see that it is quite impossible that the whole house should turn upon them as you seem to intend.

Mrs. T. I don't want the whole house to turn upon them, but I do think they should be of some importance.

Mrs. S. They are of *some* importance, of course, but one shouldn't exaggerate it.

Mrs. T. Exaggerated ! ! as if one could exaggerate their importance ! bless their darling hearts ! Edwin will never be satisfied unless they are in the room with him.

Mrs. S. I am quite sure George will be disturbed if they are constantly in his way.

Mrs. T. In that case, I really think we had better make some other arrangement.

Mrs. S. My dear Mrs. Tallett, you should exercise a little more self-control. In an arrangement of this kind you must learn to put your own fancies aside a little.

Mrs. T. (aside). Yes, so I think! (Aloud) Well, we will see when Edwin comes.

Mrs. S. Yes.

Mrs. T. Then 'babies,' I suppose, had better go on my list? (Aside) The first thing I've had on it!!

Mrs. S. (writing). Now about lamps—I am very particular about lamps. I dare say you agree with me in disliking gas in a sitting-room?

Mrs. T. No, I don't dislike it. I always think it looks cheerful.

Mrs. S. George and I both dislike it particularly. In fact, we can only read at night, each with our own lamp in one particular place.

Mrs. T. Really! How tiresome that must be!

Mrs. S. And George cannot see at all at night without spectacles.

Mrs. T. Spectacles! Does he wear spectacles?

Mrs. S. Always. They are quite becoming to him.

Mrs. T. (aside). Ugh! (Aloud) I could see quite well sitting on that chair, for instance [*Pointing to armchair*], or that one [*Pointing to rocking-chair*]—if the gas were lighted.

Mrs. S. I thought that *I* would sit on this chair with a light behind me, and George on that one, with another— then you and Mr. Tallett could have been on the sofa and used the gas, if there were no other lamps to be had.

Mrs. T. I am not sure that Edwin would like that arrangement.

Mrs. S. I feel sure George would.

Mrs. T. We will see when they come.

Mrs. S. Then perhaps I had better see about the lamps.

[*Puts it down.*

Mrs. T. In the meantime, hadn't we better have some. tea ?

Mrs. S. (looking at watch). It is only a quarter-past four. I thought five should be our tea-hour.

Mrs. T. (aside). I wish my appetite were not fast !

Mrs. S. It is so much better to settle the hours of our meals at first, and to keep to them. Breakfast, 8.15 : luncheon, 1.15.

Mrs. T. I should have preferred 1.30.

Mrs. S. Why ?

Mrs. T. Because then Nurse can have her dinner first, while I keep baby.

Mrs. S. My dear Mrs. Tallett, you must forgive me if I say that we really cannot arrange our hours to suit your nurse. As a matter of principle, I consider that we ought to lunch at 1.15.

Mrs. T. We will see when Edwin comes.

Mrs. S. Tea at five.

Mrs. T. Oh, I am so hungry !

Mrs. S. Dinner at 7.30.

Mrs. T. I do think it would be so much nicer to have supper at eight, on these lovely summer evenings ! Then we can remain out of doors till the last moment.

Mrs. S. George likes having his evening meal at 7.30.

Mrs. T. I am sure Edwin would prefer his at eight.

Mrs. S. It would be very bad for George to wait so long, as he never has any five o'clock tea.

Mrs. T. Doesn't he ? He must have altered very much since I saw him, then !

Mrs. S. What did you say ? Since you saw him !

Mrs. T. (aside). How stupid of me ! (Aloud) The last time I saw Mr. Stubbs, he did have some five o'clock tea.

Mrs. S. And may I ask when this was ?

Mrs. T. Oh, about ten years ago. It was at a tea picnic at Maidenhead.

Mrs. S. Oh, indeed! this is the first time I have heard of this! I didn't know you had met before.

Mrs. T. Oh, yes, several times.

Mrs. S. I wonder if it was not some one else of the same name as my husband! It is so very unlike him to have said nothing about it. [*Mrs. T. smiles aside.*] What was he like?

Mrs. T. Well, he was—a—a—not very tall——

Mrs. S. Quite so—not tall, but a symmetrically formed man. Fair?

Mrs. T. Yes, fair, with——

Mrs. S. Auburn hair?

Mrs. T. Ye—es, auburn hair.

Mrs. S. Then it certainly was my husband. It is very odd that he should not have told me he already knew you, as I make a great point of his telling me everything.

Mrs. T. Perhaps he forgot!

Mrs. S. No, George never forgets anything. No more do I.

Mrs. T. (aside). What dreadful people to live with!

Mrs. S. And that reminds me—I don't think we have forgotten any of the things I meant to put down in the lists, but we might just run through them and see. By the way, we must ask about the kitchen range—have you heard anything about it?

Mrs. T. (smiling aside). I have heard it mentioned, that was all.

Mrs. S. Then if you have your list, we will just tick off the things.

Mrs. T. The only thing down on my list is 'babies.'

Mrs. S. Oh, really—I thought we had divided more equally than that—but, perhaps, as I have these things down on my paper I may as well see to them. (*Reads*) Tea, marmalade, luncheon, bacon, curtains, butter, lamps, dinner, kitchen range--Oh, and I must write the list of joints from the butcher. I have no more room. I will just take your paper, as you don't want it.

[*Takes letter lying in front of Mrs. T.*

Mrs. T. (in agonies). Only, I might want to put down something more —— [*Stretching out her hand for it.*

Mrs. S. (writing). If you do, I have some paper in my bag I can give you—and I will finish my list on this one, as I have begun.

Mrs. T. (nervously). May I look at it a minute, just to see what you have down?

Mrs. S. One moment.

[*Turns over paper to go on writing.*

Mrs. T. (aside). Now then!!

Mrs. S. (starts). Why—what is this writing? It looks like my husband's!

Mrs. T. (embarrassed). Like your husband's?

Mrs. S. (springing up). It is my husband's! 'Yours truly, George Stubbs.' Mrs. Tallett! I have involuntarily read what is written on that paper—and even now I can hardly believe it!

Mrs. T. (quietly). There is nothing to believe or to disbelieve in it. It is quite simple. It is a note from your husband.

Mrs. S. Quite simple!!

Mrs. T. My dear Mrs. Stubbs, I can explain quite easily ——

Mrs. S. Explain! It requires explanation, indeed! When my husband writes to you to say that as his wife knows nothing of his having met you, you had better sink the past! Sink the past! Mrs. Tallett, what does this mean—what does it imply?

Mrs. T. (aside). Horrid little man, to get me into this scrape! (Aloud) It simply means that, as I have already told you, I have met your husband before—I see nothing so very terrible in it.

Mrs. S. Then may I ask why he writes to you to say that I am to be kept in ignorance of the fact ?

Mrs. T. Well . . . . I suppose because he thought you would be vexed, and it appears that he was right !

Mrs. S. What—you can laugh at it ! Oh, you wicked, wicked woman ! to come between me and my husband, after seven happy years of married life !

Mrs. T. Come between you and your husband ? I assure you I have done nothing of the kind.

Mrs. S. Nothing of the kind ! When he writes to you secretly, asking you not to tell me of your former relation to one another ! Oh, you abandoned creature !

Mrs. T. Abandoned !—how dare you say so ? Because I refused him ?

Mrs. S. Refused him !

Mrs. T. Refused him ! I should think so ! you don't suppose I would have accepted him ?

Mrs. S. What, my husband proposed to you—asked you to marry him ! Oh, how I have been deceived !

Mrs. T. Deceived !

Mrs. S. I thought I was the only woman he had ever loved !

Mrs. T. What difference does it make now ?

Mrs. S. What difference ? Oh, you woman with no feeling, no principle, no sense of anything you should have ! I believe the whole thing was a deep-laid plan of yours, that you might be under the same roof with him !

Mrs. T. I ! *I*, want to be under the same roof with that horrid little red-haired man !

Mrs. S. (gasping). ' Horrid—little —— '

Mrs. T. Red-haired man !

Mrs. S. (furious). Oh, that I should have lived to be insulted by an evil woman, who poisons my happiness and scoffs at my dearest affections ! but I will soon learn the rights of the matter—I will return to Leeds this instant, by the very next train, and confront him with the proofs of his perjury !

Mrs. T. Then this evening, I suppose, by exception, you will not want dinner punctually at 7.30 ?

Mrs. S. Dinner ! Do you suppose I would ever dine at the same table, or sleep under the same roof as you ? No, madam, the arrangement which you had so artfully combined is dissolved—we are a joint household no longer ! I might have known that a woman so lax in all domestic principles, so utterly wanting in regularity of habits, would be deficient in morals also—you are no fit companion for my George to associate with.

Mrs. T. There was a time when he thought differently.

Mrs. S. Fling it in my teeth as much as you like—you will not get him back !   [*Bangs out of the room.*

Mrs. T. Ha ! ha ! Exit to get her things out of the best bed-room ! Horrid, odious woman ! how glad I am she is gone ! and now I shall write to Nurse to bring the children by the early train to-morrow—and Edwin will come on Saturday—how happy we shall all be !

Re-enter Mrs. Stubbs; violently, in travelling costume.

Mrs. S. Good-bye, madam ! I hope that in the solitude and discomfort of your feckless life alone here, you may come to a sense of your guilt !   [*Exit, banging door.*

Mrs. T. Oh, I shall come to a sense of the inestimable comfort of no longer being a Joint Household !

Curtain.

AN UNPUBLISHED MS.

COMEDIETTA IN ONE ACT.

CHARACTERS.

LADY VERNON.   MRS. PAYNE.

SCENE.—*Lady Vernon's drawing-room.*

Enter Lady Vernon.

Lady V. Only two o'clock, and I have finished luncheon already ! dear me, how fast one eats when one is alone—it must be very bad for one ! I took my novel down with me, thinking that then I shouldn't hurry—but it had just the reverse effect ! as when I came to the exciting part I unconsciously devoured my meal as fast as my book—and when I had finished the chapter and came to the surface again, so to speak, I found that my cutlet was gone ! I wish I hadn't let the children go out to their aunt's—I miss them dreadfully. Besides, I am quite sure that Molly will do something dreadful at luncheon, and I shall be told afterwards how badly she behaved. Well, well, it is no good thinking about it. What a horrid time in the day just after luncheon is, to be sure—it's neither one thing nor the other—one doesn't feel brisk enough either to go on with the morning or begin the afternoon. I shall sit down and finish this absurd novel. It really is rather interesting, though one of my friends wrote it ! [*Settles herself in arm-chair with book.*] I have just got to the part where the hero, who is eloping with the heroine in a railway carriage, leans against the door in a tunnel and falls out—very embarrassing for her ! [*Reads on to herself.*] Oh dear ! her former lover, a very wicked man, jumps in at the next station . . . [*Reads on.*] Drags her to a church at the journey's end, and marries her by force ! This is indeed thrilling ! I must take breath a moment after that. [*Leans back, musing.*] Why is it that one's friends always write such very odd books, I wonder ? That reminds me of Mrs. Payne, whom I met for the first time at the Astleys, the other afternoon—poor thing, what an extraordinary creature she is ! the most flighty, sentimental, commonplace of human beings, and the most anxious to be considered a genius ! I was rather interested at meeting her, for her husband and I used to be friends—in fact, if the truth were known, he wanted to marry me ten years ago, when I was Mary Russell. What a long way off that seems, and how absurd he was, poor fellow, always beseeching me to give him the most sentimental love tokens ! a flower I had held in my hand, a bow of ribbon I had worn—once, I remember, he carried off a ridiculous old photograph of me, done when I was a girl of sixteen—a hideous old thing it was too, like most photographs done at that age ! I wish I had it now, in order to see if it is like Mary, my second girl—she is supposed to be so like me. It is too annoying of the creature to have carried off the only copy I had – I wonder if I couldn't get it back ? That is, if it hasn't been in the fire these ten years. I might write to Mrs. Payne for it if I knew her address, the piece of faded sentiment is just the thing she would like. I am told the whole energy of her being has run into the line of romantic fiction, which she reads and she writes till she thinks that everything happens in the world like it does in Arrowsmith's novels ! She is probably convinced that her husband has got something dreadful—something penny dreadful in his past—I should say he's got something much worse in his present ! I wonder if she reads him her novels, poor fellow ! I am told she is very full just now of something harrowing she is writing, about which she talks to everybody as the most profound secret, and then offers to come and read it aloud to them afterwards : she has not taken that desperate course with me yet, I am glad to say. I really don't see why I shouldn't write to Mr. Payne for the photograph, though I don't know his exact address—it is sure to be somewhere in the Temple. It will be so amusing to show it to the children, and tell them that was their mother eighteen years ago. I will. (*Writes*) 'Dear Mr. Payne, in case you should still have among your old papers a photograph of me, done when I was sixteen, it would be very good of you to let me have it again. I have no other copy, and I should like to see whether it resembles my eldest girl. Yours sincerely, MARY VERNON.' (*Addresses it*) ' Robert Payne, Esq., Temple, E.C.'—There, that will be very amusing ! curious that the thing should have come into one's mind after being out of it all these years. [*Puts letter on table.*] I wonder why the two o'clock post hasn't come yet—it is very late. [*Enter Maid with letters.*] Oh, what a nice fat bundle ! [*Opens and reads them, throwing envelopes into the fire.*] Why, all these seem to be invitations to tea this afternoon. 'Darling—come to a meeting of the Primrose League this afternoon and home to tea afterwards.' [*Shakes head.*] 'We have a most interesting Psychical séance, Mr. Myers in the chair.' No, thank you—be told a hundred well-authenticated ghost stories, and then be afraid to come home in the dark afterwards. ' Do come round this afternoon, Nurse has gone out for the day and I am keeping darling Baby.' (*Shakes head*) ' We have a few remarkable people to tea, do look in—Mr. Gladstone hasn't absolutely promised to come.' That's more like it ! Who is this, I wonder ? What a frenzied hand-writing ! [*Turns to end.*] 'Belinda Payne !' She looked as if her name were Belinda! What can she want?—'Dear Lady Vernon, you were so kind the other evening as to ask me to come and see you' (that is to say *she* was so kind as to ask if she might come and see me ! !) So, as I shall be in your part of the world this afternoon about 2·30, it will give me so much pleasure to look in on the chance of finding you. I shall have a few chapters of my last book with me [*Starts*], which I have promised to read at Mrs. Jessop's this afternoon.' [*Jumps up.*] Heavens ! I will rush and say I'm not at home.

> [*As she gets to the door the Maid throws it open and announces Mrs. Payne.*

Lady V. Too late !

Enter Mrs. Payne with a large roll of MS. in her hand.

Mrs. P. (effusively). How do you do, my dear Lady Vernon ? you received my note, I hope ?

Lady V. I was just reading it.

Mrs. P. Indeed. How curious ! I thought I should be more certain of finding you in if I wrote beforehand.

Lady V. (aside). I'm not so sure of that, if I had had half a minute longer !

Mrs. P. (takes MS.) I am a little earlier than I said, I think. My hansom drove very fast. I had at first meant to come in an omnibus, but the idea of the seething, jostling crowd repelled me—it would have been too much, I am sure, for the state in which my nerves are to-day, so I took a hansom. There is something very soothing in its rapid motion. Do you know, it is quite curious how often my moments of great inspiration are in hansoms ?

Lady V. That must be very inconvenient.

Mrs. P. But there is something very interesting in a 'bus too, don't you think so ? Has it never struck you how very like life it is ?

Lady V. (bored).   No, I can't say that it has.

Mrs. P.   Really ? how curious ! to me it is so like it.
People getting in, people getting out, jostling one another
—meeting—going away again—oh, so like it ! But the fact
is, things appeal to me in a way they don't to most people.
I think it is that my imagination is livelier—I see the
relations of things in a way that most people don't—I seem
somehow to have a knack of simile—of comparisons—
after all, everyone can't have the same sort of knack, can
they ?

Lady V.   No, and a very good thing they can't.

Mrs. P. (heartily).   Oh, I do so agree with you. I see
you think exactly as I do about things, I'm sure we shall
get on famously together.

Lady V.   I'm so glad you think so.

Mrs. P.   Oh, I feel quite certain of it ! That's another thing about me, I have such an unerring instinct
about people I meet, it's almost a divination. Now the
other evening when I met you at the Astleys, before I
had talked to you five minutes I had formed my impression of what our relations to each other were. Hadn't
you ?

Lady V.   Oh, quite definitely, I assure you.

Mrs. P.   Exactly, and I felt I could talk to you about
all kinds of things. I mean intimate, private things that I
wouldn't dream of discussing with most people—about
what I am writing, you know, and that sort of thing.

[Makes a motion towards MS.

Lady V. (alarmed).   Won't you undo your cloak ? I
am afraid it must be very hot in here, isn't it ?

[Puts roll of MS. on further table.

Mrs. P.   Oh, thank you, you really are very kind. No,
I don't take off any more, thank you, I will just remove
my boa. Why——

Lady V.   Your muff ? Here it is.

Mrs. P. No, thank you. It was a roll of papers I had in my hand.

> [*Mrs. P. looks round. Lady V. sees the letter to Mr. P. and puts it quickly in her pocket.*

Lady V. (pretending to look). Oh, this must be it, I suppose—this roll that I happened to have put down over here.

Mrs. P. (delighted). Thank you, that's it, I began to think I must have lost it on the way.

> [*Holds out her hand for it.*

Lady V. Oh, there is no hurry for it yet. You shall have it before you go away. [*Replaces it on further table.*

Mrs. P. (with a little affected laugh). I dare say you are wondering . . . . . .

Lady V. You are quite sure you are not too hot ?

Mrs. P. (impatiently). Quite, thank you.

Lady V. Because this has been such a particularly cold day—a sort of damp insidious day, and one ought to be very careful about not being overheated indoors, and then getting a chill going out.

Mrs. P. Thank you, I am glad to say I don't get over-heated indoors, neither do I get chilled going out.

Lady V. Indeed ? You are very fortunate. You are quite independent of the weather then ?

Mrs. P. Yes, I am glad to say so. You will perhaps think it curious, that a person like myself, so acutely susceptible to every mental and moral influence, so strongly sensitive to the magnetic currents of the universe around us, should not be more susceptible to the material influence of cold. That is what you were thinking, I dare say.

Lady V. Yes, I was thinking, certainly, how nice it must be not to catch cold—but since I have adopted the habit of taking ten drops of camphor on a piece of sugar whenever I feel a cold coming on, I feel almost as independent of chills as you do.

Mrs. P. (bored). Indeed ?

Lady V. But the London climate is very trying, don't you think so ?

Mrs. P. Extremely so, in several respects, but most especially in the way that it obtrudes itself into the front of every conversation, until people seem to be able to think and speak of nothing else.

Lady V. Still, people must make rather meaningless remarks sometimes, just to begin the conversation.

Mrs. P. I really don't see why—I *never* do.

Lady V. What would you have them speak of then ?

Mrs. P. Of life's dark depths, of the heart's dark unfathomable depths of sorrow . . . .

Lady V. Dear me—your experience seems to have been an unfortunate one.

Mrs. P. Unfortunate! ah! you may indeed say so ! I have tasted an agony which it is given to few to endure — while others may be assailed by the straightforward blows of visible misfortune, for which they may claim the sympathy of their fellow-creatures—I —*I*—must creep, crawl, crushed along, under the weight of a concealed and invisible sorrow. Ah me ! If the world but knew my sad story ! A dark history is mine !

Lady V. Indeed ! I am very sorry to hear it.

Mrs. P. To explain it, I must go back many years [*Lady V. sighs*], to the time when, an innocent child, I frolicked in the fields with darling Bobby.

Lady V. (surprised). Darling Bobby ? Who is that ?

Mrs. P. Mr. Payne.

Lady V. Well, but I don't quite understand. He wasn't Mr. Payne—I mean you were not Mrs. Payne then ?

Mrs. P. It is true, I was not in fact, but I already was in intention, for, childlike, we had plighted our troth to one another, and agreed that we would marry when we grew up. Alas ! for the fond trustingness of our childhood !

Lady V. Well, but you've carried out your agreement after all, since you *are* married !

Mrs. P. Ah ! but now comes the tragic part of my story. Mr. Payne arrived at manhood, went to college, and in due time began his career at the bar. My father and mother died, and I came to live with one of my aunts in London, so that Bobby and I, who had frolicked hand in hand in the fields, could now have——

Lady V. Frolicked hand in hand in the Park ?

Mrs. P. Yes, not actually perhaps, but in the spirit. It was nothing of the kind !

Lady V. Indeed ?

Mrs. P. For three years, for three long years did he keep aloof from her he loved so well, for three years she pined in secret. Now tell me—what was *he* doing these three years ?

Lady V. (startled). Why do you ask me ?

Mrs. P. I ask you, alas ! with no hope of your being able to give me an answer—but only as a human being, as one, perhaps, of that universal sisterhood of those who despairingly love—what, oh ! what was he doing during those three years ?

Lady V. Well, I imagine that he was deep in examinations. I suppose Mr. Bobby—I beg his pardon, Mr. Payne —like most other young men, was examined, before he could embrace his career, in a great many subjects absolutely foreign to it.

Mrs. P. No—no—I fear it must have been something much more potent than the law, which could engage his affections. It was, I am convinced, some artful, designing woman (perhaps even more than one !), into whose toils he fell, and who stole away the heart that should have been mine !

Lady V. Perhaps, if he *did* think of some one else during the time, the fault was not hers, but his !

M

Mrs. P. Impossible that one who had given his heart into *my* keeping should have voluntarily succumbed to the wiles of the ordinary butterfly of society. For I am conscious of being a woman of peculiar type. A man who cared for me would not lightly turn his thoughts elsewhere unless he were forcibly drawn into it. Yes, I am a strange being! I never made an attempt to allure the opposite sex—during the whole time of my probation no man ever ventured to address the smallest word of admiration to me.

Lady V. (aside). I don't wonder.

Mrs. P. I might have expected Bobby's conduct to be the same—but what good is it to talk of the past? Some day, some day I shall come face to face with those women, and taunt them with my wrongs—they shall know—the world shall know—shortly.   [*Rises, looking at MS.*

Lady V. Must you go? Well it is very good of you to have come. Remember me to Mr.——

Mrs. P. No—I need not go for a while yet. I rose to seek yonder confidante of my grief.   [*Sitting again.*

Lady V. Yonder? . . . . I beg your pardon—what is it you want?

Mrs. P. Yonder scroll.

Lady V. Oh! that roll of papers! here it is, but if you are not going just yet you don't want it.

Mrs. P. Yes I do, thank you. It will help me to tell you and others my soul's story.

        [*Sits with roll in her hand—sighs a deep sigh.*

Lady V. Perhaps you are feeling the cold? I beg your pardon, I remember you don't like to have it mentioned.

Mrs. P. The cold *I* feel is the cold, cruel, grim grasp of grief laid upon my heart.

Lady V. (aside). What a very perplexing symptom! (Aloud) I am sorry you feel uncomfortable.

Mrs. P. Ah, dear lady—uncomfortable! that were

indeed little—but stay, I will read you some papers into
which my full heart has overflowed. You will then understand the significance of my words.

Lady V. Certainly, I shall be delighted. (Aside) I
am in for it now, so I may as well put a good face on it—
besides which, the conversation was beginning to take
rather an awkward turn! (Aloud) What do you call
your book?

Mrs. P. 'The Loves of the Deceived Alinda.' What do
you think of that title?

Lady V. I think it a very good title.

Mrs. P. Ah—good—is that all? Doesn't it strike you
also as having something of yearning and sorrowful, yet
forgiving and womanly in it?

Lady V. And now you mention it I think it does.

Mrs. P. Ah! I am glad you feel it as I do. You will
tell me, will you not, if any criticism occurs to you? It
may have happened that in the soul's passionate outpouring
some minor details of style have been overlooked—though
generally speaking my style is a singularly finished and
perfect one.

Lady V. I really don't think I can promise that—I am
so very ignorant of these things.

Mrs. P. But that will make your genuine simple
remarks the more valuable.

Lady V. Very well, I will then.

Mrs. P. I fear I haven't time to go through the earlier
chapters. I have called each book by some appropriate
name. 1. Preparation. 2. Probation. 3. Expectation.
4. Revelation. That sounds well, does it not?

Lady V. Indeed, yes!—it sounds . . . portentous.

Mrs. P. Portentous—it is. (*Reads*) Book 4—Reve
lation. 'The sun was shining brightly through the
windows as Alinda took leave of her husband for the day.
"I shall be in at five then, my dear," he said, as he felt in

his coat pocket for his gloves.' I think it well to throw
in these little domestic touches, in order to heighten the
effect of the awful tragic element that follows. ' " Very
well," she replied, " the day will not seem long, I am going
to turn out the spare room." " Oh, capital ! " he answered,
heartily. " By the way, darling," she said as he turned to
go, " can you give me the key of that secretary ? There
are several drawers I must use." So unsuspecting was she !
" The key of the secretary ? " he said slowly, " I don't think
I have it—but all the drawers are open, I believe, except
one or two that have nothing but old papers in them."
" Very well," she answered with a strange calmness.
" Good-bye, dear," he said. " At five then," and went out.
Alinda stood motionless, to the eye, but with the intense
vivid perception of a moment of supreme crisis. She
remembered afterwards, when the blow had fallen, how, as
she stood there, she had heard her husband give two slams to
the hall door to make it shut, and had vaguely thought that
the first dull thud was caused by a piece of his ulster being
caught in it. Ah ! never again, never again ! '

Lady V. What, never again ?

Mrs. P. Oh, you'll soon see—that one word is a kind
of epitome of her whole bygone life, and the beginning of
a fresh era of sorrow.

Lady V. I see.

Mrs. P. 'Silently she turned—and walked upstairs
with her Fate—— '

Lady V. With her what ?

Mrs. P. With her fate—her destiny—it's clear enough
when you see it written—a big F.

Lady V. Oh—yes—but should it not be *to* her fate ?

Mrs. P. Now, now, my dear Lady Vernon, you must
forgive my saying so, but that is just where an inexperienced
critic goes astray—we of the craft know what a magical
effect may be produced by one unexpected word.

Lady V. The fact is, as you say, I am so very inexperienced, that I am afraid my criticisms will not be of much use to you.

Mrs. P. Oh, not at all, I am quite delighted to hear what you say—only you know what I mean, don't you ?

Lady V. Oh, entirely. What happened then, when she got upstairs with her fate ?

Mrs. P. 'The rest of the morning passed, she never knew how—she must mechanically have turned out the spare room as she intended, for there were odds and ends in all the chairs—seven best pincushions on the table—a heap of old cotton dresses on the floor. At length, her work done, calm and resolute, she stood in front of the secretary—she tried one drawer—then another—they yielded to her touch with glib and hollow smilingness.' Do you like those epithets, 'glib and hollow smilingness'? they are effective, are they not ?

Lady V. They are certainly, as you were saying just now, unexpected.

Mrs. P. There now, you see how quickly you could get in the way of seeing those little things, it makes such a difference to one's enjoyment of literature, you can't think !

Lady V. (resigned). I should like to enjoy some things more, I must say.

Mrs. P. 'Only the bottom drawer remained—with the heroic self-control of a martyr she tried it—it resisted her efforts, it was locked —she never lost her presence of mind— she hesitated not an instant, but, with infinite courage and coolness, she went straight to the box of keys that was in her bedroom and searched until she found one which would fit the lock—slowly she turned it—slowly she opened the drawers—transfixed she stood, and gazed at the contents.' Now what is your feeling about the situation ?

Lady V. I am wondering what she saw.

Mrs. P. Precisely. You see the tremendous significance of that awful moment ?

Lady V. Certainly.

Mrs. P. I felt sure that you would—that you must !
I resume. 'She gazed at the contents, which were arranged
and labelled somewhat after the fashion of specimens—but
they were in truth a strange museum ! for of what did
they consist ? An old kid glove—a piece of white ribbon
—a pencil—a dead flower—a photograph——'

Lady V. (aside). A photograph—that was where it was !

Mrs. P. What did you say ?

Lady V. I was only exclaiming in surprise at the
contents of the drawer.

Mrs. P. I don't wonder. 'Each of these was on a
piece of white paper, on which some initials were clearly
penned. Whose initials ?—the name of Alinda's husband
was Gascoigne—therefore A.G. might have been there—
her maiden name had been Berkley, therefore still more
might A.B. have been affixed to such relics of the past—
but no—for neither of these names, it was clear, did the
initials stand ! under the kid glove was E.H.C.—by the
ribbon, F.W.—the flower, M.M.R.—the pencil M.R. again
—there they were over and over again, the fateful hideous
characters, attached to everything ! Alinda gasped—Alinda
gazed—here, HERE, it was too evident, did her husband
keep his heart—the rest of his miserable life was but the
unstable shallowness of a dream. Oh, miserable Alinda !
alas, alas, for alone Alinda !'

Lady V. Mrs. Payne, if I may make one more obser-
vation—why was Alinda so perturbed ?

Mrs. P. Why ?!! Great Heavens, she asks why !!

Lady V. After all, even supposing that her husband—
like many other husbands—had had some so-called love
affairs—a harmless amusement enough—before he was
married, what then ?

Mrs. P. What then ? ! !

Lady V. I admit that most men don't perpetuate the recollection of their youth by tying up their relics in a drawer with neat labels—but that is not because they are more virtuous—it is because they are less methodical.

Mrs. P. Ah, cease—cease ! is it possible you can speak so lightly ? What, do you not see that it is my own story I have been reading to you—that I—*I* am the wretched, deceived Alinda—I was the wife who bade good-bye to her husband in the hall, who, alone with her sorrow, turned out the spare room—who opened the drawer of the secretary—I who have been torn by a jealous agony ever since my eye first fell on that photograph, that miserable photograph—and oh ! of such a hideous gawky girl !

Lady V. (aside). Thank you ! ha ! ha ! ha !

> [*Lady V. draws out her handkerchief to conceal her laughter—the letter to Mr. Payne falls out, at Mrs. P.'s feet. Silence. Then Mrs. P. picks it up.*

Mrs. P. It would be idle to pretend that I have not seen the name on that letter !—what—you have been writing secretly to my husband—you, to whom I have been confiding the history of my love ! oh ! shame on you—wicked, wicked woman ! while you listened with pretended sympathy to my tale, you had even then in your pocket the letter that was to estrange him from me—but you shall see—Belinda Payne is not to be tamely vanquished—Lady Vernon, we shall meet again.

> [*Puts letter down on table, prepares to go.*

Lady V. Mrs. Payne, will you oblige me by reading that letter ?

Mrs. P. *I* read it ? never ! This was meant for Bobby, not for me. I will not touch the accursed thing.

> [*Throws it into the fire.*

Lady V. I beg your pardon [*Snatches it out*]—after

the very extraordinary language you have used to me in my own house, I think you are bound to read it when I beg you to do so.

Mrs. P. I will read it—I will know the extent of your infamy.   [*Reads letter.*

Lady V. Well, it isn't so very infamous after all, is it ?

Mrs. P. This portrait, this photograph of which you speak——

Lady V. It is the one you found in the drawer, labelled M.R.—that hideous, gawky girl, you know.

Mrs. P. What ? that was——

Lady V. Myself—it was a photograph of me, and I regret to say very like me. I quite agree with you that I was very unprepossessing then.

Mrs. P. The hateful mystery grows darker and darker. How did your photograph come into his possession ?

Lady V. In the simplest way in the world. He asked me for it, and I gave it to him.

Mrs. P. He asked you for it—why ?

Lady V. Why ? I suppose because he was in love with me.

Mrs. P. In love with you ! ha ! now the horrid truth is revealed. By your own lips, in spite of your plausible words, you have convicted yourself. It is you who have rushed between me and my happiness !

Lady V. I can't be angry with you, for the whole thing is too absurd. This is simply what happened. Ten years ago Mr. Payne fell in love with me, I admit—a thing which often happens when people are young and foolish— he asked me to marry him—I refused - he then fell out of love again, a thing that happens still oftener, and there was an end of it. I had meant to tell you this in any case, after hearing your tale, just to prove to you that the imaginary being you had been conjuring up, whose malign influence hangs darkling over your life, is nothing of the

kind—that she is simply a commonplace matron sitting
quietly and happily by her own hearth, and no more concerned at what your husband is doing, or what he did ten
years ago, than he is with her.

Mrs. P. How can that be, when you this very day
have written him a letter secretly, addressed to his cham
bers ?

Lady V. Ha ! ha ! ha ! I beg your pardon—this is
really too funny ! Appearances are against me, I must
confess ! This is the plain fact—when I met you the other
day, I was reminded for the first time for many years of
Mr. Payne, and of that old photograph—another very plain
fact !—that he has. I want it, to see if it is like my eldest
girl—so, as I didn't know your address, I wrote to the
Temple, which I imagined would find him somehow—that
is the whole history.

Mrs. P. What, can this really be ? But no, there
were others yet—F.W. and E.H.C.—who were they ?

Lady V. (quietly). E.H.C. was Ethel Creswick—she
married the year after I did, and went out to India, where
she has been ever since. F.W. was Flora Williamson,
whom your husband certainly admired, as everyone else
did—she died at Mentone, poor girl, a long time ago.

Mrs. P. She is dead ? . . . . .

Lady V. Yes, F.W. is dead—E.H.C. transported for
life—and M.R., I assure you, is quite harmless—so there are
all your ghosts laid.

Mrs. P. (holding out her hands to Lady V.) Forgive
me ! I have wronged you.

Lady V. Forgive—there is nothing to forgive—the
whole thing is laughable ! But now, since we are making
friends, let me take the privilege of one, and entreat you,
who ought to be one of the happiest of women, not to insist
on being the most miserable—just take life in an ordinary
and sensible way as it comes, and you will find it a very

pleasant way of passing the time. When your husband comes in tired and worried, take it for granted that it has something to do with the day's business, and not with his early love affairs !

Mrs. P. Yes, I know he often says it is his business, but I never believed him !

Lady V. Well, I am sure that if you would turn your attention more to the endless delightful possibilities of everyday life, and neglect romantic fiction a little, you would be ever so much happier.

Mrs. P. Ah—that, I fear, I could not promise quite— neglect fiction ! no, no—I really feel it would be wrong, with a gift like mine, not to go on writing—the 'Loves of the Deceived Alinda' must be finished, but I can go more bravely to work now that I feel it is not my own melancholy history I am recording.

Lady V. Well, if you promise not to identify yourself with the heroine I must be satisfied, I suppose.

Mrs. P. And now I must be going. I have stayed an unconscionable time, but oh, I go with a lighter heart than I came with !

Lady V. (shaking hands warmly). I am glad to hear it.

Mrs. P. I may come and see you again some day, may I not ?

Lady V. I shall be delighted.

Mrs. P. And then, you know, I can read you the rest of my unpublished MS !

Curtain.

A MODERN LOCUSTA

CHARACTERS.

MRS. VERNON.   MRS. MERRINDER.

Mrs. Vernon discovered, alone.

Mrs. V. (reading the 'World'). Dear me! How dull the 'World' is this week. It's generally so delightful. I took it in first to guess the acrostics, and then when I found how entertaining the rest of the paper was, I read it regularly, from the first page to the last—but I must say I don't think this one is worth it. [*Looks up and down the columns.*] I wonder what this paragraph is about. 'It is rumoured that an eminent Q.C., in spite of the proverbial clear-sightedness of his profession, is about to be united in the bonds of holy matrimony to a lady who was once known in criminal circles as the modern Locusta.' Locusta! What does that mean? Who was the ancient Locusta, I wonder? Now this is the good of guessing acrostics. You have all sorts of books to tell you things. [*Takes a book to look it out.*] Locusta, a celebrated female poisoner in the time of Nero. A poisoner! Fancy an eminent Q.C. marrying a poisoner. I must ask my uncle about that. He will be so interested in one of his brother barristers doing such a thing. I know! I'll pretend that I think it is himself. Ha, ha, what a good joke that would be! No, I must say I can't imagine Uncle Greville ever marrying! How funny it would be! Why, if he did I should feel as if

I had a step-mother ! I wonder what she would be like ?
The very pattern of respectability, I'm sure ! And have big
grey curls here [*Touching cheeks*]. However, it isn't very
likely to happen ! He hardly ever speaks to any woman.
In fact, I was quite surprised when I saw him taking Mrs.
Merrinder about the other night at Lady Grey's, and
providing her with supper in the most *empressé* way. Probably she is a wealthy client. Well, he shall marry if he
likes, though it would certainly be a blow to me if he did.
But anything to make him happy — though, after all, it
would never make him happy to go away from Philip and
me and the baby. Why, as he has often said, he looks on
my husband and me as his own children — and the baby ! he
adores the baby, and no wonder. [*Looks at clock.*] Dear
baby ! I wonder how soon he will be in. [*Goes to window.*]
Oh, dear me, there's the sun shining, and I told nurse to take
an umbrella, because I thought it would rain. Oh no, there's
a cloud. I'm so glad. I was right, then. Oh, how nice it
is to have a baby, and a husband, and an uncle, a delightful
uncle like one in a fairy tale, always showering presents
upon one. I really am a lucky woman. The only thing is
that my nurse is going away, and she does make baby's
food so beautifully. However, I have advertised for
another, so I dare say it will all come right. I've said,
' Can anybody recommend a trustworthy nurse ?' for I must
have her trustworthy, it would be so fearful if I couldn't
depend on her to make baby's food. How long the day is !
I wish I hadn't finished the 'World.' I think I shall put
my hat on and go and join nurse and baby in the square.

[*Exit.*

Enter Mrs. Merrinder.

Mrs. M. She is not here. How foolish I have been to
come up unannounced. What shall I do next ? Have I
not made a mistake in coming here at all — in wishing to

see for myself how she will receive my news, how she will face the fact of her uncle's engagement ? What sort of woman is she, I wonder ? Empty-headed, from what I hear, but is she empty-hearted as well ? At any rate, I need not tell her anything until I see. I fortunately have a reason ready to give for my coming here to-day—that I have seen her advertisement, and have come to recommend her a servant. Then if she is a gentle good woman, we will see. [*Looks round.*] A nice little room enough. What has she been reading ? The 'World.' [*Shakes her head.*] Perhaps she is not a prude, then. No, she may be all the same. A baby's toy ! Ah, that should mean a woman with a gentle heart. Here she is.

[*Mrs. V. comes in singing, her walking things on. She stops, surprised at seeing Mrs. Merrinder.*

Mrs. M. I hope you will forgive me, Mrs. Vernon. This is extremely indiscreet of me, I feel—I am Mrs. Merrinder.

Mrs. V. Oh yes, I think I saw you the other evening at Lady Grey's.

Mrs. M. At Lady Grey's ? Yes, I was there. I saw your advertisement in the 'Times' yesterday, and I thought you would allow me to come and tell you of a nice woman I happen to know.

Mrs. V. Oh, thank you. Do you think she could make Ridge's Food ?

Mrs. M. Ridge's Food ?

Mrs. V. Yes, for baby, you know, one has to be so careful to boil it long enough.

Mrs. M. Oh ! Yes, I dare say she could.

Mrs. V. I think on the whole Ridge's Food is the best. What did you feed your children on ?

Mrs. M. I never had a child.

Mrs. V. Oh, I am so very sorry for you. I think it

must be terrible not to have a baby in the house—quite terrible.

Mrs. M.   Is yours a great delight to you?

Mrs. V.   Indeed he is: he is the greatest darling! and he is *such* an intelligent child.

Mrs. M.   Really? How old is he?

Mrs. V.   Eight months to-morrow.

Mrs. M.   Eight months? that is very early to show such intelligence.

Mrs. V.   Isn't it? That is what I say. It's wonderful— quite wonderful. Just imagine what he does. When his father comes into the room with a great noise, and says 'Baby, where's papa?' he looks round immediately. Now I call that quite extraordinary, don't you?

Mrs. M.   Quite.

Mrs. V.   I'm so glad you agree with me. Do you know I told that story to one of my husband's cousins the other day, and she didn't see anything surprising in it? Wasn't it funny of her?

Mrs. M.   Very. One's relations are very trying at times, no doubt.

Mrs. V.   They are indeed. I have very few, I am glad to say. I have only, let me see, a great-aunt (in the country, so she doesn't count), and that cousin of my husband's— and an uncle of my own, but *he* is worth a whole family put together.

Mrs. M.   Your uncle?

Mrs. V.   My uncle, yes, indeed. But you know him, I think. Surely I saw you with him the other evening?

Mrs. M.   Yes, you did. I know him.

Mrs. V.   And don't you think him very charming?

Mrs. M.   Yes.

Mrs. V.   And he is as good and kind as he is delightful.

Mrs. M.   You are very fortunate.

Mrs. V.   I am. I can't tell you what he has been to

me My parents died when I was quite a child, and my uncle has been father and mother in one to me. Then, when I married, he quite adopted my husband too, and now I'm sure he is more devoted to dear baby than either of us. So altogether, we are the happiest family in the world.

Mrs. M. You are indeed fortunate. It isn't every-one who is so happy.

Mrs. V. I have no patience with people who are not happy. I think it is so silly of them.

Mrs. M. (aside). There is nothing so merciless as youth and prosperity combined. (Aloud) But perhaps it isn't always in their own power.

Mrs. V. Oh, more or less, I think it is !

Mrs. M. To begin with, some people don't marry.

Mrs. V. Oh, that is a great mistake. I think every-one ought to marry.

Mrs. M. Everyone ?

Mrs. V. Certainly, if they want to be happy.

Mrs. M. In that case, there would be no bachelor uncles.

Mrs. V. I shouldn't like my uncle Greville to marry, of course.

Mrs. M. Why not ?

Mrs. V. I should feel as if I had a step-mother, and I shouldn't like that at all.

Mrs. M. I see you have made up your mind to the worst already.

Mrs. V. But the whole thing is too absurd to think of. Of course he will never marry.

Mrs. M. Why of course ?

Mrs. V. For one thing, he is too fond of us.

Mrs. M. Why shouldn't he be happy because he is fond of you ?

Mrs. V. Oh, it isn't a question of *his* happiness.

Mrs. M. Not if he were to marry ?

Mrs. V. He won't.

Mrs. M. Let us suppose it possible, and that you heard it was going to happen. What would you say, what would you do, I wonder ? I am really curious to know.

Mrs. V. Oh, I think first of all, I should burst into tears.

Mrs. M. Into tears ?

Mrs. V. Yes, I am sure I should. I should sob, and feel that I had lost my best friend, and that baby was going to be slighted and neglected, and altogether I should be very wretched indeed.

Mrs. M. But suppose you found he were going to marry some one who only longed to make friends with you — who would care for you and your husband, and instead of neglecting your boy, would love him too ?

Mrs. V. That would be delightful, of course, but it is so unlikely to happen. So very few people would be as kind as you were just now about dear baby, or would understand his mind so well.

Mrs. M. My dear child !

Mrs. V. (surprised). Mrs. Merrinder !

Mrs. M. I should like to care for you and yours if you will let me.

Mrs. V. Let you ? Why, it would be charming. Do let us be friends, I should like it so much.

Mrs. M. (takes her hand). If you knew what it is to me to have a warm, womanly hand in mine—to feel I am no longer alone ! Do you really mean you would like to be friends ?

Mrs. V. Indeed, indeed I do, from the very bottom of my heart.

Mrs. M. Then let me tell you something I came to say, something I determined you should only hear from my own lips, that I might read in your face what your answer was. No, now it comes to the point, I am afraid.

Mrs. V. What is it? What can you mean?

Mrs. M. Can you not guess? When I tell you that I have the right to ask you for your friendship, your love, and to offer you mine? Now do you know?

Mrs. V. (shakes her head).

Mrs. M. You saw me with your uncle, you said, two nights ago.

Mrs. V. (starting). With my uncle? Is it—no, it is not possible that——

Mrs. M. That he has asked me to marry him? Yes, he has.

Mrs. V. To marry him—my uncle! Oh!

[*Bursts into tears.*

Mrs. M. (aside). There's nothing like carrying out one's programme! (Aloud) You see, your worst previsions are realised. I fear I need not ask what your answer is.

Mrs. V. Forgive me—forgive me! The fact is, I was so taken by surprise, that I hardly knew what I was saying—but you will not take his love from us, will you?

Mrs. M. No indeed, I have told you that I won't. (*Meaningly*) You do not wish, then, to take his love from me?

Mrs. V. No, no! How can you think so?

Mrs. M. And yet, if I am not mistaken, it is a great blow to you to hear of his engagement?

Mrs. V. Yes, of course. Then when I found it was to you, that was different. [*Mrs. M. strokes Mrs. V.'s hand.*

Mrs. V. I hope you will be very happy.

Mrs. M. Don't you think that everyone is happier married?

Mrs. V. It's very nice to be married, certainly.

Mrs. M. Yes, indeed you are happy! You look as if you had never known what it was to be otherwise. Is that so?

Mrs. V. Yes, I must admit that I have always been

N

very happy, and now I am more so than ever since I have
had dear baby.

Mrs. M. (smiling).   And in consequence, doubtless, you
have a kind of feeling that when others are not so happy,
it is their own fault for losing the chances that life has to
offer them ?

Mrs. V. (confused).   No, no, not that exactly.   I am
sorry for them.   I feel pity, compassion.

Mrs. M.   Pity, compassion—yes, I know what that
means. The shadow cast by compassion is called—contempt !

Mrs. V.   No, no, I assure you I should like everyone
else to be as happy as myself, if it were possible.

Mrs. M.   If it were possible, yes, but you hardly feel
that it is ?   You are a little surprised that other people
should fall in love, and wish to live their own lives, instead
of living in other people's.   Is not that so ?

Mrs. V.   Well, of course one doesn't realise that other
people feel the same as one does oneself.

Mrs. M.   No, I have noticed that it appears to be
difficult.

Mrs. V.   And I shall soon get accustomed to the idea
of my uncle's marrying.   In fact, only this morning, just
before you came, I was thinking how strange it would be
if he married.   Something—a paragraph—in the ' World '
put it into my head.

' *Mrs. M.*   A paragraph in the ' World ?'   What was
that ?

Mrs. V.   Here it is.   Haven't you seen it ?   About an
eminent Q.C.'s engagement.

[*Puts paper into her hand.   Reads the paragraph aloud.*

Mrs. M.   And what did you think when you read that
paragraph ?

Mrs. V.   I thought how interested my uncle would be
when he saw it—and that as he is a Q.C. himself, he would
probably know who the people were.

Mrs. M. Do you want to know who the modern Locusta is ?

Mrs. V. Yes, I should like to know who she is, and what she did.

Mrs. M. I can tell you what she did.

Mrs. V. Can you ? How very interesting. Do !

Mrs. M. She ran away from her first husband with a man whom she afterwards married, and then, so it was said, tried to poison.

Mrs. V. Oh, what a horrible woman ! Is she alive now ?

Mrs. M. Yes, I believe she is.

Mrs. V. And what was done to her ?

Mrs. M. Nothing—nothing, that is, according to the law. The jury disagreed upon their verdict. They contented themselves with dismissing her into the world with an indelible shadow hanging over her name.

Mrs. V. And she deserved it !

Mrs. M. You think she did ? without knowing anything more of her history, any of the grounds of her defence, you condemn her at once ?

Mrs. V. Well, a woman who runs away from one husband, and poisons another, can't be a nice woman.

Mrs. M. 'Nice'—perhaps not ! One of the accusations against her, that of trying to poison her lover, I believe to have been false. It's true she ran away from the first one, but we cannot tell on whose shoulders rested the responsibility of that crime. She may have been flying from misery greater than she could bear.

Mrs. V. Oh no. A woman is always in the wrong who runs away from her husband.

Mrs. M. Ah, that is your hard and fast code ! That is how the world is governed, doubtless.

Mrs. V. And a good thing too.

Mrs. M. Oh, how merciless you happy and virtuous

women can be to those whom you think not so good as
yourselves !

Mrs. V. But don't you think that's right ? That's
how we help to keep other women straight, by turning our
backs on them when they behave badly.

Mrs. M. By turning your backs on them—a Christian code indeed !

Mrs. V. I feel quite sure my uncle would agree with
me. He's so intensely particular about women.

Mrs. M. You don't think he would have a wider
tolerance and more lenient judgment – that he would
readily hold out his hand to an unfortunate woman against
whom fortune has set her face ?

Mrs. V. Oh, I think his kind heart would be sorry for
her, grieved for her—but I know quite well how very
strong his views about women are, for he is never tired of
repeating them.

Mrs. M. Indeed ? and what does he say ?

Mrs. V. Oh, he has the most exaggerated and high-
flown sentiments. My husband often tells him that he
carries it a great deal too far. He would never have a
woman's name mentioned at all outside the domestic circle.
The very idea of criticism, of discussion, by those who are
not her nearest and dearest, is repugnant to him.

Mrs. M. Repugnant to him ?

Mrs. V. Yes, in fact he often says, partly in fun, of
course, that he is so glad that I am never likely to be
famous—to do anything clever, you know, that would have
made people talk about me. He wouldn't have liked it
at all.

Mrs. M. I see. (Aside) That must be a delightful
certainty.

Mrs. V. Do you know what his nickname is—what he
is called among his friends ?

Mrs. M. No, I don't indeed.

Mrs. V. He is called The Guarantee, because people always say, 'Oh, Mr. Greville's name is a guarantee for everything!' For justice in a cause—for honesty in a servant—for innocence in a client——

Mrs. M. For a good name in a woman!

Mrs. V. Exactly! so that you see that to be his niece is a very great privilege.

Mrs. M. Still more, then, I imagine, to be his wife?

Mrs. V. (starting). His wife!—yes—of course. I beg your pardon—I was forgetting. Some people grumble at him for being such an oldfashioned Puritan, but I think it's a good thing.

Mrs. M. Very!

Mrs. V. For it is horrid for a woman not to be nice, isn't it?

Mrs. M. (with veiled sarcasm). Oh yes. A woman, of course, must be 'nice' before everything. (Aside) Oh, to think that public opinion is made by such intelligences as these!

Mrs. V. You do agree with me, don't you?

Mrs. M. Oh, entirely, of course!

Mrs. V. (relieved). That's right. Do you know I was afraid you didn't—and I was so surprised, knowing so well what my uncle's opinions are!

Mrs. M. Your uncle, then, would not have been likely to marry the lady who is known as the Modern Locusta?

Mrs. V. (in fits of laughter). My uncle! Oh, how very funny! What an extraordinary idea! Oh, I never heard anything so funny. I shall die of laughing—I really shall.

Mrs. M. It is indeed extraordinarily amusing.

Mrs. V. I tell you what is making me laugh now—the thought of what immense fun it would be to pretend, for a joke, that I thought this man mentioned in the 'World' was himself.

Mrs. M.   Or to pretend that it really was he.

Mrs. V.   How do you mean?

Mrs. M.   To tell him that *I* am the Modern Locusta.

Mrs. V. (in fits of laughter).   Oh, the idea is too delicious, really!   You will kill me, I know you will.

Mrs. M.   I dare say I shall, before I have done with it!

Mrs. V.   Now I tell you what would be amusing.   Let's rehearse what we should say when we told him, and what he would say.

Mrs. M.   What *he* would say—yes!

Mrs. V.   I should begin, ' Uncle, you are going to be married?'   'Yes,' he would reply, 'to a very charming woman.'   'I know it,' I should say, 'I have seen her.'

Mrs. M. (with a little smile of acknowledgment).   Thank you.   But go on : you have not yet come to the interesting part.

Mrs. V.   'Ha, ha, uncle!' I should say, 'I know something about her that you don't.'   Then he would be surprised, wouldn't he?

Mrs. M.   Undoubtedly.

Mrs. V.   'Something about her past life.'   Then he would begin to be startled and rather anxious.

Mrs. M.   Startled—yes, and anxious!

Mrs. V.   'Do you know who she is?' I would say.   Of course, he would say 'Yes,' and then I'd say, 'But do you know who she *was*?'   That's my great point, you see.

Mrs. M.   Yes.   Who she *was*.   That's an important point, certainly.

Mrs. V.   And then——Do you think I had better prepare him more?

Mrs. M. (endeavouring to smile).   Oh no, I should think by this time he would be sufficiently prepared.   I would tell him at once.   It would come to the same thing in the end, I fancy.

Mrs. V. Very well. Then I would tell him, in the words of that paragraph, in the most tragical tones, 'She was a lady known in criminal circles as the Modern Locusta!' Ha! ha! Now wouldn't that be good?

Mrs. M. Excellent! But now what does *he* say? That seems to be the important part.

Mrs. V. First he turns white, as white as a sheet. Then he recovers himself, and says. 'You are laughing at me.' I tell him I know it for a fact.

Mrs. M. By the way, you have not told him how you are supposed to know it.

Mrs. V. Oh, I know it, because you've told me.

Mrs. M. Ah, because I've told you. Exactly. Go on. And then?

Mrs. V. Oh, I don't know. I haven't imagined all that yet. Of course there is a great tragical scene, when he finds that, as they say in books, he is linked to the vilest of her sex.　　　　　*[Mrs. M. starts.*

Mrs. V. He is broken-hearted, and in despair. He struggles between his love and—— *[Hesitates for a word.*

Mrs M. And his honour.

Mrs. V. And his honour—exactly. And—and—but I am not clever enough to imagine the rest of it. You must go on now.

Mrs. M. Perhaps I had better imagine what *I* should be saying and doing in the meantime.

Mrs. V. Ah yes, just so. What would you be saying?

Mrs. M. I would say to you—What, can you, a woman, thus lightly brand another with being the vilest of her sex? Can you judge her, and dismiss her to everlasting ignominy, without another thought—hardly even knowing of what she is accused?

Mrs. V. (interrupting). 'No, no,' I should say. 'I do know that she ran away from one man, and poisoned another——'

Mrs. M. You know that was what people said—but what if it were not true? What if the woman you are ready to destroy were far from being the vilest of her sex? —with a heart beating to passions such as you cannot even understand—with a mind tuned to emotions that you cannot reach—what if she were persecuted, ruined, by the villain who at last drove her from his house, and were afterwards falsely accused of having caused the death of the one being whom she cared for on this earth—what then?

Mrs. V. Oh, go on. You do act splendidly!

Mrs. M. (recovering herself). Ah—yes—I do—act splendidly! Now it's your turn.

Mrs. V. What a pity! You do it so much better. Then we would say—my uncle and I, you know——

Mrs. M. Your uncle and you—yes.

Mrs. V. Then we should say, of course, that it was impossible, that a woman who could have those things said about her, whether they were true or not, could never be a fitting wife for him, that the whole thing was a terrible misfortune, and—and—that would be the end of it, I suppose.

Mrs. M. The end of it? No, that would not be the end of it. I would still plead her cause. Suppose, I would say, that this woman, whom you spurn from you with such ruthless cruelty, whose youth was wrecked by an unpitying fate, suppose that she at last conquered in the struggle with destiny, and that she has since led a pure and stainless life, far from the world which has now forgotten even her name—what then? May she never again take her place among her kind? May she never stand with head erect among her sister women?

Mrs. V. Oh, but my uncle couldn't bear a woman who had been talked about. The woman who has had those things said about her couldn't be a nice woman, you know.

Mrs. M. A nice woman—ah! Your uncompromising

pettiness passes the bounds of my endurance. What can a nature like yours have ever known of passion, misfortune, of repentance - of anything which throbs in the life of a great heart? You, who would father your imbecility upon one of the noblest of men—pretending that you fulfil his ideal! His ideal indeed! You must well nigh have destroyed it, by cramping all his nobler impulses—bounding his larger views with your miserable horizon—binding him with the petty chains of a sleek and canting domesticity! oh, that it should be you, and such as you, who are the arbiters of such as I am! Good God!

Mrs. V. Mrs. Merrinder, you frighten me! you say all that as if it were true.

Mrs. M. It *is* true! [*Mrs. V. starts—Mrs. M. stops her with a gesture.*] Listen to me! If you have been capable of understanding one word of what I have been saying, listen to me now, while I tell you it is true—that it is my own cause that I have been pleading—that I—I, do you hear—am the woman who was driven from her home—that it was I who sought shelter with the man of whose death I was accused, but of which, as I stand in sight of Heaven, I am innocent!

Mrs. V. You—you!

Mrs. M. Ah, shrink from me as much as you like—you need not fear that I shall draw near you again. My dream is over. Fool that I was to have cherished it, even for a moment!—to have dreamt that after a life of loneliness and regret I might yet become the wife of a good man, and be welcomed to share the lives of happy women! fool indeed! I see now to what I am doomed. You need no longer fear that my shadow will fall across your spotless life. No, I renounce my last chance of happiness. I will not condemn the man I love to be the guarantee for my good name. Do not fear that you will ever see me again. [*Goes towards door.*] I have humbled myself in the dust before you, it is true, in one moment of delusive hope, but I could not, I know it now, pass my life in ashes before you, in one long expiation—expiation of what? Of the chance—the luck—the fate that gave you happiness, and me [*Standing in doorway*] . . . . misery!   [*Exit.*

Mrs. V. buries her face in her hands.

Curtain.

THE 'SWISS TIMES'

COMEDIETTA IN ONE ACT.

CHARACTERS.

MRS. GORDON, a rich widow.
MRS. JACKSON.
MRS. PROUT.
CARRIE, Mrs. Jackson's daughter.
ALETHEA, Mrs. Prout's daughter.
HELEN MAYNE, an orphan.

SCENE.—*The Hôtel du Lac, Zurich. The public sitting-room. Upright piano, R. Ditto, L. Small table at back L.C. Chair by it. Table in front R.C. Couch, L. Chairs, &c.*

Enter Mrs. Gordon with books, work, &c.

Mrs. G. No one here—how delightful to find a public sitting-room at an hotel unoccupied! But it is too good to last, I fear, for in a few minutes all the rest of the inhabitants will come in from the long, hot table d'hôte, and fill the room with their meaningless talk. [*Looks at watch.*] Seven thirty, and the post goes out at eight! I must finish my letters. I'll just read over this letter to see if I've left out any words—I usually do! [*Reads*] 'Thursday, July 20, Hôtel du Lac, Zurich. Dearest Susan—I wish you were here—for it is so dull being at an hotel by oneself! Where is the enjoyment of meeting ridiculous people if you have no one to whom you can say how ridiculous they are? Never mind, in a few days I shall have a companion, I

hope, for what do you think ?   I have advertised for one !
in the "Swiss Times" !   I dare say you have never heard of
that periodical—it is an English paper published at Berne
for the use of tourists. This is what I have said: "Wanted,
for a tour on the Continent, a young lady as companion,
age between twenty and twenty-five.   Must be bright,
intelligent, a good linguist, and a good musician.   Apply
personally at the Schweizerhof, Lucerne, on Saturday, July
the 22nd." Don't you think that sounds attractive ? There
must be many a young woman who would be too delighted
to come for a tour round Europe. The only thing is that I
must find exactly the right person. As you know, I unfortunately have a great many fads and fancies—I should like
my companion to have some too, provided they chime in
with mine. For instance, I should hate some one who would
borrow my scissors, or lend me her thimble, or cut my
magazines, or wander about the room with a distracted air
looking for something when I am talking, or read me scraps
of news out of a paper, or tell me the end of a book I am
panting over—or on the other hand, I should hate her just
as much if she jumped up from her chair and offered it to
me when I came into the room, instead of leaving me a cool
unrumpled seat, or who would give me up her footstool, and
generally lead a life of outward and visible mortification of
which I should feel with impotent rage that I was the in-
voluntary cause !   Oh, if I were Ibsen, and had to regene-
rate society, I would quickly write a companion play to the
" Pillars of Society "and call it the "Caterpillars of Society,"
in which I would hold up to ignominy and reprobation all
those who insist on creeping through life and being down-
trodden by their fellow creatures ! No, my ideal companion
(may Fate send her to Lucerne on Saturday !) is a quiet,
simple, yet dignified young girl, cultivated and intelligent,
who is always pleasantly occupied, who can knit and who
can read, and who is equally happy doing either or both,

and above all who cannot only play patiences, but who likes doing them on her own account instead of mine! There now, dear Susan, that is the person I want—if you know of such a one, telegraph, and I will rush rapidly across Europe to find her. Ever your affectionate friend, Jane Gordon. P.S. Harry writes to me from India that his love affair is off, I am grieved to say. I am dreadfully sorry—I had had visions of all that a daughter-in-law might be to me—and yet when I reflect how impossible it would be that my son should ever find anyone approaching to good enough for him, the thought of his marriage makes me anxious.' [*Fastens letter.*] There, now, that is done. And now, to write to Harry—I really don't know what to say—where is his letter? [*Reads his letter to her.*] 'As to what I told you of in my last letter, dear mother, it has come to an untimely end, for the moment at least. She has left—gone back to Europe. She has been very badly treated by the people she is with, but it is no use saying anything more about it now. Next year I shall go on leave, and then—we shall see.' Well, I don't understand all this. I must wait till he comes, I suppose—dear boy! I *shall* be glad to see him! and then he will show me that wonderful patience again, the 'Mystery of the Skies,' that no one can do but himself. I have forgotten how to do the beginning of it. [*Voices heard outside.*] Dear me, what a bore! I hope a crowd of horrid English people won't come in here—people who take away the newspapers, and move the ink, and play the piano, and monopolise the lamp, and altogether make life unbearable while they are in the room.

[*Sits and writes at table.*

Enter Mrs. Jackson and Mrs. Prout talking.

Mrs. J. My dear Mrs. Prout, how you can say that the cooking is good here, I don't know. Why we've had veal cutlets and salad every day for a week!

Mrs. P. Perhaps, yes—but they are very well cooked, and quite tempting to my poor appetite.

Mrs. J. I didn't know raw salad with garden mould in it was considered a good diet for invalids.

Mrs. P. And I quite enjoyed the stewed fruit.

Mrs. J. Ah, if you like the sauce thickened with glue, I don't wonder you did.

Mrs. P. Oh, I think you are mistaken, really—I must have noticed if anything had been wrong. I am obliged to give a great deal of attention to these things—I am not really equal to travelling and knocking about.

Mrs. J. I see. (Aside) Such humbug! the woman is as strong as she can be! it is only that she is so greedy, she thinks of nothing else but her food.

[*Mrs. Prout has walked to the window and is looking out.*

Mrs. P. I wonder where those dear girls of ours are? I do hope Alethea will not go on to the grass with thin shoes.

Mrs. J. Does she catch cold easily?

Mrs. P. Oh, she is the frailest of creatures, though perhaps she doesn't look it. She is all intellect, all mind— no body at all, so to speak.

Mrs. J. (aside). No wonder her dresses fit so badly.

Mrs. P. It is really for her sake I am travelling—she is so anxious to complete her education by going to Rome. She has been at Girton for two years.

Mrs. G. (aside). They have each got a daughter. I wonder if either of them would do for me!

Mrs. J. (coming up to the table where Mrs. Gordon is reading the 'Swiss Times'). Oh, I beg your pardon . . .

Mrs. P. (turning round and laying down the paper). Were you speaking to me?

Mrs. J. (pouncing on paper). Oh, thank you, yes. I

was only going to say had you seen the 'Swiss Times'?
This is it, thank you.

> [*Draws lamp towards her and sits down to read.*

Mrs. G. (aside). I do think that is the very rudest
woman I have ever seen!

Mrs. P. (coming up to table). Oh, I beg your pardon,
I think I saw the ink there—yes.

> [*Takes away ink, pens and blotting-paper from before
> Mrs. G., retires to the other table, at back, L.C.*

Mrs. G. No, I think on the whole *that* is the rudest.

Mrs. J. (who has been reading paper, gives a shriek).
Oh, I wonder where Carrie is! Here is exactly the thing
she wants. (To Mrs. P.) Just listen to this.

> [*Mrs. Jackson stands by Mrs. Prout's table and reads
> to her Mrs. Gordon's advertisement.*

Mrs. P. (excited). The very thing, of course.

Mrs. J. (pleased). Exactly. I see it strikes you as it
does me. It is the very thing for——

Mrs. P. Alethea.

Mrs. J. (taken aback). For Alethea? No—I meant
for Carrie.

Mrs. P. For Carrie—for your daughter?

Mrs. J. And why not for my daughter, as well as
for yours? May I ask?

Mrs. P. Firstly, because it says she must be intelligent.
That seems to apply more to Alethea.

Mrs. J. Yes—but it doesn't say she is to be pedantic.

Mrs. P. (outraged). Pedantic?

Mrs. J. Yes—pedantic. That is what I should say the
characteristic of your daughter is.

Mrs. P. I suppose that is because she doesn't dance
breakdowns in the public room of the hotel like Miss
Jackson.

Mrs. J. Breakdowns indeed? Carrie danced a reel

the other night, if that is what you mean. And very well she did it. I like a girl to be lively.

Mrs. P. Lively, yes, but not acrobatic.

Mrs. J. (aside). It's quite evident her girl can't dance a step—those girls never can. (Aloud) I see that candidates are requested to apply at Lucerne. Curiously enough, we had arranged to be at Lucerne on Saturday.

Mrs. P. Indeed? It is singular that we should have settled to do the same thing.

Mrs. J. Oh, really! We shall meet there then, that will be very agreeable.

Mrs. P. Particularly so.

Mrs. J. (lays the paper down). I wonder where Carrie is!

Mrs. P. I do wish Alethea wouldn't remain out so long.

Mrs. G. If you have done with the paper, may I have it for a few minutes? I had not quite finished reading it.

Mrs. J. Oh, certainly, certainly. It is very dull: there is nothing in it.

Mrs. G. (aside). That is what people always say when they hand you a paper they have read from the first word to the last.

Mrs. J. There is one thing very interesting in it, to me, at least—an advertisement for a companion—there, on the third page.

Mrs. G. Yes. I have seen it.

Mrs. J. (confidentially). I thought that would do so well for my daughter.

Mrs. G. Indeed—does your daughter wish to be a companion?

Mrs. J. Well, I don't know that she wishes it particularly, but it seems to me to be the only thing for her to do. I thought she would have been married before this. We were at Southsea last year, and she had the greatest success with the officers there, but somehow she is still at home. And now Pa says——

Mrs. G. Who ?

Mrs. J. Pa—that's my husband, you know. He says that with the four other girls we have growing up, and two boys to provide for, he can't afford to keep them all, and that Carrie must provide for herself in some way, either by teaching or by going out as a companion. Now as to teaching, I'm not sure that she has the patience for it : and though she is as clever as she can be, perhaps her cleverness is not quite in that line—it is more the kind of cleverness that can—that can——

Mrs. G. Amuse officers at Southsea.

Mrs. J. Exactly. Now this is the sort of thing that would suit her excellently. For she is certainly bright and intelligent.

Mrs. G. Is she good-tempered ?

Mrs. J. Yes, I think so. With strangers, certainly, she would be good-tempered enough, and she picks up all the new songs, and sings them with quite a dash. Oh, she would be an acquisition anywhere, I'm sure. Ah, there she is passing the window, I must go and talk to her about it. [*Exit quickly.*

Mrs. G. (shaking her head). No. I am afraid that is hardly my ideal !

Mrs. P. (advancing confidentially). Did I hear Mrs. Jackson talking to you about her daughter ? I thought so. You know I can't help thinking she is making the very greatest mistake in wanting her to apply for that post of companion which is advertised in the 'Swiss Times.' You see, it isn't as if the girl were like mine, or even like that little Miss Mayne, though *she* is commonplace enough— the person whom it would suit exactly is my Alethea.

Mrs. G. Does your daughter wish to be a companion ?

Mrs. P. I won't say that exactly, but she particularly

wants to travel, and I really have not the strength nor
the means to take her. I was ill for a week, I really was,
after we spent a day at the Palace of the Cæsars in Rome.
It is all very interesting, I dare say, but we were not
taught about those things when I was a girl. I don't
know the difference between one Cæsar and another, and I
don't want to know which of the Seven Hills we were
walking upon. I could see it was the steepest and the
muddiest, and that was enough for me. However, I am
told they are levelling all the hills in Rome now, so that
will make it less tiring both to the mind and to the body.
But what would suit me would be a quiet country life
in England, near the village of which my dear husband
used to be rector, and if I felt that Alethea could find
some one to travel with, who would know all about the
Cæsars and that sort of thing, it would be a great comfort
to me.

Mrs. G. I see.

Mrs. P. So we shall try to make an early start for
Lucerne early in the day—that is, if I have had a good
night, but I am such a wretched sleeper! Then we shall be
beforehand with other people.

Mrs. G. Yes, I dare say that would be a good plan.
Then what about that other girl you mentioned—Miss
Mayne? Will she be one of the competitors too for this
post?

Mrs. P. Oh, well, if she is, she won't be a formidable
one.

Mrs. G. Will she not? I always thinks she looks
interesting. She is certainly very pretty.

Mrs. P. Pretty? Well, if you call having regular
features, pretty—it is intensity of expression I look for,
more like Alethea's, you know.

Mrs. G. I haven't had the pleasure of seeing your
daughter yet.

Mrs. P. Ah, then, that is why you think Miss Mayne pretty. As for her being interesting, I should have thought her the dullest little person : she is always knitting, or reading, or something of that kind. And she does patiences by herself in the evening : so unlike a girl, I call that !

Mrs. G. (aside). Knitting, and reading, and doing patiences ! I like the sound of that.

Mrs. P. Here she is, coming in. Pretty and interesting indeed !

> *Enter Helen, her knitting and a book in her hand. She strolls to table, looks at books, &c. Mrs. Prout goes back to writing.*

Mrs. G. (watching Helen). Were you looking for this paper ?   [*Handing the ' Swiss Times.'*

Helen (pleasantly). Oh, thank you very much—that is, if you don't want it.

Mrs. G. Not at all.   [*Helen reads paper.*

Helen (smiling). I think I am taking all the lamplight.   [*Pushes lamp towards Mrs. G.*

Mrs. P. Tiresome woman to go and give her that paper to read ! she will be packing up and going to Lucerne too.

Helen (suddenly interested). I wonder if this is anyone's paper, or if it belongs to the hotel ?

Mrs. G. It belongs to the hotel, I think. Why?

Helen. Only that there is something here that I should have liked to cut out—an advertisement. But it doesn't matter, I will copy it.

> [*Goes to table at back. Mrs. Gordon looks on and smiles aside, as Helen copies the advertisement.*

Enter Mrs. Jackson and Carrie.

Carrie. Really, mother, it is a shame to bring me in on this fine evening, just when we were having such fun out of doors.

Mrs. J. I wanted to speak to you. Besides it is much better that you should sit in here with me, rather than be running about the garden with a crowd of strangers.

Carrie. It wasn't with a crowd, mamma, I assure you, only one person—Monsieur Barette, that young Frenchman who sat opposite us at the table d'hôte. I was teaching him how to hop.

Mrs. J. How to hop! my dear! I really think that that is a thing which girls need not teach young gentlemen to do.

Carrie. Why not, mamma? we can do it so much better than they can! you see the mistake most people make when they hop is that they hang their spare foot out behind, and then rock their shoulders about, so. [*Hops round.*] The real way to do it is to put your foot out in front, and go round lightly like this—then you are like a bird.   [*Hops.*

Mrs. J. Like a bird, indeed! The bird you are like is a goose! hopping about, neglecting your most important interests!

Carrie. Important interests? I didn't know I had any.

Mrs. J. But you have though. There is a place of companion which is waiting for you, if you choose to take it.

Carrie. Do you really mean it? Where? Anything should like?

Mrs. J. I should say you would like it extremely. It is an advertisement in the 'Swiss Times.' Here it is. Oh,

I beg your pardon, you were not reading this paper, were you ?   [*Taking the paper out of Helen's hand.*

Helen.   Oh dear no !

Mrs. J. (reading advertisement to Carrie).   There, you see, that is just what you want.   It will suit you exactly.

Carrie.   Yes.   It would suit *me* exactly, I dare say— the question is, whether I shall suit the advertiser exactly.

Mrs. J.   Why shouldn't you ?   You are bright, intelligent, between twenty and twenty-five——

Carrie.   Oh yes, I'm all that.   Now go on.

Mrs. J.   You are a good linguist.

Carrie.   A good linguist !   My dearest mother, pray draw it mild !

Mrs. J.   Carrie !   How often must I beg you not to use those slang expressions !   Nobody will want you as a companion if you talk like that.

Carrie.   Except M. Barette—he wants me dreadfully ! I see the poor thing panting with impatience in the garden at this minute.

Mrs. J.   Now just oblige me by listening to me a minute. Do you mean to tell me you are not a good linguist ?   Why, what was the good of your going to Madame Blancbec's at Fontainebleau for three months ?

Carrie.   Madame Blancbec's was an exemplary establishment certainly—the only drawback to it was that we learnt no French.

Mrs. J.   But why was I never told this before ?   Why in that case did all our neighbours at Croydon send their daughters to the same place ?

Carrie.   That was always a mystery to me.   We used to talk French to each other, certainly, but it seemed to me that to send several English girls abroad to learn French from one another was rather like the inhabitants of the Scilly Isles taking in each other's washing.

Mrs. J.   I must say I never heard anything like that ! I am sure Pa will be furious when I tell him.

Carrie.   Then don't tell him, dear mother.

Mrs. J.   There's Mabel Price, who only went to Berlin for two months, and she has spoken with a German accent ever since.   That is the sort of thing Pa would have liked, and it shows at once that a girl has been abroad.

Carrie.   Dear mother, I'm very sorry—you should have sent me to the same place.   Perhaps the French accent is not so adhesive.

Mrs. J.   Well, now about the music.   Do you think you are a good musician ?

Carrie.   Yes, I should have thought so.   What do you suppose they mean by a good musician ?

Mrs. J.   I should think some one who could play in the evening when people are talking, or sing a bright little song after dinner, Milton Wellings or some one of that sort.

Carrie.   Oh yes, I could quite well do that.

Mrs. J.   There now, you see the whole thing would suit you exactly.

Enter Mrs. Prout and Alethea.   Alethea in an æsthetic gown carrying several large books.

Mrs. P. (with paper open in hand).   Now don't you agree with me, darling, that it is exactly the thing for you ?

Aleth.   Well, of course, the question would have to be considered.   I don't know enough about it yet to give an opinion.

Mrs. P.   No, no, of course not, my dear.   But it would be such an opportunity for you to see the world, wouldn't it ?

Aleth.   No doubt that *quâ* social opportunity it might be a good one—*quâ* opportunity for self-improvement it is more doubtful.

Mrs. J. (to Carrie). You see, we could leave here at eleven thirty on Saturday.

Carrie. Yes, and I could travel in my fawn colour to look decent when we arrived.

Mrs. P. All that is wanted you could do so well ! you are bright and intelligent——

Aleth. Yes, doubtless.

Mrs. P. You are a good linguist——

Aleth. I should like to know more accurately what is meant by a good linguist. If it means to chatter French slang more or less fast, that is one thing, and I don't pretend to it—if it means to have a thorough critical, philological, and etymological knowledge of foreign tongues, so as to be able to read the masterpieces of France, Germany, and Italy with intelligence and understanding, that is another. That, I think, I should be qualified to do.

Mrs. P. Really, Alethea, you always seem to go so deep into things ! much too deep for me, I'm sure.

Aleth. There you are mistaken, mamma. It is impossible to go into things too deeply.

Mrs. P. (aside). It really would be very nice if she had some one to travel with.

Mrs. J. (to Carrie). And what I feel about this is, it might lead to something else.

Carrie. What sort of thing ?

Mrs. J. You might meet some one abroad who—who—oh ! well, all sorts of things may happen.

Aleth. (to Mrs. Prout). Of course there is no doubt, that did I obtain this post, my horizon would be infinitely widened.

Mrs. P. Of course, dear, of course, and that is so nice for young people !

Aleth. (sharply). It is most unfortunate, mamma, that I cannot succeed in making you see my point of view.

Mrs. P. Oh, yes, dear, I quite understand--you think,

as I do, that it would be a good thing if we went to Lucerne on Saturday.

Mrs. J. (to Carrie). I shall give notice then that we don't need our rooms here after Saturday morning.

[*Both couples advance and lay papers on table at same moment.*

Mrs. G. Well, have you come to any conclusion ?

Mrs. P. and Mrs. J. (together). Yes, the post mentioned in this advertisement will exactly suit my daughter.

Mrs. G. So many people seem to want companions just now—I have a friend who is looking for one.

Mrs. P. Oh, indeed ! Her place might suit Miss Jackson.

Mrs. J. I was going to say that it might do for Miss Prout.

Mrs. G. Are you sure you don't want to apply too, Miss Mayne ?

Helen. On the contrary, I should like to very much indeed.

Mrs. J. Oh, I hardly think you would find either of these would do for you.

Helen. Do you think not ? Why ?

Mrs. J. Oh, well, you know——

Mrs. P. The fact is, you see——

Mrs. J. In the meantime, Carrie, don't you think it would be a good thing if you were to freshen up your music a little before Saturday ?

Carrie. I think it would.   [*Looking round at piano.*

Mrs. P. (hurriedly). Alethea, darling, suppose you were to practise a little ?

Aleth. Yes, that might be advantageous.

Mrs. J. (aside to Carrie). You make up to this lady while we are here, and show her what you can be in the way of a companion. Then if by any chance you didn't get the other—see ?

Carrie. I see, mamma—I wasn't born yesterday, thank you. I know my way about.

Mrs. P. Alethea, dearest, suppose in case the other idea came to nothing——

Aleth. Came to nothing, mamma ? Why should it come to nothing ?

Mrs. P. Oh, well, because you might not like it, you know.

Aleth. That is possible, of course.

Mrs. P. Suppose you were to make yourself agreeable to this lady here ? Her friend might suit you better.

Aleth. Yes, I agree with you, mamma, that such a plan appears to offer many advantages.

Mrs. J. (to Carrie). You ask her if she likes music.

Carrie. Or I might sing a song that would show her what I can do.

Mrs. P. (to Alethea). If I were you, my dear, I would go and play.

Aleth. Yes, that would not be undesirable.

[*Gets up and goes to piano, L.*

Mrs. J. (looking round). Good gracious ! She's going to play. We really can't have her monopolising everybody's attention in this way, Quick, Carrie ! Don't keep in the background, pray.

[*Carrie jumps up and rushes to the other piano, R., just as Alethea is going to begin. Carrie makes a spring on to the music stool and begins a song. Alethea looks round, much surprised: Carrie goes on as if she saw nothing.*

Aleth. Oh, I beg your pardon. [*Carrie goes on.*] I beg your pardon ! perhaps you didn't observe that I was just going to play.

Carrie. Oh, what a pity, I'm so sorry you should be disappointed. [*Carrie sings. Alethea plays.*

Mrs. G. (loud, to Helen).   It is a pity there is not a third piano for you to play upon at the same time.

Helen.   Yes, it is a great pity—I might have shown you some of my accomplishments.

Mrs. G.   My dear, I am only so thankful that if you have any accomplishments you keep them to yourself.

Mrs. J. (from piano).   What do you think of that, Mrs. Gordon ?

Mrs. G.   Do you mean of hearing two different things at once ?   I am not sure that I think it quite answers.

Mrs. J.   No, I mean my daughter's singing.   She's considered to have a most effective style of singing.

Mrs. G.   Yes, I should think it was most effective.

Mrs. P. (to Alethea).   Say something to show how much you know about it—do put yourself forward a little more, my dear !

Aleth. (from piano, to Mrs. Gordon).   You doubtless have observed that what I have been playing is one of the best examples of Beethoven's second period before he altered his manner.

Mrs. G. (aside).   I wish she would alter her manner !

Aleth.   Perhaps if Miss Jackson doesn't wish to sing any more just now, I might play you the last movement of this—it is a typical rondo, characteristic of that form in its highest development.

Carrie.   Or I was just going to suggest that if Miss Prout didn't wish to go on playing I might sing you Linda Wright's last composition—the words are so touching as well as the air.   It is called 'The Ninth Love is the Love that endures.'   Shall I ?

Mrs. G.   I am so very much obliged to you both— but to tell you the truth, I have a slight headache this evening—I think I am not up to listening to any more music.

Mrs. J.   A headache !   Oh, dear me, Carrie knows just

what to do for a headache—don't you, Carrie? Let her get you something for it.

Mrs. P. Alethea will fetch you something.

Mrs. J. Carrie will get some menthol—run quick, dear!

Mrs. G. No, no, please don't do anything of the kind.

Carrie. Oh, please do let me—a headache is such a wretched thing, I know. I so often have them myself! where did you put the menthol, mamma?

Mrs. J. The menthol? I put it into your hand.

Carrie. Oh, yes, I remember—and I dropped it in the garden, when I was hopping. Dear me, I'm afraid I didn't pick it up again!

Mrs. J. Just like your carelessness, Carrie.

Mrs. P. Alethea, you know what to do for a headache, don't you? She has been a martyr to them herself, poor girl! It is all that study of course—it would be surprising if she didn't have them.

Aleth. (to Mrs. G.) I wonder what sort of headache yours is—whether it arises from some general constitutional disturbance, or if it is purely nervous? Is it over the brow, or do you find one side affected more than the other?

Mrs. G. Thank you, I really couldn't say what class of headache it is, except that it is really not worth paying any attention to.

Aleth. My headaches, the worst ones, generally begin over the left eye and go gradually round the head.

Mrs. P. Ah, my dear, you take after your poor Aunt Eliza—hers, I remember, used to do just the same thing. They were not quite as violent as yours, perhaps, but that was not surprising, as she was not nearly so clever.

Mrs. J. My headaches always come on just at the top of my head.

Carrie. Mine come on just here.

Mrs. G. Why, what afflicted people you all are ! Have you no headaches, Miss Mayne ?

Helen. No, I am sorry to say I haven't. In fact I am quite unequal to the occasion when headaches are talked about, as I never have any.

Mrs. G. (aside). What a delightful person !

Mrs. J. (aside). I never saw such a silly little creature as that girl is.

Mrs. P. She has none of the poetry of feeling that belongs to ill health.

Mrs. J. Look here, Carrie, why don't you get a foot-stool for Mrs. Gordon—or do something ?

Carrie. I don't know where there is one.

Mrs. J. Look then ! Let her see how energetic and useful you are.

> [*Carrie fusses round, while Mrs. Gordon is talking to Helen, to Mrs. Gordon's manifest annoyance.*

Mrs. G. (to Helen). So you never have any headaches ? what an agreeable companion !

Mrs. P. Companion ! Surely she's not thinking of her !

Helen. Yes, I'm a very sturdy person.

Mrs. G. Sturdy, are you ? I should hardly have thought it from your appearance.

Helen (smiling). Oh, yes, I am though—I dare say the reason you think I look pale is that I have been a long time in India.

Mrs. G. In India ? Have you ? Where ?

Carrie (who has been looking about for footstool). There—under the table !

Mrs. G. (worried). There, what ?

Carrie. Oh, only a footstool.

Mrs. G. Do you want a footstool ?

Carrie (with an engaging giggle). Oh, it was for you I wanted it.

Mrs. G. For me, was it? Thank you, I have one already—I never use a pair.

Carrie. Oh, I see—I beg your pardon. (To Mrs. Jackson) Mamma! Why did you tell me to get a foot-stool?

Mrs. P. (to Alethea). Mind, my dear, you never offer to get anything people don't want.

Aleth. Well, really, mamma, I should have thought it was hardly necessary to say that to one who has studied the most elementary laws of supply and demand.

Mrs. P. I see, my dear, I see! (Aside) That girl always has an answer for everything. It *would* be a good thing if she could find some one to travel away with! Do do something more to make yourself agreeable, my dear.

Mrs. J. (to Carrie). Why don't you do something a companion does? it would be the best possible practice for you.

Aleth. (to Mrs. P.) What shall I do?

Carrie (to Mrs. J.) Do? What do companions do?

Mrs. P. Oh, you might do a hundred things! people read aloud——

Mrs. J. They pick up stitches in knitting——

Mrs. P. Write letters——

Mrs. J. They suggest things for colds in the head—all sorts of agreeable things.

Aleth. Well, I can read aloud, I dare say, if that would do?

Carrie. I could pick up her stitches, if that's all.

Mrs. P. Well, try, dear—don't stay in the background! it is such a mistake for a girl to be in the background— Aunt Eliza used always to say so.

Mrs. J. (to Carrie). Do suggest something—don't let that stupid little creature engross her attention in that way!

Mrs. G. (to Helen).   I am very much interested in India—we must have a long talk about it.

Aleth. (advancing with a book).   This is an essay on the comparative method of enquiry as applied to the researches of modern science.

Mrs. G. (bored).   Oh indeed !   Well, Miss Mayne, as we were saying——

Aleth.   I thought perhaps you would like to hear some of it read aloud.

Mrs. G.   I am afraid I should hardly understand it. But pray don't let me interrupt you—Miss Mayne and I can go on chatting in a low voice without disturbing anyone, can't we, Miss Mayne ?

Aleth.   Oh, it was only for your sake I was going to read aloud—I think reading to oneself is a much more fruitful method of study.

Mrs. J.   Now, quick, Carrie, you say something !

Carrie.   Oh, I think it *is* so sociable just to talk and to work !   (*To Mrs. Gordon*) May I see what your work is ?   What lovely knitting !   It is beautiful—quite a work of art !

Mrs. G.   I am glad you find it so.   I should have thought it was a very ordinary object.   [*Holds up long woollen stocking.*]   It is a pair of winter stockings I am knitting for a charity.

Carrie.   Oh, I am so devoted to knitting !   If you drop any stitches you will let me pick them up for you, won't you ?

Mrs. G.   Thank you, you are too kind—I don't often drop any stitches, I am glad to say.   Perhaps that is because I have knitted vigorously for twenty years past.

Carrie.   No wonder you knit so beautifully then.   But you will let me help you whenever you need it, won't you ?

Mrs. G. Oh, thank you, thank you, yes. (Aside) Dear me, this torrent of solicitude from everyone is becoming maddening ! I wish there were some other place to sit.   [*Gets up and goes to window, Alethea follows her.*

Aleth. Does not the light in the middle distance recall to you what Ruskin says in one of the recent numbers of 'Præterita?'

Mrs. G. (turning back from window). No, I can't say that it does.   I dislike Ruskin particularly.

Carrie (enthusiastically). Oh, do you dislike Ruskin ? I'm so glad ! I can't abide him—at least I can't understand a word he says ! never could !

Mrs. G. (aside). This is getting unbearable ! But this evening will save me the trouble of making my choice at Lucerne.   [*Takes a pack of cards out of her bag.*

Carrie. Oh, are you going to play at cards ! How delightful ! I love cards ! Oh, you should hear me play a Nap ! I scream—I can't help it—I quite scream !

Mrs. G. I don't think you will be called upon to scream over my cards—I am going to do a patience.

Carrie. A patience ! Oh, I shall love that of all things ! I do like watching a patience—only that I never can understand why people want to arrange the cards in a particular way.

Mrs. G. It must interest you immensely to watch it then.

Carrie. I'm such a silly creature about that sort of thing !

Aleth. I shall be very glad to see how a patience is done—I have always understood that it is a most desirable form of recreation for an over-taxed brain.

Mrs. G. (to Helen). Are you also intensely interested in patience, Miss Mayne ?

Helen. Indeed I am ! in fact I hope you won't be

shocked at me if I tell you that I do a patience every evening before going to bed.

Mrs. G. (pleased). Indeed? how delightful! Then I am sure you will be able to teach me some I don't know.

Helen. I dare say I might, I learnt a good many in India—they were a great resource in the hot weather, when we were obliged to stay indoors for so many hours. I know one most delightful one—shall I show it you?

Mrs. G. Pray do.　　　　　　　　　[*Helen shuffles.*

Mrs. J. (to Carrie). How is it that you can't play patience or do any of these things?

Carrie. Because you never took me to India, of course! it is not my fault if you will remain at Croydon all the year round.

Mrs. P. (to Alethea). How is it *you* don't know any patiences, Alethea? I thought you knew everything.

Aleth. I have never had any leisure to spend in acquiring mere pastimes.

[*Helen lays out cards—the others look on.*

Helen. This is a rather complicated one, I am afraid, but very interesting.

Mrs. G. I wonder if it is in the handbook for Patience?

Helen. No, I should think not—in fact I have only met one person who knows it—the one from whom I learnt it.

Mrs. G. (excited). Why, surely I know this—what's the name of it?

Helen. It is called 'The Mystery of the Skies.'

Mrs. G. That's it then—it's my boy's patience!

Helen. Your boy?

Mrs. G. My son Harry—Major Gordon.

Helen. Major Gordon!

Mrs. G. Yes—was it from him you learnt it? Yes, I see it was—I see it in your face!

Helen.   It was—yes, it was !

Mrs. G.   You came across him in India then ?   Come, put these cards down for a moment and tell me all about it.

Mrs. J.   What an intriguing girl !

Mrs. P.   Very—and *so* plain !

Helen.   I was with some people called Stewart— Colonel and Lady Alma Stewart—Colonel Stewart was a great friend of my father's, they were in the same regiment.

Mrs. G.   In the same regiment !   Was your father Colonel Mayne ?

Helen.   Yes, he was—did you know him ?

Mrs. G.   He was one of my oldest friends !   But now tell me about Harry.   It was at the Stewarts' you saw him ?

Helen.   Yes, it was.

Mrs. G.   Then what made you leave India so suddenly ?

Helen.   I can't tell you, Mrs. Gordon.

Mrs. G.   You need not—I know it already.   Harry fell in love with you, and you, instead of returning it, fled to England and left him disconsolate.

Helen.   Dear Mrs. Gordon, since you know so much I had better tell you the rest, that you may not think worse of me than I deserve.   Lady Alma has a daughter, Geraldine, a very nice girl indeed, and a great friend of mine. I think that at first the Stewarts thought—they hoped——

Mrs. G.   That Harry was going to fall in love with Geraldine ?

Helen.   Yes, I think so.   And then, when they found that—that—he liked me, Lady Alma was vexed, and she told me I was ruining your son's prospects, and all sorts of things, and I couldn't bear to stay any longer.   So I came away to England.

Mrs. G.   And left my poor boy in the most miserable frame of mind.

P

Helen.   I am so sorry, Mrs. Gordon.

Mrs. G.   Well, we shall see what you will say when he comes back to Europe next year, to look for you.

Helen.   Next year ?   Is he coming next year ?

Mrs. G.   Do you mean to say you didn't expect him ?

Helen.   No, no, I didn't, I assure you ! I had meant to take a situation as companion somewhere and vanish.

Mrs. G.   I know that when Harry has set his heart on a thing he commonly obtains it.

Helen.   Oh, Mrs. Gordon !

Mrs. J.   A dangerous girl, very.

Mrs. P.   I never liked her face.

Mrs. G.   Still, if, on the other hand, you have set your heart on being a companion, suppose we make a compromise —come and be mine.

Helen.   Mrs. Gordon, how good you are !

Mrs. G.   Good, not at all ! You will be doing me an immense service, for I wanted a companion so badly I was compelled to advertise [*lowering her voice*] in the 'Swiss Times' !

Helen (starting).   What, you ?

            [*Mrs. G. nods.   Both laugh.*

Mrs. P.   Oh, what rude people !

Mrs. J.   What an ill-mannered girl ! (To her daughter) Carrie, go and join them, can't you ? You can laugh so very loud.

Carrie (to Mrs. G.)   Are you not coming back to your patiences ? We are dying to see them, quite dying.

Mrs. G.   You must be, I'm sure.

Mrs. P.   Now, Alethea, do put yourself forward, or what's the use of being so clever !

Aleth. (looking from window—to Mrs. G.)   Curious atmospheric effect of clouds that is—most interesting ! you see there are distinct specimens of three of the great cloud groups.

Carrie. What, *three* great cloud groups ! dear me, that looks bad for the picnic to-morrow.

Aleth. What an unintelligent rejoinder !

Mrs. G. Are you going for a picnic to-morrow ?

Carrie. Well, it was to have been for Saturday, but if we are going to Lucerne that day, we had better have the picnic to-morrow.

Mrs. J. (to Mrs. G.) We are going to Lucerne, certainly, to see if my daughter likes the lady who has advertised for a travelling companion.

Mrs. P. I am afraid your daughter will be disappointed, as Alethea is thinking of taking the post. It is so important that she should travel as much as possible. Oh, dear, I hope she will get it !

Mrs. G. Dear ladies, I must not let you go to Lucerne under false pretences. That post offered in the 'Swiss Times' is no longer vacant.

Mrs. P. No longer vacant !

Mrs. J. How do you know ?

Mrs. G. For the best of reasons. The advertisement is mine !

Mrs. P., Mrs. J., Carrie, Aleth. Yours !!!

Mrs. P. Well, I must say I think it was rather shabby to steal a march on us in that way.

Mrs. J. Yes, to have an interview with us before we had one with you, so to speak.

Mrs. P. The shock of discovery might have been fatal to me in the weak state of my health.

Mrs. J. (aside). Of your intelligence, you mean !

Mrs. G. After all, I wanted a companion—I advertised for one.

Mrs. J. But why don't you want one still then ?

Mrs. G. Because since I arrived here, I have found exactly the companion I wanted—Miss Mayne has kindly consented to come to me.

Mrs. P.   What—you have taken Miss Mayne, when you might have had Alethea !

Mrs. J.   Or Carrie !

Mrs. G. (to Al.)   No, my dear young lady, I am afraid you and I would never have suited each other. You are far too learned to be contented with me.

Mrs. P.   Oh, but Alethea likes ignorant people sometimes, don't you, Alethea ?

Aleth.   Never, mamma !

Mrs. G.   Thank you, I am infinitely obliged, but I am afraid it wouldn't do.

Mrs. P.   Oh dear, I wish she had some one to travel with !

Mrs. G.   And as for you, Miss Jackson, I think the sort of person who would suit you would be some one who required a thorough knowledge of hopping, in all its branches.

Carrie.   I quite agree with you. I'll go back to the garden and teach M. Barette !   [*Exit rapidly, hopping.*

Mrs. J.   Carrie—Carrie, naughty girl ! Oh dear, what shall I do with her? (To Mrs. Gordon) I can only suggest, madam, that in future you shouldn't send people running about Europe by advertising in a newspaper for somebody you don't want.

Mrs. G. (looking fondly at Helen).   I hope I can promise this at any rate, that in the future I shall not need to advertise for a companion in the ' Swiss Times ' !

Curtain.

LAST WORDS

DIALOGUE AT A CARRIAGE WINDOW.

CHARACTERS.

LAURA.   PAMELA.

SCENE.—*Supposed to represent the platform at a railway
station. One end of a railway carriage is seen, slanting
to the audience, so that the faces of the person inside the
carriage and of the outside are equally well seen. (The
carriage may be represented by two chairs if necessary.)*

Enter Laura—she is looking back impatiently.

Laura. It is a blessed moment when one finally comes
to see people off at the station! I have heard there is a
Chinese proverb which says, 'When the guest is gone, the
host is glad.' It is very true! The Chinese must be a
remarkably sensible people. They don't know the meaning of the word hospitality, I believe. They keep their
towns and their houses closed against strangers—or they
used to, at any rate. Very wise of them. It is a pity,
though, in some ways, for I should like to send some
English people I know to China very much. [*Looks at station
clock.*] Dear me! nearly twenty-five minutes still before
the train starts! It was a short-sighted policy on my part
to hurry our dear Pamela off to the station so soon, and
then have to wait with her here; but the fact is, I felt
anything was better than our sitting solemnly in the
drawing-room together, with our things on, ready to start,
exchanging the agonised parting trivialities that people

fall back upon on these occasions. Why do they, I wonder?
It perfectly amazes me sometimes to hear what people are
saying to each other, at the window of a railway carriage,
for instance—and yet I am conscious of being just as
idiotic myself when I am in the same position! [*Looking
round.*] What can that girl be doing? She has been five
minutes at least taking her ticket. Perhaps she has been
telling the booking clerk one of those long stories about
herself she indulges in! Listening to her conversation is
like being in the maze at the Crystal Palace. You go
rambling round and round, and backwards and forwards,
without having an idea where it is all to lead to—then you
suddenly find yourself in the middle just when you least
expect it, and it is impossible to get away from it again to
anywhere else! She has never listened to one word that
I've said, the whole week she has stayed with me—perhaps,
if the truth were known, that is why I don't enjoy her
society as much as I might. But, after all, I shouldn't
have told her anything about myself, for I do not mean
to let anyone into my confidence about—about—Colonel
Percival yet! Eventually, of course, the whole world
must know it, when I have consented to marry him—but
not yet. Here she comes!

> *Enter Pamela in travelling costume, putting her ticket
> into her purse, counting change, &c. She goes to
> the carriage.*

Pam. (getting in). Good-bye, then, dear. I've had
such a delightful visit. I can't tell you how much I've
enjoyed it, and all our delightful talks! good-bye!

Laura. You needn't have been in such a hurry to get
in: we are rather earlier than I thought. The train won't
be starting for twenty minutes yet.

Pam. Oh, really! I thought you said we had no
time to spare. This is very nice, isn't it?

Laura. Very !

Pam. We shall have plenty of time to talk.

Laura. Yes. [*Pause.*] . . . . I hope you will have a pleasant journey.

Pam. I'm sure I shall. You've been so kind, and settled everything so well for me.

Laura. You have your ticket all safe ?

Pam. Oh, yes. It is in my purse—and I have put my purse safely in my leather bag, which is locked—and the key is in this little velvet bag. So, you see, I know exactly where to fish for it.

Laura. I see—most convenient ! [*Pause.*] Your luggage will be in the van—the guard will get it out when you arrive. (Aside) There now ! I knew I should begin saying this kind of thing. I must make up my mind to it, I suppose !

Pam. Give my love to your little brothers and sisters. I do hope they'll remember me.

Laura. They won't have forgotten you by the time I get back to the house, at any rate, for it won't be more than an hour since you saw them.

Pam. No, no, of course not—and they're so quick and clever besides ! Mind you write to me and tell me how they get on.

Laura. . I'll be sure to do so.

Pam. And tell me when Jacky can cut up his meat for himself, and whether they say anything amusing at dinner.

Laura. Yes, I will. (Aside) Here we are in full swing ! I *do* hope nobody is listening to us !

Pam. And, oh ! mind you don't forget to let me know the very moment Molly can say ' potato.'

Laura. I won't forget. She very nearly managed it this morning, didn't she?

Pam. Oh, very ! I was so excited ! [*Pause.*] . . . *Mind* you don't repeat the things I've said.

Laura. Indeed I will not. (Aside) I wouldn't attempt such an effort of memory !

Pam. I dare say I shall have a great many more stories to tell after I've been to Woodlands. It is a pity I shall have no opportunity of telling them to you for so long, isn't it ?

Laura. Yes, a great pity.

Pam. There is going to be an immense party in the house, you know—the two Compton girls, and Major Weevle, and Harry Barrington. We shall have the greatest fun in the world. .

Laura. The Compton girls play lawn tennis very well, don't they ?

Pam. Well, yes—I suppose they do, though I can't say I think them so very remarkable. But they always have lovely tennis gowns, and that is a great thing.

Laura. What Mr. Barrington is that—the one who acts ?

Pam. Yes, indeed it is—and I hope they'll get up some acting. I do love it so !

Laura. Why, Pamela, I never knew you acted !

Pam. Oh, yes ! I acted once in some charades at school. And then I have a sort of feeling about it that makes me think I could do it. People do have that sort of feeling about acting—don't you think so ?

Laura. That they most certainly do, and it leads to the very wildest results. Most people have a sort of lingering idea about many things, that they *could* do them if they were to try.

Pam. (satisfied). Yes, that is exactly what *I* feel. But then, you know, perhaps it is different for me, for I can't help feeling sure that I really *should* be able to act.

Laura. Then, when is the play to come off ? For there isn't much time, it seems to me.

Pam. Oh, some time next week, I suppose. Carrie

Beverley said something about it when she wrote—the end of the week, I dare say.

Laura. The end! I should hope so! Why, this is Wednesday already, and the play is not even chosen yet!

Pam. I don't think that matters much. We shall know it quite well enough, I dare say—it isn't like professionals, you know.

Laura. No, that it certainly is not.

Pam. Oh, dear me! there are some people coming this way. I do hope they're not coming in here——

Laura. I'll block up the doorway, and pretend I'm just going to get in and take up the other five places!

Pam. (leaning out and watching). No, it's all right—they've got in somewhere else.

Laura. Why, Pamela, they're the people we met on the sands the other day, that you thought looked so very nice!

Pam. Yes, so they are. Never mind—it's quite different in the train. People who look very nice on the sands are monsters as soon as they try to get into one's carriage, I always think.

Laura. One comfort is that they hate us just as much probably, and are longing to avoid us too!

Pam. Oh, do you think so? That hasn't occurred to me. But of course it isn't quite the same thing, you know!

Laura. Why not?

Pam. Oh, because—because—just because one *is* different, you know, from other people.

Laura. But perhaps *they* don't think so.

Pam. That's a horrid idea. [*Pause.*] How long have we now before the train starts?

Laura. Only ten minutes now.

Pam. Oh, I'm sorry. I'll tell you why, Laura. I had such an interesting letter this morning, that I wanted to tell you about.

Laura. Then, why haven't you told me all this time, instead of waiting until now ?

Pam. Because I've been so busy this morning, ever since the post came in, that I really haven't had time. It is too long to begin upon all in a minute—but it really is *most* interesting ! I dare say you've noticed that I've been rather preoccupied and incoherent this morning ?

Laura. No, I don't think I have. (Aside) Not unusually so !

Pam. Well—the fact is—the fact is —now you *promise* you won't tell anybody, Laura ?

Laura. Of course I won't. You know quite well I never do.

Pam. Yes, but this really is important. It isn't like anything else I've told you.

Laura (aside). I'm glad of that ! Be quick, then, or I shan't have time to hear it. Some one has written to propose to you, I suppose ?

Pam. Not at all, quite the contrary.

Laura. What !—to refuse you, then !

Pam. No, no—don't be so tiresome, Laura.

Laura. I beg your pardon. Go on, then.

Pam. First, I must tell you something that happened two years ago. [*Laura heaves a sigh.*] No !—was it then ? Yes—of course—this is July—the 15th, so there has been one July since ——

Laura. Two, you mean.

Pam. No, no—*one*—one 16th of July, I mean.

Laura. Oh, very well, if you must needs be so particular as to the sixteenth of a month—like people who must always measure exactly to the sixteenth of an inch ——

Pam. (impatiently). Well, never mind that now. I was staying abroad with my sister, Mrs. Dagonel—and there - I met—a young man.

Laura. Dear me! what a dangerous place to stay at!

Pam. And, when I had been there about ten days, we became engaged to each other.

Laura. That was very prompt.

Pam. Yes, it was—too prompt, perhaps—for I must tell you that before leaving England I had just refused some one else. You know what a sad wicked creature I am in that way. I can't help playing havoc with the men's hearts, as they tell me, wherever I go!

Laura. But why should your having refused one man make it difficult for you to accept another? I should have thought the contrary would have been the case.

Pam. No—you shall see. The one I had refused just before I left England—what shall I call him?

Laura (bored). That depends on what his name was.

Pam. No, no—because if I tell you his name, you'll know who he is.

Laura. I'm afraid that's undeniable.

Pam. Well, I'll call him A., as they do in the sum books. Don't you remember the sums we used to have to do at school—if A. has fifty pounds and spends twopence halfpenny a week, and B. with fifteen hundred spends three and ninepence a day, which will be in the work-house first?

Laura. Yes, I remember. But, **Pamela**, we only have eight minutes longer—you'll never get to the end of your story at this rate! if P. has fifteen sentences to say, and stops every two minutes to put in an extra one, when will she get to her story's end? Never, I should say.

Pam. Because you *will* keep interrupting me, dear! Well, as I was saying, I had refused A. in England, and accepted B. at Brussels.

Laura (smiling at a recollection). Brussels! It must be a dangerous place. A friend of mine was once in love there too.

Pam. Indeed ! But now, Laura dear, you must let me tell my story, or you will never hear it.

Laura. Very well. Go on. It's like playing at ' I love my love.' We'll call him B., and he lives at Brussels.

Pam. Yes, yes—now listen. The dreadful thing was, that when I saw A. I thought I liked him best, and so—I broke off my engagement to B.

Laura. And what did B. do ?

Pam. He broke his leg.

Laura. What, as well as his engagement ? what a very unexpected result ! Was that from grief ?

Pam. No, no ! It was because his horse stumbled with him the day after I saw him. He was taken to a hospital at Brussels, where he lay for two months, and I never saw him again.

Laura. But what became of A., then ? He had remained in sound health all this time, with no broken limbs, I hope ?

Pam. Yes, he had—but there was something very mysterious about A.'s behaviour altogether. He didn't know, of course, that I had changed my mind—and I didn't like to tell him—and so he went away without saying anything more about it.

Laura. But why do you call that mysterious ?

Pam. Because it was so odd that a man who had proposed to me in London a fortnight before should meet me in Brussels and not propose to me again !

Laura. I must say I don't find it so odd. There must come a moment when a man who has been in love with a girl leaves off proposing to her.

Pam. Yes, when she marries him, or when she marries some one else—not till then !

Laura. But, my dear Pamela, you are attributing most unusual constancy to mankind ! Besides, it isn't every woman who can inspire such a lifelong passion !

Pam. (satisfied). No, of course not. I know it is not *every* woman! . . . Well, as I was saying—but what o'clock is it?

Laura. You have six minutes more.

Pam. Oh, that's all right—I shall have plenty of time, for I'm just coming to the interesting part now.

Laura (aside). I'm glad of that!

Pam. I must tell you that the day I became engaged to B. was the 16th of July, and on that day we did a very silly thing—we tore my programme in two——

Laura. Your what?

Pam. My programme. Oh, I forgot to tell you we were at a ball, at the Legation—and we each said we would keep the halves of the programme all our lives.

Laura. Of course! And did you?

Pam. No, no—wait—you'll see. And then he said, 'The 16th of July will always be imprinted on my heart, as it is on this programme.' That was very nice, wasn't it?

Laura. Very—and original, too!

Pam. And then he said, 'Whether I am far from you or near you, remember that in my thoughts I shall always be with you, on the 16th of July.' He said it so sadly, poor fellow—he seemed quite to have a presentiment that the engagement would be broken off!

Laura (aside). Perhaps he had heard something of you before!

Pam. Now I come to the wonderful part of my story. Do you know what day this is?

Laura. You reminded me just now—it is the 15th of July.

Pam. (triumphantly). And to-morrow therefore will be the 16th. Did you ever hear of anything so extraordinary?

Laura. I really don't see that. I've known it happen once or twice before.

Pam. Laura, you are so unsympathetic! You don't at all realise what a wonderful coincidence it is that *this* morning, of all mornings, I should turn the old torn half of my programme out of a pocket in my travelling bag, and that on the top of that I should get a letter from Carrie Beverley, telling me they expect Colonel Percival at Woodlands to-morrow!

Laura. Colonel Percival!! Is *that* his name?

Pam. (covering her face with her hands). Dear me! Yes—it is. Now I've let the cat out of the bag, and you'll laugh at me, I know! What a silly thing I am, to be sure!

Laura (aside). Can it be *my* Colonel Percival? (Aloud) Then, how long is it since you have seen him?

Pam. Why, Laura dear! what a memory you have. I've just been telling you how long it is—not since July 1880 — two years ago!

Laura. And you have never met him since?

Pam. Never!—though I assure you I've thought of him, often—on the 16th of last July, of course, and many other times besides, whenever I've felt lonely and had nobody else.

Laura. What was he like when you knew him?

Pam. Ah, now I see you're beginning to be interested in him. I was sure you would be, poor fellow—because one can't help feeling sorry for him, you know, after all.

Laura. Why?

Pam. Oh, having his engagement broken off—and then his accident—and then——

Laura. But, as to his accident, he is as well now as ever he was—that is—(*checking herself*)—I imagine he must be, since it is two years since it happened—and, as to his broken heart, that may have been healed also since you saw him.

Pam. It *may*, of course—but I don't think it is very

likely. However, I shall soon see—for —but mind, Laura, you have promised not to tell anyone this !

Laura (impatiently). Of course, of course ! to whom should I tell it ? I could find no one who would be as interested in it as I am.

Pam. (effusively). What a sweet thing you are, Laura dear, after all ! Well, where was I ? Oh, I know. I was saying, if he is at Woodlands, I mean to show him my half of the programme, and ask him for his—and then—and then—(*archly*)——

Laura. And then, what ?

Pam. (coquettishly). Well, then, I suppose—then—we shall become engaged again, and perhaps married. I have not quite made up my mind, but very nearly.

Laura. Your mind, perhaps—but what about his ? How can you tell whether he is of the same mind still after all this time ?

Pam. I don't think he is likely to have changed, unless he has perhaps taken a passing fancy for some one who reminded him of me. Of course, those things do happen sometimes.

Laura. But now just let us suppose, for the sake of argument, that it has happened. Let us imagine that, after he came out of the hospital at Brussels, he returned to England, and in the course of time made acquaintance with some one else—whether like or unlike you it matters not—that he gradually found that the old love had faded from his heart, and the new taken its place—that his affection was returned, and that now two people are on the road to happiness—what should you do ?

Pam. The case isn't worth discussing. I can't think of anything so unlikely.

Laura. Still, it is a good thing to be prepared for any emergency—I feel quite anxious to know what you would do ?

Pam. If I found out he really were such a wretch as that, I should think I were well quit of him. I should then make up my mind, I suppose, to marry Henry Smythe.

Laura (astonished). Henry Smythe !!

Pam. (laughing). Oh, dear ! giddy thing that I am, I've done it again ! I forgot I hadn't introduced him to you before, so to speak. Henry Smythe is the other individual in my story—the one we called A., that I refused before I went abroad.

Laura. Not Henry Smythe of Blandover ?

Pam. Yes, of course ! do you know him ?

Laura. How long is it since you have met him ?

Pam. Oh, about a year, I suppose—not that—nine or ten months, perhaps.

Laura. Then it *must* be the Harry Smythe of Blandover who is to marry my cousin Nellie Cartwright next week !

Pam. What ! It can't be ! There must be some mistake !

Laura. I don't think there is, for I am going to the wedding.

Pam. What an unprincipled, heartless creature ! Did you ever know anything as false and wicked as men are ! It really is shameful ! Well, now, of course, my mind is made up—there is nothing left for me to do but to marry Colonel Percival.

Laura (taken aback). To marry——?

Pam. Colonel Percival.

Laura. But suppose he doesn't ask you ?

Pam. Oh, Laura ! I never knew any one as blunt and unkind as you are. And just now I was thinking you were being so nice about it all !

Laura. I am only trying to make you understand that it doesn't at all follow, because you threw over a man two years ago, that he will propose to you again next time you meet. Suppose by this time he is engaged, or on the eve of being engaged to some one else?

Pam. We'll soon see that. I know Rupert Percival— I know that when I meet him to-morrow, on the day which first consecrated our love, I can, if I choose, bring him back to my feet.

Laura (indignantly). What, Pamela! out of a mere caprice—you know it is nothing more—you are going to remind the man who once loved you of the power you had over him, and perhaps arrest him at the crisis of his fate! He may now be on the eve of declaring his passion to some one else, and your interference may destroy the happiness of two lives. Think before you stretch out your hand for that which now belongs to another, and which if you had it you would not value. Pamela, you know you don't care for him!

[*During the whole of the above Pamela has been fussing about, looking in her bag, &c.*

Pam. (absently, still looking about). Yes, yes, Laura dear—I know! you are always so romantic! You get so excited over little things! it will all come right, never fear. I'm afraid I've not paid as much attention as I should have liked to what you were saying, for I'm beginning to feel worried about my ticket. I think I hear the man coming. *Where* did I tell you it was? Oh, I know— in my bag.

Laura. Never mind the ticket—it won't be asked for yet. Just listen to me a moment, Pamela.

Pam. 'One moment,' indeed, dear Laura! It's all very well to say 'Never mind the ticket'—but, if it were lost, I should have to pay 17*s.* 6*d.* at my journey's end. [*During this time she has produced her key out of her little bag, unlocked the big bag, taken out the purse, and opened it.*] Why, here it is, of course! How stupid of me! And I remember now, they don't clip the tickets till the next station, so I've had all this trouble for nothing. Now, what was it you were going to say?

[*A paper has fallen from the purse when it was opened, outside the carriage door, at Laura's feet.*

Laura. It is too late now—the train is just starting.

Pam. What a pity! You must tell me another time. Why, where is it, Laura? I've lost that bit of my programme! Oh, look! there it is—quick—quick—give it me!

Laura. Is that it?   [*Pointing to paper on ground.*

Pam. Yes, it is. Oh, make haste, give it to me! What should I do without it?

[*Laura picks it up, and stands a minute looking at it. Pamela holds out her hand.*

Laura (throwing it into Pamela's lap as the train is supposed to move off). Take it! May it do all you expect!

Pam. Thank you! Good-bye, dear!

[*Waves her handkerchief.*

Curtain.

A WOMAN OF COURAGE

MONOLOGUE.

SCENE.—*A Hotel sitting-room. Door R. Window with closed curtains R.C. Door L. Table, chairs, &c.*

Mrs. Trembleton standing at the door with bag in her hand, speaking to some one outside.

Mrs. Trembleton.—No, I want nothing else to-night, thank you : this room will do quite well. I should like to be called at half-past seven, please. [*Comes forward.*] So here I am at my journey's end, actually in a hotel by myself, for the first time in my life. It feels very strange ! I wonder if I did right to come ? What will my husband say—my dear George ? Will he be pleased, or displeased, at the bold step I have taken ? At any rate he will not be able to taunt me again with being a coward, afraid of my own shadow, as he is so fond of saying, afraid of stirring a step unless he is there to support and guide me. For it was most daring of me to leave home in his absence— to come up to London alone, bringing the diamonds my dear mother left me, to lodge them at the banker's. It is what he has been wanting me to do ever since we had them in the house, mainly on my own account, as there have been so many burglaries round us at Richmond that every unexpected sound I hear I think is a murderer in the dining-room. When George is at home I don't mind so much, as he is always ready to tell me how foolish I

am, like a dear, good husband, and to suggest some plau
sible explanation for the sounds that fill me with terror.
But during the last week, since he has been in France, I
really couldn't stand it any longer.   I am a little ashamed
of myself, I must admit, but after all, we all know that
women are not as brave as men : it isn't expected of them,
it would be unfeminine if they were.   George always
laughs at me most unmercifully for my want of courage—
indeed, it is quite a standing joke with him.   After all, it
is perhaps rather a good thing that a husband should have
some innocent little standing jokes at his wife's expense,
it does her no harm, and makes him think he is a very
witty fellow—but I have often pointed out to him that he
has never seen me in any real emergency, brought face to
face with a visible danger : then of course it would be very
different.   I should approach it in quite another way, I
am sure.   I have often felt that in some tremendous crisis,
some unexpected occasion for heroism, I should be equal to
anything—that then would be the moment for me to draw
on that store of strength which no one has suspected till
now.   When it is an every-day sort of peril, and George is
there to defend me, I naturally turn to him—if I see a
spider on my dress, for instance, or a daddy-longlegs flies
round the lamp at night, near my head, or if the furniture
gives a great creak suddenly when I don't expect it.   It is
true, perhaps, that I am a little nervous about uncanny
things—ghosts, darkness, the tales of the Psychical Society.
I know that after sitting next to Mr. Myers one night, at
a dinner-party, I hardly dared to go home afterwards, and
that after reading ' Dr. Jekyll and Mr. Hyde ' I couldn't
sleep in the dark for a month.   But still, as I tell George,
it really doesn't signify so much, only being afraid of things
that one doesn't meet with.   It would be much worse if I
were like my sister, for instance, whose fears find opportunity in every instant of her daily life—who dares not

walk through a country lane for fear the cow grazing on
the other side of the hedge should turn out to be a mad
bull—who, if a puppy comes gambolling along the road towards her, already sees herself under the care of Pasteur—
who, if the wind blows at night, lies quaking, prepared to
receive her neighbour's chimney-pot on her devoted head—
or, still worse, if she happens to have heard of some illness
a friend is suffering from, develops the symptoms of it all
complete, and prepares for approaching death. No, that
sort of terror is foolish. Now, it is quite a different thing
to be afraid of a burglar. Burglars really do exist, there
is no doubt about it—there are too many well-authenticated cases of their appearing in the flesh. Therefore I
feel it would be a misplaced lion-heartedness to keep those
diamonds any longer locked up in my wardrobe. I have
tried every means possible to tranquillise my fears by
keeping a watch over them. First I made my maid sit
with them while the other servants were at dinner, as
though they were the baby and mustn't be left—the result
of that was, that the third night the cat jumped out from
behind the window-curtain, and the maid went into
hysterics from sheer terror, thinking he was a man in a
mask, while I, hearing the noise, fainted in the drawing-
room, thinking that the maid was being murdered. Then
we tried having a watch-dog, but he regularly went to
sleep at sunset, and snored so loudly that he kept us awake
all night—snored so that the most timid house-breaker
must have been encouraged to come in. Then we put a
spring rattle in the hall to summon the police, but it was
such a difficult thing to work that I am sure it would have
required the united strength of three stout burglars to
spring it—so on the whole it will be quite a relief to me to
know the diamonds are out of the house, though it was a
terrible responsibility having them on the journey. I did
not like to cling too closely to them, for fear of arousing

suspicion—but oh ! how my heart beat when that man got
in at the first station, that dark-browed man with shiny
boots and a large scarf-pin ! I know swell-mobsmen always
wear shiny boots and a big pin. When he came in, I
instinctively took the bag from the netting above my head,
and placed it by my side—then I thought it would be
better to behave as though there was nothing specially
valuable in it, and I put it up again. Oh, how frightened I
was when he jumped up and said, ' Will you allow me to
do that for you ?' How foolish I felt I had been—how I
vowed never to be so rash again ! I wonder where that
man went to ? He lifted his hat in an offensively friendly
manner as he left, and I am sure I saw his eye fall on my
bag. Oh, how fearful it would be if he had guessed its
contents, and were to track me to obtain possession of it !
Such things have happened, they happen every day.   I
wish I had gone into one of the rooms below, even though
it was more expensive, and noisier. They told me that on
the first floor every room was occupied except one. I
should have felt happier, I think, surrounded with people—
here I feel very lonely : I don't believe there is anyone on
this floor but myself, it all sounds so quiet. [*Looks round
her nervously.*] I will lock the door at any rate, then no
one can attack me unawares. [*Locks door.*] Now I feel
happier ! But perhaps I had better double-lock it, that
would be safer still. [*Turns key again.*] There, that was
twice, I think. [*Tries to turn key back again.*] I will unlock it and see. Oh, dear, how stiff this lock is to turn !
I can't turn the key back again. [*Makes great effort.*]
That is once at any rate. [*Tries it.*] Yes, it is still locked.
[*Tries again, the key comes out.*] What a stupid lock !
[*Tries to put key in again.*] Why, what is the matter ?
The key won't go in ! Good heavens ! Suppose I can't put
it in again ! Here I am locked in—locked in at the roof
of the house ! Oh, how horrible ! [*Tries again.*] No, it

is no use, the key is bent—I have hampered it somehow. What shall I do? Oh, of course the waiter must have a key. I will ring. [*Runs to the bell-rope, which comes down in her hand.*] Why, the whole house is coming to pieces. Oh, what shall I do? My last hope is gone! I may be shut up here for days. No, after all, I said I was to be called at half-past seven, so I have that hope, at any rate, but until then? What a dreadful thought that here I am, locked in, helpless, at the mercy of anything that may happen! My hair will turn white, I know! Oh, why did I come? And yet, here at last is real danger : now this, if ever, is an occasion for presence of mind, for courage, for heroism even : now my courage will rise, it will be equal to the demand on it! Let me consider, first of all, what might happen, so as to be prepared for my fate. The most likely thing, of course, is a fire—the great point is to know exactly beforehand what one will do. [*Reflects.*] Let me consider it calmly, solemnly! I see it all in my mind's eye—the first alarm, the running to and fro of terrified men and women, the fire-engine rattling through the streets, coming nearer, nearer—heralded by the shouts of its brave riders, it dashes into the yard, the fire-escape is put up to the walls, the spray from the engines dashes against them : like lightning the gallant fellows tear up the steps, they emerge with lifeless female forms in their arms—down the netting to the ground—back again to the top—on to the roof like a cat—down again—up to the top once more! Am I forgotten? No : the steps of my rescuer draw nearer. Breathless, blackened by smoke, he leaps into the room, where, almost suffocated, but still calm and collected, I await him with a damp handkerchief tied carefully over my mouth—one moment more—the window—the dark—the frantic crowds below—one wild leap into the blackness of space——[*Covers her face with her hands, gasps shuddering.*] Ah! Where am I? I really believed I was doing it ! But it is well to be prepared, calmly and resolutely prepared, to face a hideous peril. [*Lifts the candle, looks round her nervously—shrieks.*] Ah ! what is that ? A black thing crawling on the ceiling ! a beetle ! No, no, it is the shadow of the extinguisher ! I am afraid of looking round me, there seems to be something behind me at every step I take. [*Whirls round quickly and looks behind her, goes round the room cautiously, opens door R., looks in.*] The bedroom is tiny, I am glad of that : it somehow doesn't seem as likely that an apparition should be doubled up in such a small space, like a Jack-in-the-box. [*Walks round, comes to window curtains R.C., whence a pair of boots protrude. Staggers back speechless with fright, pointing at them.*] A pair of boots ! [*Whispering.*] A pair of shiny boots ! ! ! I am lost ! It is he ! He has tracked me here ! I am locked in with him—I am at his mercy ! I dare not call out of the window—at the slightest sound of alarm I make he will spring on me. I remember the cold glare of his eyes as he looked at my bag in the train ! I dare not look, I know too well it is he ! But how is it that since I came in he has not moved, not sprung on me ? Ah ! it is too clear why. He thinks he is concealed, he does not know I have discovered his secret ! He waits until I have put out the light, then, under shelter of the darkness, he will make his escape with my mother's diamonds in his hand—the diamonds she wore on her wedding-day ! Ah ! how little she thought what would be their fate ! (*With a sudden thought*) But if he did succeed in taking them, he could not get away—the door is locked, locked, hopelessly locked ! No, no : of course he must have a key—a false key—malefactors always have— or how could he have come in ? There is but one thing to be done. I will play a desperate game : I will put out the light and let him think I am asleep. Under cover of the

darkness he will steal away with my bag, but my life, at
any rate, will be saved! Oh! George, George, if you
could see me now! Oh! mother, mother dear, forgive
your child! Oh, my innocent children, sleeping in your
beds at home, if you knew the horrible peril in which I am
placed! Good-bye, all my dear ones, I may never see you
more! [*Carries candle to bedroom door, blows it out, opens
door, pretends to go in, and shuts it with a loud noise—sits
motionless by bedroom door, listening with agonised face—
after a minute clock strikes twelve.*] Midnight! Oh! I
cannot stand it any longer! Come what may, I must have
a light! The air is thick with horrors, the spectres of
midnight are everywhere—light, I must have a light!
Where is the candle? Where are the matches? My
hands tremble—I scarce can hold them! [*Drops them.*]
Ah! [*Covers her face with her hands.*] Where are they?
I thought I heard a mocking laugh behind me—dreadful
faces look at me out of the darkness. Oh! where is it? I
cannot find it! [*Gropes about, finds the candle.*] Here is
the candle, but the matches, where are they? A measure-
less darkness is round me—I am giddy—I am lost—I no
longer remember where I am! I am afraid to move, for
fear I should go near him, and rouse him to violence and
madness! [*Gropes about, finds matches, draws a deep sigh
of relief.*] Ah! at last, the matches! I hardly dare to
strike one, the flame will light up some hideous thing
peering out of the darkness! Oh! George, George, why
did you ever leave me? Oh! if you were here now!
[*Strikes match, and lights the candle with trembling hands,
then looks furtively round her, sees the boots, she is close to
them—starts away again at finding herself so near them,
and darts to the other side of the room.*] Is it possible he
has not heard me? He must be asleep, worn out by the
excitement of his wicked project. I have heard that so
the American Indians sleep at the stake—he can sleep

between one dark deed and another ! [*Watches the curtains.*] I saw a rustle—I am sure I saw a rustle. He is
waking—now, now the moment comes. Oh ! for courage
to inspire me ! I must try to put him off the scent.
[*Speaks loudly and cheerfully, looking furtively at curtains
at intervals.*] What a very nice hotel this is ! What a
charming room ! I am very glad I came here, very glad
indeed. The whole thing has been so pleasant : a journey
without a hitch, then the arrival here, all so comfortable !
and I don't feel the least lonely, with so many people sleeping near me. I see the rooms on each side of me are in-
habited—and just now, when I looked into the passage, I
saw two waiters on duty there, and I noticed a burly
porter walking up and down, too, with a thick stick in his
hand, so I only have to open the door and call if I want
anything, or ring the bell. (Aside) I only wish I could !
(Aloud) Besides, how comfortable it is being without any
luggage ! I feel so independent ! for, of course, as I am
going back to-morrow, it was not worth while to bring
anything but my things for the night—they just fill up my
hand-bag, it is so convenient. It is so light I can carry it
quite easily myself, so I am not afraid of its going astray—
not that it would matter if it did, as there are no valuables
in it. So that I really have nothing at all to think about.
That is what makes my expedition so thoroughly delightful ! Oh ! I *am* enjoying myself ! [*Looks round.*] Now,
if he is awake, he must have been completely lulled to
security. Yes, I am sure he is awake. His feet seem to
me to have changed their position—the right foot is a shade
more forward, I am almost sure, as if he were going to step
out into the room . . . and yet no, it looks stiff, inert, as
though it were—Ah ! [*Starts up, catches her dress in the
chair, shrieks, covers her face with her hands without looking behind her.*] Ah ! what is it ? Yes, I am your prisoner,
I am at your mercy ! Take it, take the bag, take every-

thing I have, but oh, unlock the door and let me go from here unharmed ! [*Looks round.*] Why, I was caught on a nail ! I thought I already felt the cruel hands dragging me to my fate ! But oh, if he would not prolong my torture – if he would leap out on me in savage exultation and take my heart's blood ! I could not defend myself, there is no weapon at hand—yes ! What is that ? [*Looks at the fender.*] A bottle—an empty bottle. Ah ! it is labelled laudanum ! now, now I know it all ! This is the meaning of the stillness, the horrible stillness of that form behind the curtain—it is the stillness of the dead ! It is not with a robber, a murderer, I am shut in here at midnight —it is with a corpse—a cold corpse—the corpse of one who has died by his own deed—who died by poison here in his lonely room under the roof ! There he stands, hidden by the curtains behind which I dare not look—I dare not draw the curtain which shelters that horrible inmate ! This, then, was the reason why this room oppressed me with horror from the moment I came into it, why I shrank from the sight of these walls which had received the dying look of the suicide—the air was heavy with crime—this is the room that witnessed his last struggle—with his last effort he drew that curtain before his convulsed features ! Oh, how little I realised till this moment the tragedies of which we daily read ! Now I am face to face with one— alone with suicide and death. Oh, what must I do ? What shall I do ? I shall go mad ! [*Leans forward on the table with her head on her arms.*]

[*Knocking at the door. She starts up and stands quivering. More knocking. She whispers close to the door hoarsely.*] Yes, what is it ?

Voice (outside). Sorry to trouble you, ma'am— gentleman leaving at four o'clock in the morning has left his boots here, he says.

Mrs. Trembleton. Left his boots here !

Waiter. Yes, m'm, behind the curtain.

Mrs. Trembleton. Left them behind the curtain ! [*Looks round.*] What ! oh ! Can it be ? [*Rushes at curtain and draws it aside.*] A pair of boots ! Oh ! how foolish I have been ! [*Waiter knocks again.*] Yes, the boots are here, but I can't open the door. I have hampered the lock somehow. Will you get a key, please ? Thank you—and, waiter, when you come back, I think I would rather go into the room below—never mind if it is noisy. [*Puts on bonnet, &c., takes bag.*] Oh, what an hour of agony I have passed ! if only I had known there were no legs inside those boots, how much suffering I should have been spared ! still, I am not sorry to have had this experience—this terrible experience ! and after all, I don't know that I have come out of it so badly. [*More knocking at the door.*] Is that the key ? Thank you. Open the door, please. [*The door is opened from the outside.*] And I really believe [*Going out*] that when I tell George how I confronted the perils of a hotel at midnight, he will at last agree that I must be A Woman of Courage !

A HARD DAY'S WORK

MONOLOGUE.

Oh dear, what an exhausting day I have had! Since this morning when I first went out, until this evening when I returned from a dinner-party, I have been on the move all day, mentally as well as physically, about other people's business. Perhaps it is partly my own fault that there are so many claims upon my time—but there, I can't help taking a keen interest in all that surrounds me—I am too impressionable, too clear-sighted, too sympathetic! It would be better for me, I dare say, if I spared myself more, and did not allow myself to be troubled about other people's trials and difficulties, but then I feel it would not be right of me to refuse to help them by my advice, when I always see exactly the thing to be done—it would be hardly fair for me to stand aloof and let people settle their affairs the wrong way, when a word from me would set them right—but still, it is very trying, *most* fatiguing! Poor Fanny Howard! I wonder how *she* has settled her difficulties! I met her in Knightsbridge this morning, as I was going out to shop the first thing after breakfast. I saw she looked preoccupied, and in a hurry, so I stopped her at once to ask what was the matter with her, and then I turned back to walk with her, which I felt was only kind.

'I'm going for the character of a nurse,' she said, in her usual flurried and nervous way, 'a perfect paragon I've heard of!'

('A paragon !' I thought to myself, 'that sounds bad !—
I don't believe in other people's paragons !')

'I must make haste, for the lady I am going to is just
leaving town—such splendid references I've had with this
woman—and I've had a personal interview with everyone
she has lived with, except Mrs. Tyler.'

'Mrs. Tyler !   Not Mrs. Henry Tyler ?' I cried.

'Yes, Mrs. Henry Tyler—she has just gone to Switzer-
land, and they don't know where a letter will find her—
besides, the nurse was only there three months, for she said
it was impossible to bear with Mrs. Tyler's temper.'

'But, good heavens ! my dearest Fanny, if the woman
was only there three months, Mrs. Tyler is exactly the one
you should have seen —you must really communicate with
her at once ! I know her very well, and I know, too, that she
had a French nurse the other day, who was the most dreadful woman ! I shouldn't be surprised if this were the very
one.   Jeanne Duval, did you say her name was ?'

'No—Mathilde Laborde.'

'Ah, well—still it is the same, you may depend upon
it !'

'Oh, Geraldine !' cried Fanny petulantly (she certainly
has become very irritable lately—poor thing, it must be the
fault of that husband of hers, one of the most tedious men
I ever met). 'Now you have quite unsettled me again,
just as I had made up my mind at last !'

'But how very fortunate it was that I happened to meet
you now, dear Fanny, before it was too late !'

I wished I could have remained longer with the poor
thing, to have helped her out of her difficulties to the end,
but I really had not the time to spare, as I had promised
Lady Agnes Merton to look in during the morning.   So I
was obliged to leave poor Fanny, although my heart smote
me for doing so.

When I saw Lady Agnes, I felt at once that something

unusual had happened—she came in, her face wreathed with smiles, bubbling over with happiness.

'My dear friend, what do you think ? Nita is engaged !'

'Nita, your daughter ! I *am* glad to hear it ! To whom ?'

'To one of the most delightful young men I have ever met.

('Of course !' I thought. I never yet knew a mother who did not say the same thing of her daughter's *fiancé*.)

'We have not known him very long, but he seems to be in every respect exactly the husband we could have desired for her. You know him too, I dare say—Bertie Erskine.'

'Not Bertie Erskine about whom there was that sc—— ' I checked myself in time.

'What did you say ?' asked Lady Agnes quickly.

I hesitated.

'Well, really . . . My dear Lady Agnes, it may not be true, you know, but there certainly was some story about his being turned out of his club last year—that Lady Gordon was mixed up in it somehow. I really forget exactly what it was, but I dare say I could find it all out for you.'

'Bertie Erskine !' repeated Lady Agnes slowly—she certainly is stupid at taking in things sometimes. 'Can it be possible ? However, it is not too late—he will be here this morning.'

'Exactly ! and then he can tell you all about it himself —so much nicer—and after all, an engagement is not such an irrevocable thing' (*cheerfully*). 'Good-bye, dear Lady Agnes ! I am so glad I just happened to come in this morning !'

By the way, I heard from a friend I met in the afternoon, that it was not Bertie Erskine, but Billy *Fitz*Erskine, the story was about.

I wonder if Lady Agnes has found that out.

I dare say she has. At any rate, I am afraid I shan't have time this week to go and tell her, and I never like putting that kind of thing in a letter—I am always so afraid of spreading scandal—but certainly for the next few days I shall not have a minute to spare. Really, I can't think how I live through all I have to do—I am quite worn out with it sometimes. I got to Lady Greville's to-day, where I have a standing invitation to luncheon, quite faint and exhausted. I was rather surprised there to find no one but Sir Charles Porter in possession of the drawing-room. Nice youth, Sir Charles Porter—at least he will be when he is older. I don't know how it is, boys of six or seven and twenty are not nearly so interesting as they used to be—perhaps it is the difference in education—everything is changing nowadays.

Sir Charles seemed to be in a state of nervous anxiety, quite unlike his usual light-hearted manner—and started when he saw me come into the room, as though when the door opened he had expected to see some one else. I, seeing he was unwilling to talk, took the whole burden of the conversation on my shoulders as well as I could, but it was very uphill work, and I finally had to fall back upon a photograph album, which I never do unless I am positively at my last gasp.

Sir Charles seemed quite listless at first, but he gradually woke up into paying more attention, as I told him about all the people whose portraits we were looking at. I have a way of running on, I suppose, that makes people listen to me somehow—they seem to think I have a happy knack of putting things, a sort of sparkling way with me, perhaps—and so, I began telling him all about everybody. The first two portraits in the book were of course Lady Greville's father and mother. The mother is a most extraordinary-looking old lady, and, as I said to Sir Charles, is certainly a warning to her daughter of what *she* will be like—and

still more to Blanche Greville, her granddaughter, for the
girl is as like her grandmother as she can be. Sir Charles
had not noticed the likeness until I pointed it out to him.
Then there came a portrait of General Chaloner, Lady
Greville's brother, Blanche's bachelor uncle, who, it is said,
means to leave his niece all his fortune. He is a most
splendid, soldierly-looking creature, and, as I told Sir
Charles, likely to live for thirty years longer, for all those
Chaloners are a wonderfully long-lived race. Their name
is legion—and their photographs are legion too! And as
for the Greville family, I got quite tired of looking at all
the representations of them, depicted in every stage of
growth and fashion! Sir Charles, poor fellow! evidently
thought it his duty to please me by looking at every one of
them scrupulously, as if they were the most interesting
things in the world to him—it was too funny! I couldn't
help feeling, and saying, as we turned over page after page,
' Really, I don't think I ever saw such an uninteresting
family—they are all one worse than the other. Don't you
think so, Sir Charles ? '

' Well, I don't know, it hadn't occurred to me,' he said,
in a constrained voice—his manner certainly has altered
incredibly for the worse since I first knew him !

' Let us go on to something more interesting,' I said,
turning over the pages. ' Ah, this is better—do look ! this
is really a very amusing juxtaposition of people! Guy
Paget, Henry Fitzwilliam, Captain Morgan and Charlie
Lennox—all of them Blanche's admirers ! What a good
idea to put them on the same page, isn't it ? '

' Very,' said Sir Charles grimly.

' Captain Morgan was a great friend of mine,' I continued, determined to amuse my gloomy companion if I
could. ' He was ordered out to Africa at the end of last
summer, as I dare say you know. During the whole season
he had been very intimate with some friends of mine. I

won't tell you their names, as I don't think it would be
quite fair.   I hate spreading gossip—but I dare say you
will guess ! He had more especially seen a great deal of the
daughter, a very intimate friend of mine, who had certainly
looked very kindly on him, as young girls too often im-
prudently do.   Ill-natured people said—though I am not
sure that I *quite* believe them—that when Captain Morgan
was ordered to Africa, he was not sorry of the opportunity
it gave him to say good-bye to Miss—— (never mind who)'
(*archly*) 'before arriving at a further stage of friendship at
which a farewell might perhaps be more difficult, though
more dramatic—so accordingly the night before he sailed,
he went to say good-bye to her, and found her, by the most
curious chance in the world, quite alone.   What do you
think happened ?   Either she was unable to restrain her
feelings, or else she had the most wonderful presence of mind
—I have never known which to call it—but when the fatal
word ' Good-bye ' passed his lips, she burst into an agony
of tears, and well-nigh sank on the ground at his feet !
This threw him into the greatest perturbation, poor youth !
which was still further increased when the door suddenly
opened, and Lady Greville, finding the young couple in the
touching situation I have described, gave them her bless-
ing !'

' *Lady Greville !* ' shouted Sir Charles, in a state of un-
accountable excitement.

' Dear me, yes—now I have let the name slip out, like
the stupid thing I am !   How very absurd—but however,
I dare say you had guessed it already ?'

' Guessed it ? No, indeed ! by heavens, I had not !
What ! Do you mean to say that the heroine of your story,
the girl who fell at the feet of—of—Captain Morgan, was
Miss Greville ?—Blanche Greville ?   It is impossible !'

' No—I assure you the story is quite true, perfectly true
—Captain Morgan, I need not say, went away from here

that night—for it happened in this very room—an engaged man.'

'But then, if it is true, why did he not marry her ?'

'Ah, now you come to the dramatic part of the story. Affection, they say, depends upon propinquity. So, when. one person is in Grosvenor Square, and the other in Africa, affection is perhaps apt to languish ! At any rate, when Captain Morgan had been away six months, Blanche thought that Sir Henry Smythe, with 20,000*l*. a year, would make a more desirable husband. So she wrote to break off her engagement to Captain Morgan, who, they say, was not at all sorry to be released—but now a dreadful thing happens. Sir Henry Smythe, who, as you know, is always going round the world when he has nothing else to do, turns out to be engaged to a girl in Japan, the daughter of the English Minister there—and so, poor Blanche is left mourning !'

Sir Charles certainly is a most extraordinary person, he had suddenly awoke out of his lethargy into a state of violent passion, like a child who is roused from its sleep, and begins to scream—he began striding about the room like a madman (I shouldn't be surprised if *that* happened some day, he is so very peculiar sometimes), and then said abruptly :

'I find I must go—I'm afraid I can't wait till Lady Greville comes in. Will you tell her that—that I had an appointment at half-past one, in the City ? I had forgotten it,' and off he went.

Of course I, who, when I am shown one sentence of a story, can always reconstruct the rest of it, now saw the state of things, which indeed I should have discovered in any case a few minutes later, when Lady Greville arrived, very much surprised to see *me*, and me only.

'What, Geraldine ! you here ! How long have you been here ?' and she looked round the room vaguely, as if she expected to see some one else.

'Yes, dear,' I said, 'I thought I would come in to luncheon with you to-day, and as I was told you would be home at half-past one, I waited—but I have not been at all dull. Sir Charles Porter has been here, and I found him most entertaining!'

'Sir Charles Porter! Is he gone, then?'

'Yes, he was obliged to go—he told me to tell you he had an appointment in the City at half-past one.'

'How very odd—why that is the very time he appointed to come here! He wrote to me last night to ask if he might come to speak to me at 1.30 to-day. Of course I knew what for—for, between ourselves, he has been paying a great deal of attention to Blanche lately, and in fact I have wondered a little at his not declaring himself before. Blanche had already settled to go out driving with Lady Castleton this morning, but I expect her in every moment. Sir Charles, I dare say, will turn up here presently.'

However, I don't believe that Sir Charles did turn up, or what is more, that he ever will, in that particular way— but I did not remain to see, for I made my escape as soon as I could after luncheon, as I had to get to the other end of London by tea-time. I had promised to go to tea with Mary Woolner, dear good creature! She is one of those people whose children are always at a crisis of their education when you go to see them. She is always *just* making up her mind to have a holiday governess for Mary, or to take Jack away from school for a year, with a tutor, or to send Nellie to Queen's College, and so on. Accordingly, when I got there this afternoon, I found the customary state of things—namely, that Mary was quite rigid with agitation at having decided to send Lucy to Heidelberg for six months, to live with a former governess of her own who takes in six young English ladies, who have the privilege of speaking German to her, and their mother tongue to each other, for the sum of 120*l.* a year. I felt when I first heard

of it that the whole thing was inexpedient and absurd, and
that the plan could never answer, but I don't like meddling,
so I held my peace, until Mary so pointedly asked my
advice that I was obliged to tell her what I thought. I
said, 'I don't think I can give an unbiassed opinion about
Heidelberg, for I happen to know two or three things about
the place that would quite prevent me from ever sending a
daughter of mine there.'

'Good heavens, Geraldine, not really?' Mary exclaimed.
'Why, I have just posted my letter to Fräulein Zimmern,
making all the final arrangements, and saying Lucy will
cross next Tuesday. *Do* tell me what you have heard!
What sort of thing do you mean?'

'Well, on the face of it,' I replied, 'a university town
is not quite the place to send a girl to. The students make
it very disagreeable in many ways, and I believe at Heidelberg it is not at all an uncommon thing for them to kiss
their hands to girls in the street. Now I consider that
shocking!'

'Oh, extremely so, no doubt—but still, if that is
all——'

'All! But, my dear Mary, how much more do you
want? Besides, it is *not* all—far from being all! There
are all kinds of stories about the place, and I believe it to
be an undoubted fact that last winter no less than three
English girls ran away from boarding-houses with German
students. Now, how would you like *that* to happen to your
daughter?'

'Not at all, I must confess. Still, I don't think it very
likely that Lucy——'

'*Lucy!* but after all, Lucy is in *some* respects, I imagine,
like other girls! I know, of course, how carefully you have
trained her, and what excellent principles she has, what
charming manners—but girls will be girls, you know, and
you can't expect her to be quite unlike the rest of her sex.'

'Well, we will see what my husband says,' Mary answered, as that kind of woman invariably does—and as it happened, just at that moment the door opened, and Mr. Woolner walked in.   Now, he is exactly the type of man I have a perfect horror of—a great, bluff, matter-of-fact sort of creature, priding himself on his common sense and know-ledge of the world, and always settling things in an off-hand manner which he considers infallible, without an idea of the more sensitive perceptions and scruples of womankind.

. 'Oh, George, I am so glad you have come in !' Mary cried.   'What *do* you think Geraldine has been telling me about Heidelberg ?'

'I'm sure I can't tell,' he answered, in his indifferent, ill-mannered fashion.   'That the university has the cholera, perhaps, or that the Schloss has fallen into the river.   Is there any tea left, Mary ?'

'No, but do listen, George !   She says there have been three elopements from Heidelberg !   What *are* we to do about Lucy ?'

'About *her* eloping, do you mean ?   She must manage that for herself, my dear.   We can't do anything for her !'

'George ! how tiresome you are—you know quite well what I mean.   Do you think that Heidelberg can be a proper place to send her to, after all ?'

'Well, all I can say is, that if it is not, London isn't a proper place either—for there were certainly three, if not four, elopements from London last year, and many other wicked things, which perhaps Lucy may take to, if she has a turn that way !   Come, give me a cup of tea, my dear, and let's hear no more of this nonsense !'

Horrid, gormandising creature, always thinking of his own comfort, and preferring his tea to his children's wel-fare !   I need not say that after his most rude and insulting words I would not stay in the room with him a minute longer.   Perhaps next time Mary is in a difficulty, she will be sorry that she has cut herself off from the chance of my help.

I dislike of all things having to dress for dinner in a hurry—the result of all this Heidelberg discussion was that I got to Lady Marie Stanhope's dinner-party a quarter of an hour after everyone else had arrived. My host, who took me down, was in rather a thorny frame of mind in consequence, in spite of his delight with his new cook—which, by the way, he most naïvely imparted to all his guests ! though, as I told him, I don't think she is as good as the last. But he doesn't care what anybody says, he is the sort of man who always thinks he is right. I got quite exhausted by the end of dinner, after vainly trying to prove to him on several occasions that he was wrong !

He said only one thing that interested me, and that was, that he had met Sir Charles Porter this afternoon, who said he was going to the East. I am glad of it—he will be out of the way of that flirting Blanche Greville.

Heigho ! *I* should like to go to the East, or to the West, or somewhere at any rate a long way off, beyond the reach of people who come to me for advice and sympathy—but I really don't like to do it. I don't feel as if it would be right to leave all my friends for so long. But there is time enough to think of it, after all—I won't trouble my head about it to-night, as I have a busy day, and an early start, before me to-morrow. I promised I would go to Lady Walmer's in the morning, to help her to choose the new paper for her dining-room—I know if I don't go that she will take that horrid greenish-grey one she has set her heart upon, and which I detest ! And now, to bed—for I am quite worn out, in mind and in body, by my hard day's work !

Curtain.

THE RELIQUARY

MONOLOGUE.

Alice. It is done ! I have written to accept him ! There is the letter, the fatal letter, that carries my destiny within its folds. I am almost afraid of it, it seems to me such a terribly important document ! It is very odd—from the moment I had written it I felt less and less inclined to send it. What a curious thing, to be sure ! It doesn't always happen, I suppose : people can't always feel like that about the letters they've written, or we should never receive any at all. Correspondence would cease, postmen would starve, the Dead Letter Office would be the only one we should need.

But I am talking vainly—this is an idle dream ! there lies the letter, it is written, stamped and sealed, and therefore, in accordance with a stern and unvarying law of nature, it must now go to the post—there is no help for it, I suppose. Still, it cannot go until to-morrow morning, that is one comfort ; for it is past midnight, and time all good letters were in bed. And yet, if I could only have had it posted now there would have been an end of it, and I should never have seen it again. I should have heard of it, though, often enough, for I know what the result would be—Frank would come rushing round here the first thing after breakfast, and then I should never be left in peace again. I really don't think I could stand it.

Have I done right, I wonder ? What a silly creature he must be to give me all this trouble—to write to propose to me, instead of asking me straight out when we were together, and getting my answer then and there. It would have been so much better ! I should have been surprised into saying something—I'm sure I don't know what—and there would have been an end of it. He has had heaps of opportunities, I am sure, for doing so. We were together at Lord's on Monday, and stood on the top of a little shed for ever so long after luncheon, while he was explaining the cricket to me—what could have been better than that ? Or the night before, at Lady Montague's, when we were crushed into an alcove on the stairs by three dowagers, for ever so long, why couldn't he have done it then ? not to mention all the other places I've met him at in the last fortnight, for he has been absolutely my shadow ! Bazaars, where I've sold him rose-buds for fifteen shillings, and cups of tea for a pound—private theatricals, where he's had to stand on the landing all the evening and look through the chink of the door—recitations in the afternoon, where he has sometimes been the only man in the room, poor dear, such was his devotion !

Ah, well, it has been a pleasant and peaceful time, without fiery emotions of any kind, and now he must needs write me this idiotic love-letter, and put an end to it ! put a beginning, I suppose I should rather say—which is it to be ? Perhaps if I sleep upon it I shall feel happier in the morning. 'Night brings good counsel,' the French proverb says. I suppose I can't be so *very* much in love with him, or I shouldn't hesitate at all. I should like to ask somebody's advice about it—some one of my own age, who knows exactly what it is to be in love, who has had the complaint recently, like my aunt and her friends, who are always comparing experiences of their last illness—but I don't quite know whom to ask. Not Rose Leigh, for I

believe she is more than half in love with Frank herself —
I don't know that *that* matters, though — she might be all
the better able to judge. Not Carrie Macdonald, for *she*
has the most extraordinary ideas. I've heard her say that
one can only be in love once in a lifetime — now I know
for a fact that isn't true !

Well, well, I must struggle out of it myself, I suppose,
as best I may. At any rate, if I am on the eve of such an
important crisis in my life, I think that before going to
sleep I ought to put my papers in order — how grand that
sounds ! Yes, I must turn out my secret drawer — my
drawer of relics — all my precious souvenirs that have been
lying there and accumulating with astonishing rapidity for
the last five years, since my eighteenth birthday ! — and
now I am going to tear them up, throw them away, forget
all the love affairs I've ever had, and subside into an ugly,
commonplace matron. Oh, how many things ! I declare
I've almost forgotten what they all are. I wish I had
written their names on them when I put them away, as
mamma does on her jams in the summer.

What on earth is this ? a piece of broken pencil. That
must be here by mistake. I'll throw it away — no — stay —
surely I remember something about it — what was it ?
Oh ! (*laughing*) oh — I remember — it must be Bertie
FitzWilliam's ! Poor Bertie, what a dear good creature
he was, and *how* stupid ! a great immense fellow, with a
deep voice, and no more ideas than — than a soldier generally has ! and so shy, *so* shy. *Declaring* his love was an
expression which could by no possibility be applied to him.
He insinuated it, perhaps, hinted at it, made distant allu-
sions to it, but as to declaring it, it was a great deal too
much for him, in spite of his being six feet two.

I shall never forget him, that last evening — we were
staying in a country house, where there had been a lawn
tennis tournament in the afternoon — he and I were drawn

to play together—he put me in the corner of the court and took everything himself, and we won. I *was* so proud! In the evening there was a great ball—I danced nine times with him, I remember—and then I discovered that the poor creature actually thought I cared about him! We were sitting in the conservatory. after a waltz—he certainly did waltz most divinely! when he suddenly said, blushing violently, in a very hoarse, deep voice, 'Miss Beverley, I have something to say to you.' 'Indeed?' I said, smiling sweetly, 'I am very glad of that.' 'Yes— I have something to say to you.' 'I should not have thought it,' I replied, after waiting a moment to see if anything came. 'Can't you guess what it is?' he said, becoming more and more strangled. 'Certainly not,' I answered, airily. 'Can't you really guess, Miss Beverley?' 'Haven't an idea!' and I suppose the entire blank of my expression must have quenched his hopes at once and for ever—for, after sitting for a moment, speechless, like a design for an image of misery to be executed on a colossal scale, he seized my ball programme, saying, 'Give me something that has belonged to you—something that has touched your hand: give me this.' Such was his agitation, and such the size of his hands, that he broke the pencil in two, and left this half of it in my lap, and then— he fled! Poor Bertie, he is married now. . . . . I *hate* those sandy-haired women with light eyelashes! No, I don't think I can throw away that pencil, after I've had it all these years. [*Puts it back.*

What is this? [*Taking up letter.*] 'My own dearest darling'—that sounds affectionate! [*Looks at signature.*] O'Grady—Captain O'Grady, of course!—he was a lieutenant then—I had forgotten his very existence! [*Looking over letter.*] This is exactly the way he used to talk— I fancy I can hear his Irish brogue now! [*Reads*] 'My own dearest darling,—I am leaving you, it may be for years.' (That's an original expression !) 'I am going to India, to win honour and renown—but oh, my darling, the fiercest sun that ever blazed in the East is but cool compared to the burning, consuming flame of love that fills my heart ! The wildest tiger that ever leaped in the jungle is tame compared to the unconquerable ardour of my passion ! Think of me, dear, when you are at home at ease.' (Another original remark !) 'Think of me beneath the scorching sun of India, scaling the snow-capped Himalayas, track-ing the wary crocodile, subduing the mighty elephant— think of me, braving every hardship, every danger life can afford, that I may gather fame, riches, and glory, to lay them at your feet !' Ha, ha ! he never did produce any of them to lay at my feet, poor fellow. Perhaps the wary crocodile was too much for him after all ! [*Puts the letter back with the others.*] I don't think I can tear it up, for if I were to find he had been eaten by a tiger, I should never forgive myself !

What is this printed paper ? Royal Institution—a list of lectures ! It looks much too learned for the company it is in. I wonder how I came to get hold of it, for I don't think *I* ever attended one of those lectures in my life. With all my faults, I don't think I ever went through the phase of suddenly taking a deep interest in some learned or artistic subject that I cared nothing about, and pursuing it hotly for a season at a time, as I have seen various of my friends doing ! [*Looks at paper.*] And yet there must be some reason for my having this. [*Sees name on it.*] Ah, I see. Professor Schmitz was to lecture—it was that funny little German who took such a fancy to me ! Nice little man he was, and most amusing to listen to, with his broken English and foreign expressions, until he became so silly about me : *then*, of course, all the sense went out of him.

The fact is, I never can keep my men friends, because

just as we have got to know one another well, they fall in love with me, propose to me, I refuse them, and there is an end of it! I am always so unfortunate in that way. I wonder why? It isn't that I am so *very* pretty—rather pretty, perhaps, but not enough to account for everything —and I'm quite sure I'm not clever, for even the Professor, who was in love with me, used to be in despair because I couldn't understand his learned talk. Perhaps there is a 'charm' about me! Yes, that must be it! That is what people always say when they wish to praise a woman who is neither pretty, nor amusing, nor anything else— 'there is such an indefinable charm about her!'

Why, here is a letter from the Professor, put away with the programme—in such a funny little cramped German writing! [*Reads*] 'Honoured Fräulein!'—why do Germans always put a note of exclamation after the beginning of their letters, I wonder? perhaps it is because they are astonished at finding they can write one at all—and I don't wonder, with the crabbed little characters they use!—'I send you the programme of a soon-to-be-delivered-and-I-hope-a-little-interesting-to-you lecture at the Royal Institution. She treats of a subject of whom certainly you have heard, and which I think will to you in the highest pleasure and interest bring. Her name is "The Unconscious Cerebration of Tadpoles, and the Influence of their Brain Development on the Intelligence of Man." She has been through-translated into English by one of your learned Herr-Professors, by reason of the English technical words, in which it fails me of readiness, spite my being able, as you well know, in daily life English to speak like German.' (That is very true—no one can deny *that!*) 'I hope then, dear Fräulein, that you will make me the honour of hearing my lecture. I have been having the pleasure of speaking her already last Thursday, before a numberfull and mixed-up audience. I hope then, dear

Fräulein, that you will come, and that you will bring some of your friends with, to listen also.'

Ha, ha !—I don't think I *can* wade through any more of this effusion, especially all this romantic nonsense at the end. Oh dear, how funny it is—'any of your friends with ' —so exactly what he used to say ! I fancy I can see him now, at my mother's afternoons, handing about the five o'clock tea in a state of cheerful bustle, and saying in an insinuating manner with his head on one side, 'Some shucar with ?' 'A leetle milk with ?' Poor little man ! I never saw him again after I received that letter !— he never forgave me for not attending his lecture ! I shall keep the programme and letter, though—to show how foolish even a wise man can be when he is in love !

[*Turns over papers—takes out a photograph, her face changes.*

Ah !—what is this ? an old photograph of me, with two words written across it : '*Until death !*' Until death, indeed, it was ! the sight of it gives me a stab—I feel my heart-string stighten as I look at it— my poor Fred !—why, why was I so foolish—why was I so weak—why did I let them send him away from me, because, forsooth, he was poor ! Ah, if it were now, when I am older, braver than I was then, I would have *insisted* on my right to choose him— to follow him to the end of the world ! Ah, it is very well to say, as I foolishly said just now, that we can love many times—No, it is not true, no, we cannot— not with the overmastering passion that comes to us but once ! I may have cared, in a way, have thought myself in love with this one or that one—but *Fred*—Fred was myself—he belonged to me, and I to him, from the first moment we met—it was as natural as that the sun should shine, or the trees bud in the spring. . . .

Fred, Fred ! Ah ! that day, the last day we ever had together—the day they sent you from me ! we had been so happy that afternoon- we had walked under the trees like

two children, hardly conscious of the world around us,
except to feel what a beautiful world it is, and what great
happiness there is in it for those who love—and then, my
father came home—you went to him—oh, he laughed at
your tale—he laughed at your youthful passion—he bade
you leave me for two years. Oh, Fred, I almost wish you
had not come back to me that day, to whisper to me yourself what our fate was to be, for whenever I think of you
I see you with the white, stony, despairing face I saw
then. . . . [*Speaking low and rapidly.*] He went away—
to Africa—he fought there—he rushed purposely into the
thickest of the fight at Ulundi—he was found there after
the battle, lying dead amongst the dead—the portrait of
me on his breast, his hand resting on it as though with his
latest strength he had striven to take it out, to look on it
with those dear eyes, that could no longer see. No, no,
this I cannot destroy—'until death,' too, it shall be mine—
and yet I must not look on it again, for the sight of his
writing, the mere thought of his name sends a quiver through
my whole being. . . . [*After a minute rouses herself, turns
over papers listlessly, then pushes them away.*] No, I cannot look over these to-night—my merry mood is gone—they
have lain here so long, they may e'en remain a little longer,
and yet I shall no longer be free now [*Half-shuddering*]—
is it safe to leave the ghosts of my past life to rise at any
moment? No, I will destroy them all. I will burn the
whole heap of them without looking at one of them again,
lest some tender recollection should bid me stay my hand.

[*Pushes them into a heap.*

And yet, what a pity it seems——[*A paper falls from the
heap at her feet—she picks it up*] What is this? Why, here
is the letter I had this morning from Frank. I wonder how
it got in here? I need not keep *that*, I suppose—for if—
if I send that letter of mine [*With a sigh*] I shall hear often
enough from him for the next few months, and then—and
then—oh, I know exactly how it will be.

Maggie Brice used to show me the letters she had from her husband when they were engaged—such long delightful letters, eight or ten pages, full of poetry and passion, and all that kind of thing. I have seen some of those he writes to her now, after they have been married two years—half a sheet of note paper. 'I shall be home on Wednesday by the nine train, and shall want supper,' or 'The man forgot to put up my dress clothes, send them after me—dusty journey—the sandwiches were stale !'

Good heavens ! it is enough to make the gods weep ! Can it be that *this* is the sort of thing that awaits *me* ? that this is the bondage into which I am so madly rushing ? No, no, my every conception of life would be turned upside down. I should have to grovel where I have commanded. *I*, who all my life have been petted and adored, would have daily to minister to the comforts of some one else ! oh, the thought is *too* fearful ! I simply couldn't endure it ! To think that I, with my own hand, should have signed away my freedom ! [*Takes up the letter she has written.*] Happily the letter is not sent yet—it can be recalled—it *shall* be recalled ! *this*, and no other, is the letter I will destroy— this shall be the burnt-offering I will make to the past ! [*Tears up letter—throws pieces on ground—stands a moment looking at them.*] There, I can again feel I belong to no one but myself ! it is delightful, of course, to be free—oh yes— I am glad I have done it, very glad. I can't help feeling a little flat, though, all the same.

I should have been happy with Frank, I am sure, very happy indeed—and after all, even if he did write to me to order his meals for him, I think—I think I should have enjoyed doing it for him, I really should—it would be so much more satisfactory to feel there is some one in the world whose existence revolves round one's own. I should hate to feel I was not first with *anyone* in the world. . . . And after all, I can't go on refusing people for ever—it isn't as if they went on being in love with me either, it wouldn't matter so much then—but the moment I've refused them, they go and marry somebody else. I never saw anything like it! if I don't marry in self-defence I shall degenerate into an aunt—absolutely only an aunt. Oh, no! That would be worse than anything! I should have no one to take care of me, to look after me.

Frank would take care of me, I know—he always does now, at least. How nice he was at that picnic at Maidenhead the other day, when he carried my wraps, and helped me across the stream! I wonder if he would do that after we were married? Yes, I'm sure he would. And yet, I remember noticing that day that Mrs. Merewether had to cross the brook by herself—*her* husband was helping Mrs. Humphrey, while Mr. Humphrey was taking charge of Lady Scott! still, I don't think that could ever happen to me, for Frank is not like anyone else in the world—no, no, he certainly is not.

I have thrown away the chance of happiness that lay beneath my hand. I have torn my letter up. How *could* I?.. After all, why should I not write it over again? No one need ever know I hesitated. I will tell Frank, perhaps, some day, but nobody else . . . yes—I will write it again!

> [*Takes a sheet of paper quickly, to write—as she does so, pushes the whole heap of papers, &c., she has been looking at into a basket beneath.*

Curtain.

S

THE WATERPROOF

A MONOLOGUE.

Ah! Now I have got home I can take off this miserable waterproof of Mrs. Mowbray's. I do hate wearing other people's things. I can't think why she insisted on my borrowing it, except that there are some people who always will lend you things you don't want to have. 'Oh, you really must have a waterproof,' she kept saying—'it is going to rain heavily, and you will get so wet jumping in and out of hansoms.' Cat! After all, she wouldn't have had a carriage herself if Mr. Mowbray had not made all his money in tea—and he looked so exactly that sort of man, with a red face, and little sandy-grey whiskers! Why she should have made such a fuss about him after he died I can't imagine.   [*Laying cloak on chair.*

There, now I've got rid of that horrid thing. Some one was saying just now—who was it? Oh, I know, it was Mrs. Mowbray herself: that woman is always trying to say something learned—that menkind are divided into groups by the shapes of their heads. That's the kind of thing that is quite useless to know, and I consider it indecent to talk about in a drawing-room. I am sure that womenkind are divided into groups by the shapes of their waterproofs—and when I see a woman with one of those hideous, old-fashioned, round shiny things on, I know exactly what she would say—if I were to talk to her, that is ; but I never would, for I don't want to hear about the outbreak of whooping-cough at Jacky's school, or how much more susceptible to infection Minnie is than Polly. On the other hand, I dare say that the woman who wears a waterproof with silk outside, and a hood lined with red, would be more dangerous in some respects, though perhaps more agreeable. As to Mrs. Mowbray, she is neither the one thing nor the other; she is half-way between the dowdy and the dangerous. [*Looking at cloak.*

I can't quite make her out. It is very odd, but I don't believe she likes me. I wonder why not? I hate the woman myself, of course : to me she is a most dreary creature. She never has anything interesting to say about people, only the most meaningless praise. I am told that everyone confides their private affairs to her. There are some women who have that sort of mission—to be a sort of friend of all work, as it were—a kind of aunt to the human race. Well, those people are useful sometimes! Just at this juncture I rather want a confidante, for I asked Major Symonds for two days for reflection. This is the second—what am I going to say to him? Why do I hesitate, I wonder? Why did I not say yes at once? He is pleasant—oh, certainly pleasant enough—I don't like people who are oppressively intellectual—and his sister has told me that he is not nearly so passionate as he used to be. He doesn't look very soldierly, perhaps, but I don't mind that—in fact, I think a warlike air is misplaced in a drawing-room. He looked quite presentable at Lady Brightwell's At Home, I thought. We were coming downstairs together—at least, we were not together at that moment, for I was coming down alone, and I saw him also alone. And it is so odd for a soldier, he sometimes has those fits of shyness. I don't know what else it could have been, he seemed really afraid to meet my eye. He was turning his head away, as though he didn't dare to speak—but of course I saw how it was, and felt it would

be only kind to come to his help, so I suggested to him
that we should go in to supper together. I saw how grateful he was to me. Then, while we had supper, we began
talking about all sorts of things I thought would please
him—about the sadness of being lonely, and of wanting a
companion—and I told him I saw he was lonely sometimes,
and that I was sorry for him. And then he said, 'Mrs.
Story, you are quite right, indeed, you are right—it is a
terrible thing to be alone at my time of life.' Such nonsense to speak in that way—his time of life, indeed! He's
much too young to talk like that—I don't consider that
people arrive at a 'time of life' till they're well over sixty,
certainly not at fifty-two. He said, 'I have made up my
mind not to be lonely any longer. Do you think—would
it be possible that I could find anyone to share my solitude?—that a battered old soldier like me would have
any chance?' A battered old soldier, indeed! If he is
battered, it's nature and the east winds in the streets of
London that have done it—I don't believe he has ever
been further afield than Wimbledon Common. 'Battered!'
I exclaimed. 'Oh, my dear Major Symonds!' He looked
pleased, certainly—pleased and soothed. There are some
women who know exactly the right thing to say, and I am
one of them. 'Well,' he said, trying to look modest, 'I
must say I thought the other day, when I was with Mrs.
Mowbray——' and he stopped. 'With Mrs. Mowbray!'
I cried. 'But what has she to do with this question?'
He said nothing. He smiled rather inanely, I must confess. I saw at once how it was—he had been making a
confidante of that woman, and telling her about me. It
was indiscreet of him, of course, but I don't know that I
minded it—in fact, I was rather pleased, as I am quite
sure it must have annoyed her.

At this moment we were interrupted by two dowagers
looking for seats, who came and stood behind us, until

they positively lifted us from our chairs by the force of
their glare, so we could say nothing more. 'I will give
you an answer the day after to-morrow,' I said hurriedly,
as we went out through the hall. This is Monday, come
to see me at five o'clock on Wednesday.' He said nothing—I left him looking absolutely vacant, as I must say
he does sometimes. I suppose he was taken aback at the
delay. And now, this is 4.30 on Wednesday—what am I
going to say to him? Let me look back into the past.
Ah, I have too many broken hearts on my conscience to
dare to bear the burden of another!

There was Douglas Benson, a barrister, brilliant and
successful—what a life to have ruined! There was no
doubt about his feelings. Whenever he was in my society
he was a prey to the deepest melancholy. I never shall
forget that night that we dined at Maidenhead with the
Tollemaches. I felt I must endeavour to dispel his gloom,
and after dinner I offered to go with him for a row on the
river. I saw his inward struggle—he dared not expose
himself to the fatal temptation—but I nerved myself to
the effort for his sake. It was no use : the cloud settled
darker, darker on his features. He could not trust himself to speak. We never met again after that evening.
What became of him I dared not ask ; I was haunted by
the thought of those dark, lowering features!

Then there was Lionel Talbot. What a handsome
fellow he was!—the very type of a British sailor. Ah,
that time at Portsmouth, when they gave a farewell dance
on board his ship ! I saw what he wanted—what he was
evidently longing to suggest, and let him understand in
covert terms that I would overcome my dread of the sea to
gratify his parting wish. But he was too noble, poor
fellow, too heroic. He replied that there were 'some
things too precious to expose to the fury of the elements.'
Ah, he was right there ! It was his last voyage. His

ship was lost in the midst of the Pacific Ocean, and he died, breathing my name—at least, I have no doubt he did breathe it, though I shall never, never know.

But why should I melt my heart by dwelling on these tender memories, instead of steeling it to be firm and valiant? It is an awful thing to have to make up one's mind. I could almost be sorry to-day that I have no chattering female friends to whom I am in the habit of telling everything. Like my Cousin Lucy, for instance—I know as a fact that if any interesting crisis happens in her life, she has to sit down and write it to eleven intimate female friends, with whom she has sworn to exchange every thought. And there is Mrs. Mowbray, who is in the same position as regards Mrs. Fanshawe. I have heard that not only do these two tell each other everything, but they also send each other all the letters they receive from other people. In fact, I believe that if one of them were to receive a proposal, she would send it to the other to know what she was to say. I call that really immodest.

Ah! [*sighing*] and that brings me back to the question I ought to be considering all this time. What must I say to Major Symonds? What must I do? Ah! I fear I have no doubt I have most foolishly suffered myself to be melted by dwelling thus upon the past. I must accept him—yes, I must—for I couldn't break another heart, I really couldn't.

[*Is going to dry her eyes.*

Why, where is my handkerchief? Oh, of course, I must have left it in the pocket of that wretched waterproof.

[*Feels in pocket of waterproof—pulls out two letters with handkerchief.*

What are these? These are not mine. [*Looks at one.*

'DEAR MRS. MOWBRAY,—' It is in the handwriting of Major Symonds!

[*Closes her hand on it, and stands for a minute irresolute.*

It is as I thought—he evidently wrote to her about me. Well, one can hardly blame him, poor fellow, for seeking a friend's advice at this crisis—this most momentous crisis! Oh, I really must read it. I shall like to see how he speaks of me to others.　　　　　　　*[Opens it with a coy smile.*

'DEAR MRS. MOWBRAY,—You will know—you must know—the subject on which I am writing to you——'
　　　　　　　　　　　　　　　　[Reads on—shrieks.

Ah, the base treachery! That wicked, deceiving woman! Oh, my poor friend, that he should have been caught in her toils. Ah, how powerless a man is when a designing, shameless woman entraps him! This, then, was why he turned despairingly to me that night—he sought for succour, for rescue, and I, cold-hearted, cruel that I was, refused it. Ah, why did I not answer him then and there? Why did I not cleave to my place, though all the dowagers in England stood behind it? Well, well, his destiny would have been different with me. He has, in despair at my seeming coldness, proposed to another woman out of pique —his manly heart has been caught at the rebound. *[Sighs.*

It is as well, perhaps, for in a moment of yielding I might have fettered myself for ever.

　　　[Walks up and down—her eye falls on the other letter.

Ah! I had forgotten this one. I wonder what surprise *this* contains.　　　　　*[Picks it up—looks at signature.*

'Lina Fanshawe.' Of course—it is one of the dozen letters she sends to her dear friend every day.

'DARLING MABEL,—' Ugh! that makes me quite sick, it really does! 'I return Major Symonds' letter, which has amused me excessively.' Coarse, insolent woman. 'Imagine his proposing to you! I am so glad you refused him—how could he ever think you would do anything else?' What, she has refused him! Refused! well, so much the worse for her. She has not caught him at the rebound then—

his heroic sacrifice has not been accepted. Let me see what else she says. ' I only hope he won't be as broken-hearted over it as Douglas Benson was. Do you remember that night you refused him at Maidenhead ?' What, I drove him too into madness by my cruelty ! It's well for him she refused him. What an escape he has had !

[*Reads.*

' And now I must congratulate you, dearest, on the good news you tell me—the return of——' What! 'Lionel Talbot !' His return ! ' What a hero he will be when he comes back, after being supposed to be drowned : such a hero that I imagine that you will no longer hesitate to '—ah, it is impossible !—' to announce your engagement.' Lionel Talbot alive—not dead—and engaged to Mrs. Mowbray ! Well, I dare say even *that* is better than lying at the bottom of the Pacific—and yet, no, I am not sure that it is. Oh, what shipwreck of all his hopes ! Alas, how many lives have I ruined ! But there is one person, at any rate, to whom I can make amends. It was I drove Major Symonds to the desperate sacrifice he attempted, and I will reward him for it. This decides me. It was I who well-nigh seared and blighted his life—I will console him myself !

Curtain.

'OH, NO!'

A MONOLOGUE.

I was a young girl once—not so very long ago—a *very* shy young girl—I smile now, as I think of the agonies of timidity and embarrassment which I used to go through every day—every hour almost—with such very inadequate cause! When I first 'came out'—when I began to go to balls, receptions, afternoon teas, garden parties—positively everyone who came to speak to me was a fresh source of terror—another alarming incarnation of society, before whom I felt more utterly speechless and awkward than words can describe. My very heart used to quail when I saw good-natured friends of my mother's come up to me, out of sheer kindness, I am sure, to make small talk to me —when some courtly young man would advance to put my cup down, or some still more polite youth invite me to dance—I was pleased, of course—but oh! the suflerings I underwent! I was so shy on these occasions that I could absolutely utter no word—and the more I tried to think of something to say, the more utterly did speech, thought, intelligence and everything else appear to have departed from me! At last, unable to bear it any longer, I confided my sorrows to my mother one evening, as we were going out to a ball, and asked her to help me. 'My dear Violet,' she said, smiling, 'girls of seventeen are not expected to be very eloquent—if you can listen agreeably when people talk to you, and make some trifling rejoinder every now and again, that will do quite well for the present.'

'But that is exactly my difficulty—I can't think of any

rejoinder—I am so shy, all my ideas go away the moment
people speak to me ! '

'But surely you can think of saying *Oh, yes*—or *Oh, no*
—as the case may be—that is not a great effort of imagination ! '

'But I should never know which to say—I should
invariably say *Yes* when it ought to have been *No*—if I
only had *one* answer that would always do, then I shouldn't
have to think about it at all.'

'Well, I am not sure that it would be a good plan
always to answer *Yes* to everything that is said to you—
you might find it inconvenient sometimes ! '

'Then I will say *Oh, no*—that can never commit me to
anything.'

'Very well,' said my mother, laughing—'you had better
try it to-night, and see how it succeeds ! '

So, thus provided with a fund of conversation, I arrived
at the ball a little happier in my mind than I generally felt
on these occasions, but still with some misgivings, as usual.
We were received in the drawing-room by our hostess, Mrs.
Fenwick, one of the kindest-hearted women in the world,
who was at once anxious to find me a host of partners.
'Now, my dear, you've come prepared to enjoy yourself, I
hope—you don't mean to sit by your mother all the evening,
as some strait-laced young ladies I know do ? '

'Oh, no ! '

'You must let me introduce a great many partners to
you.'

'Oh, no ! '   [*Deprecatingly.*

'Nonsense—of course I shall—there is my nephew just
arriving—Arthur, you know Miss Graham—Violet, I need
not introduce Captain Gosset to you.'

'Oh, no ! '

'May I have the pleasure of a waltz ? or is your card
quite full ? '

'Oh, no !'

'That is delightful—let us have a turn now, before the room is too crowded'—and off we went. 'I don't think I have ever had a better waltz in my life,' he said as we left off. 'I won't ask you if you have enjoyed it too—that would be conceited of me !'

'Oh, no !'

'We have not met for such ages—I was wondering if I should ever see you again—not since that day at Maidenhead, have we ?'

'Oh, no !'

'How delicious it was on the river in the evening—and what a splendid little canoe that was I rowed you in ! nothing so jolly as a canoe, is there ?'

'Oh, no !'

'I dare say, though, you've been on the river hundreds of times since, and have forgotten all about that day ?'

'Oh, no !'

'What a pity—there is the end of the waltz—you must give me another presently—let me see, there is No. 4—give me No. 9 and No. 13—may I put my name down for those —you don't think that will be too many ?'

'Oh, no !'

'It isn't enough, *I* think !'

'Oh, n——'   [*Checks herself.*

'Let us go out on to the balcony—or are you afraid of being too cold ?'

'Oh, no !'

I don't know how long we remained on the balcony —I am afraid, a long time. Presently Lucy Fenwick came out, with Mr. Le Marchant—by the way, I believe it was settled when they were children, by their mothers, that Lucy was to marry her cousin, Arthur Gosset, when they grew up—people say that Mrs. Fenwick is very anxious, now, to bring it about. I don't care about Lucy

very much—she talks and giggles so much, no one knows
what she is going to say next. 'What, Violet ! is this
where you are ?' she cried. 'Mrs. Graham has been
wondering what had become of you—is this where you
have been all the evening ?'

'Oh, no !'

'She says it is more than half an hour since she has
seen you !'

'Oh, *no* !' I said indignantly as I rose.

'This is our dance, I believe, No. 9,' Captain Gosset
said, as we stepped back into the room.

'Oh, no !' I said, incredulously, rather horrified at finding that actually *four* dances had passed while we were on
the balcony.

'Indeed it is, I assure you,' he said ; 'don't let us
waste any more of this delicious music ! . . . . not so nice
as it was before—too many people now—let us go on to
the balcony again !'

'Oh, no !'

'That is very cruel of you—mind you don't forget that
you have promised me No. 13.'

'Oh, no !'

By the time No. 13 came round, I was quite tired out
with dancing, and besides, the room was so hot and crowded
one could hardly move. So Captain Gosset suggested that
instead of dancing we should go into the conservatory,
which was delightfully cool, and quite empty. 'Jolly
place, a conservatory !' he said—'fountains plashing,
Chinese lanterns burning—flowers smelling — and — all
that ! no place like it when you want to talk, is there?'

'Oh, no !'

After this remark, however, Captain Gosset relapsed
into silence, instead of at once breaking into the irresistible
eloquence he had led me to expect—and we both sat for
some minutes contemplating the fountains, the flowers and

the Chinese lanterns—which at last appeared to have the desired effect—for he suddenly said, 'Miss Graham !—Violet !—do you mind my calling you Violet ?'

'Oh, no !'

'I am going to India next month—it may be years before I see you again——'

'Oh, no !' I said, reassuringly.

'I cannot leave England without speaking to you, without telling you of my love—for you must know, you must have seen what I feel for you—have you not guessed it long ago ?'

'Oh, no !'

'Nay, I am sure you have ! Violet—could you, would you endure the idea of going out to India ?'

'Oh, no !'   [*Decidedly.*

'What—you would not ?—but surely you must care a little for me—you could not have been to me as you have been, if you did not feel something more for me than friendship ?'

'Oh, no !'

'Think over what I have said, then—do not reject the idea at once—give me a little hope ! I am not displeasing to you, am I ?'

'Oh, no !'

'Do you dislike a soldier's life ?'

'Oh, no !'

'My darling ! how happy you would make me——' At this moment Mrs. Fenwick appeared in the doorway.

'What, Violet, my dear child ! are you not afraid of a chill, sitting in this cold place ?'

'Oh, no !'

'Have you had any supper ?'

'Oh, no !'

'Arthur, how neglectful of you—do take Miss Graham in to supper.' And so we went into the supper-room, where there was an immense crowd, and where Lucy Fenwick kindly insisted on giving me up her seat, between two female friends of her mother's—and after supper we went home.——Captain Gosset went to India, the next month. You will ask whether I ever went there too? Oh, no! Time and absence, new friends and fresh scenes, turned the current of his thoughts, and brought healing to his grief. His heart did not break—neither did mine. He is now, I believe, happily married—so am I—so is Lucy Fenwick—and we are none of us as foolish, or as shy, as we were ten years ago—Oh, *no*!!

Curtain.

NOT TO BE FORWARDED

A MONOLOGUE.

SCENE.—*A sitting-room in chambers. A pile of unopened letters, papers, &c., on the table.*

Enter Dick Stanley hurriedly, in travelling costume, with a bag in his hand.

Dick. Ha! what a comfort to be back again in my own chambers! this week that I have been out of town has seemed to me an eternity. What an enormous pile of documents is awaiting me! That is the result of saying nothing is to be forwarded during one's absence. It is quite a mistake, not to have things forwarded. That was old Brown's idea. When he heard I was going out of town for a few days' change, he said at once, 'Well, my dear feller, if I were you, I would say nothing is to be sent after me, otherwise your holiday will be no holiday. You can't think what a feeling of perfect peace it gives one to be beyond reach of the post!' I was fool enough to believe him, and to act on his advice—but it didn't give me a feeling of perfect peace at all—quite the reverse! It gave me a feeling of perfect fever. I was the whole time wondering if my correspondence, just this week, might not contain something of vital importance, that was now awaiting me at home—if the crisis of my fate might not have been reached, and if by my idiotic folly I might not have missed the road to Fortune! not that I had any

reason, from past experience, to expect that such a thing
would happen, for up to now I have been singularly free
from any crisis in my fortunes.   I have enjoyed a complete
immunity from the feverish emotions which beset those of
my friends who achieve unexpected success.   Yes, there is
no doubt about it, I have been unlucky from the beginning. First of all, nothing could be more unfortunate than
having 500*l.* a year to live upon—it is neither the one
thing nor the other—it is too much or too little.   In
secure, inglorious possession of that unworthy pittance, I
have been debarred from all the incitements of heroic
poverty.   I have never known the joy of coming to London
with a crust in my pocket, determined to make my fortune
or starve uncomprehended in a garret.   No, mine has been
the prosaic, vegetating existence of one whose daily wants
have always been supplied, and no more—whose income
is sufficient for one, but not enough, alas! for two.   For
two . . . yes, there is the rub!   It is no good denying it —
unless I can double my income by my own exertions, I am
condemned to a life of hopeless celibacy!   I shall see the
woman I love carried off under my eyes by a more successful rival, while I am seeking, pining, yearning for fame
and fortune, that I may lay them at her feet.   But how
am I to do it?   I have sat for hours in chambers, waiting
for briefs that have never come.   I have written three
plays and a novel, which have all been refused.   I tried to
get on to the staff of a newspaper, which wouldn't have
me.   I went on to the Stock Exchange, and embarked all
my available means in a venture which I was told would
make my fortune . . . . it came to grief next week.   In
the meantime, the possibility of my ever winning Amy
Wilton is drifting further and further away from me—and
the worst of it is, that that fellow Fortescue, who is always
dangling after Amy, will keep on succeeding in everything
he does!   If he sits in his chambers, solicitors come to

him with fat briefs under their arms—if he were to write a
play Irving would act it to-morrow —if he were to speculate,
it is a dead certainty that his shares would immediately go
up to 100 per cent. Well—it's no good getting excited
about it—I suppose some people are luckier than others,
that is all. But it certainly is an undoubted fact, that
whenever a good thing turns up, Fortescue is always on
the spot, ready to catch it and put it in his pocket ! [*Turns
over papers.*] Six 'St. James's Gazettes' in a heap ! I've
escaped reading those, at any rate. I'll just look at last
night's, though, and see if a fresh mare's nest has been
discovered by anybody. [*Looks at paper.*] By Jove !
[*Reads aloud.*] 'An extraordinary excitement was created
in the City yesterday by a rapid and unexpected rise in
Kimberley diamond shares, brought about, it seems, by a
small band of enterprising speculators. The fortunate
individuals who were in possession of private sources of
information, and had bought a few days ago, at the right
moment, succeeded, it is said, in realising a fortune.' By
George, what a piece of luck ! That is the kind of thing
that never happens to me. [*Throws down paper.*] Why,
here's a letter from old Smithson—he's a lucky fellow on
the Stock Exchange, if ever there was one ! I've no doubt
he made something out of this Kimberley business. [*Opens
letter.*] 'Dear Dick, I can put you up to a good thing if
you like. We want three more men to join, and I thought
perhaps you would like to be one of them, as it will probably mean making some thousands apiece out of Kimberley.
Please answer by return of post, as if you don't feel inclined to risk it we must have some one else. Yours ever,
HENRY SMITHSON.' Out of Kimberley ! Why, when was
this letter written ? oh, miserable man that I am, it is
dated Wednesday, 9th, and this is Tuesday, 15th—it was
written nearly a week ago ! I wonder if there is anything else from him ? [*Turns over letters hurriedly.*] Yes

T

—here is another. [*Tears it open.*] 'Did you receive my
letter about Kimberley? let me hear at once!' and all
this time I was sitting in a punt at Twickenham, trying
to think of some way to make money! Here's another
letter from him, by hand, marked 'Immediate.' 'Send
me a telegram when you get this, or it will be too late.'
Too late, indeed! Oh, why did I ever go away? A
telegram—perhaps this is from him too.   [*Opens telegram.*

'Stanhope, 6 Paper Buildings, Temple.

'If I do not hear from you by 6 P.M. to-day (Friday),
must ask some one else.   SMITHSON.'

Friday—five days ago! I wish that punt had been
at the bottom of the river! Another telegram—I hardly
dare open it!   [*Opens it.*

'Stanhope, 6 Paper Buildings, Temple.

'Not hearing from you, have made offer to Fortescue,
who accepts.   SMITHSON.'

(Wildly) Fortescue! of course, it couldn't be anyone
else! what, he offered the shares, *my* shares, to Fortescue,
and the shameless fellow dared to accept them, and to
make the fortune that ought to have been mine! and
now Amy is lost to me for ever! . . . . . to think that at a
moment like this I was loafing about on the banks of the
Thames, listening for a foolish cuckoo, of which I might
have heard a dozen more distinctly at any clock-maker's in
Regent Street! oh, why did I ever listen to Brown, when
he advised me to go away and leave no address? Never
will I do it again. Never will I leave home for an instant,
except on Sundays when there is no delivery—I will be
on the doorstep when the postman comes, take the letters
from his hand, and answer them before I go upstairs!
But what is the good of saying so now—now, when it is
too late? when I have lost the only chance Fortune ever

threw in my way—when my correspondence is useless, and my life is a blank ? [*After a moment tries to recover himself.*] Well, I had better open these other letters, I suppose—perhaps I shall find I might have made another fortune the day before yesterday ! here is one from my little cousin, Ethel Broadstairs—she and Amy are tremendous friends. [*Opens it.*] Hallo !

'Dear Dick, I want to tell you something that I know will interest you—but you must promise and swear not to tell anyone else, because I've promised and sworn I won't tell you ! Mr. Fortescue proposed to Amy Wilton on Saturday night at Mrs. Gordon's ball '——Proposed ! I knew it ! [*Turns over page*] ——'and what do you think ? she refused him !' Refused him ! in spite of all the diamond rivers of Kimberley ! joy and victory ! well done, Amy ! and what a good little soul Ethel is, to write and tell me at once ! Come, I feel encouraged to open the others, though I can't expect to find anything much better than that ! [*Looking at an envelope.*] Commercial Union—I wonder what that is about ?   [*Opens letter.*

'Dear Sir, you told me the other day you wished to find some employment. Our secretary is obliged to leave us on account of his health, so I write to offer his post to you. If you think it will suit you, please let me hear from you without fail before three o'clock to-morrow (Tuesday).' Tuesday—that is to-day ! [*Looks at watch*] and it is only just two o'clock ! extraordinary though it may seem, for once I am still in time ! my luck has turned at last ! I will take a hansom and drive to the Commercial Union this very instant—the road to fortune, the road to Amy, lies open before me —perhaps, after all, Fate means to atone for my letters not having been forwarded !

[*Snatches up hat, and exit hurriedly.*

THE CROSSING SWEEPER

A MONOLOGUE.

Crossing Sweeper. Well, I dare say you think it very amusing, standing and sweeping this 'ere crossing all day, and no one to say ' Thank you ' for it. I don't think it is myself, and I wouldn't do it if it weren't for a reason I've got, that I'll tell you about in a minute. I haven't learnt any other trade 'cos I never had no father nor mother, as far as I can make out, to teach me one. I sometimes wonder what it must be like to have a mother. I don't know that I should care about it much—one is more free and independent-like without one. Mothers drags little boys by the hand when they're crossing the road, and says to them, ' There now, you've stepped into all that mud !' then they're so busy scolding 'em they never think of giving me a penny. I don't quite see how people can get about London if they're afraid of mud—it's a thing I never minded myself, and many a time I've been thankful I hadn't on fine boots like some of the gentlemen as crosses here, and is in a state if they dirties 'em. It doesn't matter to me if I splashes my legs, nor yet my trousers— they're all the same colour to begin with, and no one's any the wiser. I was washed once, though, and that was in the hospital for a week at a time, and I didn't like it at all, I can tell you. What's the good of wetting you all over and making you all greasy with soap and rubbing at you with towels, just to get off the dirt that's there again next day ?

there's no sense in it. Well, that time I was in the hospital was what I was going to tell you about, when I saw that beautiful lady I want to see again. It wasn't a bad time, barring the washing : there was plenty to eat, and I was as warm as warm the whole day long ; but I was precious glad to get out of it again into the streets and the mud, I can tell you. One week of keeping still is enough for me. I had got knocked down by a carriage when I was running across Oxford Street one day, to ask an old lady for a penny : that's why I was taken to the hospital. Well, so the day before I was coming out, a beautiful lady comed in and talks to all the people round about—so I looked at her and wondered if she was going to speak to me. She did, she looks at me and says, 'And how are you, my little man ?' 'I'm all right, thank you, lady,' says I, 'and I'm going out to-morrow.' 'Going out, are you ?' she says. 'Well, mind you're an honest boy when you go out.' She was a beautiful lady, and no mistake. She had pink cheeks, just like a doll that the little girl had in the next bed to me, and bright shining eyes, and a dress all sticking out and flopping about everywhere, the kind of dress that fine ladies holds up very high, like this, when they're crossing the street. Well, I came out of the hospital next day, and I met Jim Bates, and he wanted me to go with him and pick up a living, as he calls it, in the streets—the sort of living he picks up is purses, and handkerchieves and such like, if people dropped them, or even if they didn't drop 'em, and sell them to a Jew. But I thought I wouldn't do that, as I wanted to tell the lady when I met her again that I had been an honest boy, the same as she said. So I begged in the streets till I'd got money enough to buy an old broom, and then I come here and swep' this crossing, 'cause it's near the hospital, and I thought the lady was sure to come this way again some time. But I've swep' and swep' 'ere ever since—that's close upon a year now—and

I've never seen her once. I've many a time thought I saw her, and once a lady came along over there, with a dress all sticking out and a long cloak all covered with spots, and lines and marks, and I thought it was her, and I made all ready and had a beautiful clean crossing for her to walk over, and then when she came up it was somebody else! it was quite a fat old lady with a red face, and I was so angry I spluttered the mud all over her with my broom, and serve her right too. And so yesterday night I thought to myself, 'I'm about tired of this! if she don't come soon I shall just throw away my broom and go after Jim Bates, for I've had enough of this 'ere.' I'll go away to-day, this very day, I declare. I'll just wait till six people more have passed, and if she don't come then, why, I can't help it, that's all. I won't wait here for her any longer. There's somebody over there. That's No. 1, that's the old gentleman who comes down here every day. He don't give me anything, he just turns up his trousers and wears old boots, and doesn't care twopence about the mud! I won't sweep for him. There's a maid and two children, that counts for three. I see that maid often, and she never gives me nothing—so I'll just spite her and put a little pile of mud ready for the little uns to walk into. That's right, he's dabbed 'is foot right into the middle of it. It's no use your shaking and scolding him like that! serve you right, p'raps that'll make you take some notice of the crossing sweeper. There's a lady coming right away over there, who's that? No, it's only a district visitor, I know her! she's been across a good many roads to-day by the look of her—oh, thank you, lady! well, it isn't always the richest as give most! that's 5—no, that's 6. Ah—what, there's some one, yes, away over there . . . why, I believe, yes, I do believe it's a cloak, just like hers was! Yes, and it's a face like hers too, and bright eyes and pink cheeks—yes, yes, it's her after all! well, this is luck, I was right to wait this time anyhow!

and it's a good job I didn't go off with Jim Bates, else I couldn't have told her as I'd kept straight. Here she is now, quick ! I've made a nice clean place for her to walk. 'Please, lady, it's me, lady, as you saw——' Why, she's gone on ! She don't know me again. [*Stands staring a minute and then throws his broom down and runs after her.*] 'Please, lady——' What's that ? '*You go away, I never give to beggars in the streets.*' 'I ain't a beggar ! you can see that by my broom. What do you say—"Go away, or I'll call the police"?' [*Stands looking after her, then dashes his broom down.*] Well, if that's how it is, I'll just go off to Jim and make a living with him. That wasn't worth keeping honest for, that yonder !

THE VICEROY'S WEDDING

A MONOLOGUE.

OF course I wanted to go to the Viceroy's wedding ! I'm not ashamed of it—everybody did. Everyone always does want to go to everyone's wedding, especially if they're not asked. And besides, I was particularly interested in this wedding. I saw so much of the Viceroy when I was in India, staying with my sister who is in the 91st.

He was very nice to me, most particularly nice—I was quite looking forward to seeing him again over here. But people who are nice to you in India are not always the same in England : it's something in the climate, I suppose.

I must confess I was surprised when I heard he was going to marry Mrs. Stanhope, such a dull little person ! especially as in India he used to seem to like more attractive women. Ah ! I little thought of his ever being married without my being there to see ! especially as, when I heard the wedding was to be in Westminster Abbey, I gave him a hint—I wrote and asked him for an invitation. But no, nothing came, either for the Abbey or for the garden-party afterwards at the Duchess of Portlake's, from whose house the bride was to be married. And the dreadful thing was, that I had told all the neighbours that I should be at both ! It is really too inconsiderate of people not to ask one to a party that everybody expects one to go to. Then, as the day drew near they all began asking me what I was going to wear—if I was going to have a new dress, and so on. 'No,' I said, 'that is not the way I like spending my money.' Then they all admired my self-control. So did I! I don't know how I managed to hide the sufferings I underwent as the days went on. Yesterday was the last of them—I went to bed quite determined that this morning I should say that I was too ill to go after all—but Mrs. Robinson must needs send round to know by what train I was leaving, as she longed to see me dressed. Horrid woman! I believe she suspected the truth. But I was a match for her—I sent word back that I was leaving by the eleven o'clock train. I got up, dressed, and went off to the station.

The neighbours were all as excited as if I had been going to be married myself. The booking clerk, even, knew all about it. 'Westminster Bridge, I suppose?' he said, with an admiring smile. 'Yes,' I said firmly, 'Westminster Bridge.'

'Ah! you are a lucky woman,' said the Vicar, who had come to see some one off. 'It isn't often I want to go to a wedding, but I must say, I should like to see this one.'

'Well, you see, he's an old friend of mine,' I said, airily, getting into the carriage. 'Of course when people are old friends——'

'Oh, yes,' he said, 'when people are old friends——'

Fortunately at this moment the train moved on. The people in the carriage had all heard what the officious creature said.

'All this in your honour!' said one of them jocosely, as we got to Westminster Bridge and saw the flags.

'Yes, in my honour,' I said with a sickly smile, and I got out, meaning to go to Marshall and Snelgrove's and buy remnants for the rest of the morning. I felt there was a chance of my being a remnant myself by the time I got there. I never was so jostled and pushed in all my life. Rude people go to weddings—very rude, indeed. Just as I was getting to the foot of the stairs, I heard my name uttered in a piercing shriek.

'Lucy! Lucy!' I looked round. It was Aunt Eliza! My heart died within me. Now she would go with me to Marshall and Snelgrove's, choose the things I bought, and buy the things I had chosen. That's what happens when you shop with your relations.

'Hah, Aunt Eliza!' I said, with a ghastly attempt at a rapturous smile. 'Where are *you* going?'

'I was going to the Abbey,' she said, clinging to my arm convulsively.

'To the Abbey!' I shrieked. 'You're not going to the wedding?'

'I was going to the wedding, but the most terrible thing has happened.'

'Is the wedding put off?' I cried.

'Put off? No!' my aunt said impatiently, 'but I've lost Mrs. Ronner.'

'Mrs. Ronner! But still, you need not go into mourning for her—it is not as if she were a relation.'

'It isn't as if she were dead either!' said my aunt exasperated. If there's one thing that makes people more angry than not understanding what somebody else says, it is not being understood themselves.

'I mean I lost her in the crowd when I got into the train—and what to do I don't know, for I've got her ticket.'

'Her ticket!' I cried. 'Then you've got a spare one if you don't find her?'

'But I must find her!' my aunt shrieked. 'They're her own tickets. She got them, from being a cousin of Miss Anderson, who taught Mrs. Stanhope's sister-in-law's children when they lived at Prince's Gate, so I must find her. Besides, I can't possibly fight my way into the Abbey all by myself.'

'No, no, you shall not do that,' I said. '*I*'ll go with you, sooner than you should go alone.'

'But, my dear, I *must* find her,' said my aunt, not at all grateful for the suggestion. 'She must go to the wedding! It isn't as if she weren't a cousin of Miss Anderson, who taught Mrs. Stanhope's sister-in-law's——'

'Yes. yes,' I said, edging determinately towards the way out. 'She is a tall, dark woman?'

'Yes,' my aunt said, 'and dressed in——'

'A light brown silk,' I cried, 'and a black cape, and bonnet with white lace strings?' for I knew just the kind of clothes Aunt Eliza's friends wear at weddings. 'Then she's gone up that staircase.'

'Oh, you dear Lucy, you always see everything!' So with Aunt Eliza clinging to my arm we hustled up the staircase with the crowd.

'Where is she?' panted my aunt as we got up to the top of the stairs and looked round.

'There's a black cape,' I shouted, pointing in the direction of the Abbey—'not a minute to be lost!'

So Aunt Eliza, who on ordinary occasions is terrified if she is in the same street with a horse, darted after me between cabs and omnibuses, behind carts, on people's feet, and under them—still in hot pursuit of the invisible Mrs. Ronner, a fat ghost in brown silk beckoning us on. Through the crowd, along the cloisters——

'She went round that corner!' I cried, completely carried away by the excitement of the moment. Round the corner after her—on to the door of the Abbey! My heart stood still—but the rest of me didn't. To stop was impossible, with the rest of the guests surging behind.

'Each 'old yer own ticket, please,' said the distracted policeman.

My aunt pressed Mrs. Ronner's ticket into my hand. I took it silently. Mrs. Ronner's ticket? No, *my* ticket! We were inside the Abbey—I was saved!

'Oh dear, where is she now?' said Aunt Eliza gasping.

'South transept,' said I, looking at my ticket. 'Come to the south transept, and look for her there.'

'She *can't* be there,' said my aunt with one last gleam of bewildered lucidity. 'How can she have got in?'

'Come along, come along,' I said, dragging her after me. Oh dear! what a weight she was, and how I wished I were alone! There ought to be a place to leave one's aunt in when one goes to Westminster Abbey. However, we got to the south transept at last. Crowds of people there already — hot and satisfied people on the front seats — hot and angry ones at the back.

'Dear me! we shall never see Mrs. Ronner here!' sighed my aunt, as she looked round her.

'I'm afraid we never shall,' I said with great truth.

'Why, there's Mrs. Welby,' said my aunt, 'and her brother Captain Clarke, and his niece Booboo Smith! . . How delightful! We'll go and sit with them. Mrs. Welby was Mrs. Ronner's second cousin, you know—*her* mother was a Jones . . .' And she began vigorously pushing her way through the crowd towards them. The seat she was making for, exclusive of its being occupied by Mrs. Welby, Captain Clarke and Miss Smith, had no particular advantage. It was about the worst place for seeing in the Abbey. No, it was not for that I had left Wandsworth at eleven!

'There now, this is cosy,' Aunt Eliza said as we squeezed in, 'isn't it, Lucy?'

'Very!' I said. It had not occurred to me till that moment that cosiness was our object.

'I'm afraid we shan't see much from here though, shall we?' I said, and I stood on tiptoe and craned my neck. So Aunt Eliza, Mrs. Welby, Captain Clarke and Miss Smith all stood on tiptoe and craned their necks too, such as they were—and we all had a distinct view of the same thing ; that is, of the backs of some enormous people in the row in front of us. Tall people go to weddings—very tall people indeed—and I don't know how it is that the people in front of one especially, always seem to average nine feet high on these occasions. I then saw one empty chair in front.

I said to Aunt Eliza, 'I will find another seat, so that you may be less crowded here—but you stay with Mrs. Welby. It does not signify where I go, so long as you are comfortable.'

'No, no, dear,' said Aunt Eliza. 'I could not think of letting you go alone. You don't mind going, do you, Mrs. Welby ? '

'Of course not,' said Mrs. Welby, 'nor will Captain Clarke and Booboo.' And so after some delay in finding Mrs. Welby's umbrella, a most valuable adjunct at a wedding, we all five fought our way to the empty chair, on which there were already two people when we got there. I was in despair.

'Never mind the chair, I will stand,' I said to Aunt Eliza, taking up my position bravely in the gangway in front of the first row of people.

'The only thing is,' whispered my aunt, ' I'm not sure of Mrs. Welby being able to stand, she suffers so terribly from rheumatism. Do you think you can stand, Mrs. Welby ? '

'*I* can,' said Mrs. Welby, 'but I'm not sure about Captain Clarke. He has the gout so badly, you know.'

'Then, my dear,' said Aunt Eliza to me, 'we'll just go back to the seats we had before.'

'All right,' said Mrs. Welby. 'Captain Clarke, will you tell Booboo that we are going back to where we were before ? ' And they all waited in a fat row for me to lead the way.

Then I played my trump card. ' Very well,' I said,

' and I'll just go back to the door for a last look and see if Mrs. Ronner is there.'

' Oh, you good Lucy ! ' said Aunt Eliza.

I fled, without waiting for more. I looked furtively round when I got to the other side, to be sure they were not following. No, they had settled in some seats several rows farther back than they were before, and behind a large pillar. They *must* have felt cosy this time ! I saw that pursuit was impossible—went round the other way—got back again to the front. I found an old man standing on a chair—I cheerfully offered to share it with him. Then, when the crowd pushed us, later on, and he fell off, I had it to myself, and so I had a most excellent view of everything. I saw the top of the bride's head as she stood in front of the rails. I saw the back of the best man perfectly, and I almost think I heard a murmur of voices as the ceremony was taking place. So altogether nothing could have been more impressive. Then when it was all over, I picked up the favour the old man had dropped, I pinned it in the front of my gown, and went to the Duchess of Portlake's party. I ate strawberries and cream all the afternoon, and I gave my name clearly to the reporter at the door—so that now everybody in London knows as well as you do [*To the audience*] that I was at the Viceroy's wedding.

JACK AND THE BEANSTALK

A PLAY IN THREE ACTS.

CHARACTERS.

MRS. BROWN.   JACK (her son).   COUNTRYMAN.   OGRE.
GRUMPS (his wife).

ACT I.

Mrs. Brown (spinning). Seven o'clock—It's time for supper! but there's nothing to eat in the house—what I shall say to Jack when he comes in I don't know. And I know the first thing he'll say will be, ' Well, mother! what is there for supper?' Ah, there he is outside. [*Jack heard whistling and singing*]. He is a nice boy certainly, and a very good boy too sometimes, but he is a very noisy one.

Enter Jack.

Jack. Mother, what is there for supper?

Mrs. Brown. There, I knew it! Don't shout, Jack, I'm not deaf.

Jack. All right, I won't. (Whispering) Mother, what is there for supper?

Mrs. Brown. I never saw such a boy! He thinks of nothing but his meals!

Jack. Of course I do, at meal times. That's right and proper! (*sings*)

Yes, yes, my appetite
Is always good for meals at night—

You mustn't starve me quite,
You'll see me grow quite thin and white.

Mrs. Brown.   Well, well, I can't help that,
I'd rather see you pink and fat—
I don't know what to be at,
I feel inclined to stew the cat.

Jack.   Now then, let's lay the cloth.

Mrs. Brown.   You may lay the cloth on the table if you like, but there's nothing else to put on it.

Jack.   Nothing for supper !

Mrs. Brown.   Not one crumb.

Jack.   Let's buy something then.

Mrs. Brown.   We haven't any money to buy anything with.

Jack.   Let's sell something.

Mrs. Brown.   We've got nothing to sell.

Jack (making a dart at the cat).   Let's sell the cat !

Mrs. Brown.   Sell the cat !   What would you get by that ?

Jack.   We should get scratches, spits, and mews, I should think.   Ha, ha !

Mrs. Brown.   Ah !   It's nothing to laugh at ! there is only one thing we can sell, and that is the cow.

Jack.   What, mother, sell our pretty Brindle ?

Mrs. Brown.   Alas, yes !   We must part with her, there is nothing else to be done.

Jack.   How much will you get for her?

Mrs. Brown.   Well, neighbour Hodge would give me fifteen pounds for her.

Jack.   Fifteen pounds !   Dear me, how many breakfasts, dinners, and suppers I could have for that.

Mrs. Brown (going out).   Oh that I should have such a greedy, greedy boy as this !   Now take care of the house, and don't you get into mischief for once.

Jack.   All right, mother, I'll take care of it.

> [*Exit Mrs. Brown.*

Jack.   There ! Now I'm the master of the house ! Now, what shall I do next ? If I could find the cat I would tie.him up in the pudding bag. Perhaps I had better learn my spelling for to-morrow.

> [*He takes book and plays at football with it.*

Enter Countryman.

Countryman.   Good evening, young man.

Jack.   Good evening, old man.

Countryman.   You're not very polite.

Jack.   I'm not generally considered so.

Countryman.   Where's the master of the house ?

Jack.   Here.   I'm the master of the house.

Countryman.   What, do you live alone here ?

Jack.   Yes, except my mother—she lives with me, but that doesn't count.

Countryman.   Where is your mother gone to ?

Jack.   She has gone to see neighbour Hodge about selling the cow.

Countryman.   Selling the cow ?

Jack.   Yes.   We're very poor.   We haven't got anything to eat in the house.

Countryman.   Nothing to eat ! that's bad.   How much will she sell it for ?

Jack.   Oh, I don't know.   As much as she can get.

Countryman.   Pity she didn't sell her to me, I want a cow myself.

Jack.   Do you ?   Look here, what fun it would be to sell you the cow before mother comes back ! it would be a surprise.

Countryman.   Not a bad idea.   (Aside) I will deceive this innocent child, and buy his cow for nothing.

Jack.   What will you give me for it ?   You must give

U

me a great deal, you know. Let me see, more than fifteen pounds, I should think.

Countryman. I don't know that I can give you that much in ordinary money, but I have something of much more value in my pocket. [*Produces beans.*

Jack. Oh, what lovely things !

Countryman. I should think so ! it is not often you come across anything like that.

Jack. Then how many of those will you give me for the cow ?

Countryman. Well, let me see — you say you want fifteen pounds for the cow, and these are much more valuable. I will give you a dozen.

Jack. A dozen, all right. (Aside) That's a splendid bargain ! I hope I am not taking the poor man in.

Countryman. All right, that's a bargain. Where is the beast ?

Jack. There she is, outside — go out of doors and turn down the path, it is the first cow to the left.

Countryman. Your hand on it.

Jack (sings).   Then there's my hand —
      I understand !

Countryman.   To fortune 'tis the way —
      You ne'er again
      Will have, 'tis plain,
      The chance you've had to-day !

          [*Repeat together and dance.*
      [*Mrs. Brown comes in and sees the others dancing.*
Mrs. Brown. I hope I'm not interrupting you.

Countryman (still dancing). Not in the least m'am, not in the least, thank you — I happened to be calling, m'am, and as you were not in I thought I would dance a little to pass the time until your return.

Mrs. Brown. Thank you, that is very kind of you, but I am sorry to say that I have not the pleasure of your acquaintance.

Countryman. No, m'am, no, m'am, that is quite true, that is why I began to think it was time you should.

Mrs. Brown (aside). He is too polite for my taste—I never trust people who are polite.

Countryman. In the meantime your son has been entertaining me—what a charming, well-bred young gentleman he is!

Mrs. Brown. It is not often he has that said of him.

Countryman. He is just the young gentleman I like.

> [*Holds his hand to Jack—they dance together on tiptoe, Mrs. Brown following angrily after them—Countryman dances out.*

Mrs. Brown. I never saw such doings as this! as if we had nothing better to do! sit down and get your spelling book, and see if you can keep quiet for five minutes.

> [*Jack sits down with his book.*

Jack. C O W—What does C O W spell, mother?

Mrs. Brown. C O W spells Cow.

Jack (smiling to himself). Cow! I thought it did!

Mrs. Brown. Neighbour Hodge says he will buy Brindle—I wonder where she is, I must go out and see her.

Jack. Oh no, you need not, I have just seen her.

Mrs. Brown (looking out of the window). I don't see her anywhere! where can she be?

Jack. Perhaps she is sitting under a cabbage leaf, or she's climbed the cherry tree—oh no, I forgot, she is a grizzly cow and can't climb trees.

Mrs. Brown. Hold your tongue, you naughty boy! go and see where she is.

Jack. I know where she is without going to see—at least I know where she is not, and that's in the garden.

Mrs. Brown. Not in the garden! Where is she then?

Jack. I've sold her.

Mrs. Brown. You've sold her! You naughty, bad boy!

Jack. Not at all, I've saved you the trouble.

Mrs. Brown.   What did you get for her ?

Jack.   Ah, mother, you will be pleased !

Mrs. Brown.   What, have you got more than twenty pounds ?—you are a good boy !

Jack.   Well, not for more than fifteen in money. Look——   [*He puts his hands into his pockets.*

Mrs. Brown.   Be quick !   I'm dying to know what you got.   [*Jack pulls out a handful of beans.*

Mrs. Brown (impatiently).   Come, never mind those stupid things—give me the money !

[*Takes the handful and throws them out of the window.*

Jack.   Stop, stop, mother, that's the money !   You are throwing away the money that I got for the cow.

Mrs. Brown.   What !   Do you mean to say that you sold my cow for a few worthless beans ?   you wretched boy, you have ruined me !   you have ruined your mother !

Jack.   But, mother, Mr. Barleycorn said they were worth a great deal more !   a great, great deal more !

Mrs. Brown.   But he did not speak the truth—you stupid boy

Jack.   I thought grown-up people always spoke the truth.

Mrs. Brown.   Well, you'll know better after this, I hope. You stupid, stupid boy !   Whatever are we to do ?

Jack.   Well, I do think it is a pity my beautiful beans were thrown away. [*Goes to window to look.*] Why, what's that in the garden ?   Look, mother, look !

Mrs. Brown (rushing).   Is it Brindle ?   Brindle come back ?

Jack.   No, no, something far better than that—it is something growing, growing right up to the sky.

Mrs. Brown.   I do believe it's a beanstalk !

Jack.   A beanstalk ?   Yes, it is my beans growing ! Oh, mother, how exciting !   I'll climb up and see where it goes to

Mrs. Brown. No, no, don't go up into the sky in that way without knowing where you are going.

Jack. I must, mother, I must ! Good-bye ! I'll bring you back something beautiful from the clouds—perhaps another cow as good as Brindle.

> [*He climbs on to window sill and sings.*

Song.

Up, upon a beanstalk, high as a balloon,
All among the little clouds, a-sailing round the moon.

Mrs. Brown. Oh, if you are going, mind you come back
soon—
I don't like your climbing things that lead
up to the moon !

Curtain.

ACT II.

SCENE I.—*Interior of the Ogre's castle. A large kitchen.*

Enter Jack, cautiously, looking round.

Jack. Oh ! at last ! What a long beanstalk ! I thought I should never get to the top. And now that I am here, I wonder where I am ! It looked like a castle from outside. Ah ! here is some one coming.|

Enter Grumps, the Ogre's wife.

Grumps. Shsh ! Shoo ! ! Go away ! ! ! [*Waving frying-pan at Jack.*] No boys here.

Jack. But, my good soul——

Grumps. No, I ain't your good soul. Go away, I tell you.

Jack. But why ?

Grumps.   Because this is the Ogre's castle, and he will
be back directly for his dinner.

Jack.   And what will he have for his dinner?

Grumps.   You, if you stay any longer! So I advise you
to disappear.

Jack.   That's all very well, but where am I to go to?

Grumps.   Go back to the place you came from.

Jack.   But I don't know the way.

Grumps.   How did you get here, then?

Jack.   I happened to meet a fairy after I left the beanstalk, and she directed me to your house.

Grumps.   Well, happen to meet another then, and let
her direct you back. If you wait much longer you'll meet
the Ogre, and then you won't need any directions.

                              [*Ogre heard outside.*

Ogre.   Fee, fi, fo, fum!
          I smell the blood of an Englishman.
          Be he alive, or be he dead,
          I'll grind his bones to make my bread.

Jack.   What is that?

Grumps.   The Ogre—the Ogre!

Jack.   Oh! do hide me somewhere—please!

Grumps (opening oven door).   Quick, then! Here you
are. Jump in here!

     [*Jack jumps in. Grumps closes door just as Ogre
       comes in.*

Ogre (sings).   Fee, fi, fo, fum!
          I smell the blood of an Englishman.

What have you got for my dinner to-day, you useless
woman? What is there? come, tell me quick!

Grumps.   A nice little kid, that I caught on the mountain.

Ogre.   I don't believe it! There is something else!
[*Sniffing.*] What is that I smell? It's a boy—I'm sure
it's a boy!   [*Jumps up.*

Grumps.   A boy—nonsense! Where should a boy
come from?   [*Stands in front of oven.*

Ogre. I'm sure there's a boy in that oven—and what is more, I mean to look.　　　　　[*Goes to oven.*

Grumps (in front of the oven). Very well—if you open the oven now, your dinner will be spoiled, that's all —the kid won't be done enough.

Ogre. Hum, ha—well—I won't look in it till after dinner then—but mind the kid is done right, or I'll throw you out of the window. I'm going to change my seven-leagued boots, and when I come back it must be ready.

　　　　　[*Exit, singing ' Fee, fi, fo, fum.'*

Grumps (to Jack). Quick, quick ! now is your time ! [*Jack comes out.*] I don't think it would be safe for you to try to escape now, as he might see you from the window —but he always goes to sleep after his dinner—when you hear him snore go gently out.　　　　　[*Puts him behind a chest.*

Enter Ogre, singing, ' Fee, fi, fo, fum,' &c. Sits down, ties a napkin round his neck.

Ogre. Well, where's that kid ? Isn't it ready ?

Grumps. Coming – coming—here it is ! it's no good my putting it on the table to get cold while you're half a mile off, is it ?

Ogre. Silence, you horrid old woman ! or I'll eat you for my pudding. [*He dines : she waits on him. Song ad lib.*] Now then clear away, old witch—and bring me my fairy hen !

　　　　　[*Grumps goes to where Jack is hiding and gets the hen—he puts his head out, Grumps pushes him down again.*

Ogre. Now then, is that hen coming ? I never saw such a house—the hens are always late !　　　[*Sings.*

Come, make haste—make no delaying !
Do you hear what I am saying ?
If that hen has not been laying
You shall die this very day !

Grumps (bringing hen). Here she is, your call obeying —
Here's the pretty beast dis-
playing
All her talents, ever laying
Fifteen golden eggs a day.

[*Repeat together.*

Ogre. Now then, what are you standing there singing for ? Go and get my money bag ready—and my fairy fiddle—all the things I shall want [*Grumps going, Ogre calls after her*]. And Hi ! [*She turns back.*] If I should happen to go to sleep presently——

Grumps. Happen ! Why, you never do anything else !

Ogre. Hold your tongue, you monster—or I will put you into the oven ! I was going to say,—I wish you to sit on the door mat, in case anyone should disturb me if I should happen to go to sleep.

Grumps. All right. Now you have everything comfortable. Your hen and money bag—and your armchair.

Ogre. I thought I heard something behind that chest ! the dog isn't here, is he ? I won't have him left in the room.

Grumps. No, no. He isn't there.

Ogre. How do you know ? Go and look.

Grumps (takes stick and pokes behind chest where Jack is, Sh—sh !

Ogre (imitating her). Sh ! indeed ! What's the use of that ? Here, give it to me, I'll soon see if the creature is there. [*Runs at one side of chest and bangs stick down, Jack runs out at the other—and the same at the other side.*] There, that's the way to do things ! there doesn't seem to be anything there. You were right for once—so you may go and leave me in peace. [*Exit Grumps singing. Ogre strokes hen.*] Pretty creature ! And you are not only pretty—you are clever—that's better still ! and not only

clever, you are good, which is best of all! for you know
how to lay me fifteen golden eggs every day. Come, where
are they? [*Lifts her up and finds the eggs.*] Ah—that
will do for my pocket money till to-morrow—so now you
may just wait there until this evening. [*Goes to sleep.
Soft music. Jack comes out softly—carries the hen behind
the chest, and as he does so falls over something with a crash.
Ogre wakes, looks round.*] Why, what was that? I'm
sure I heard a noise—it must have been a cinder falling
out of the fire—or I woke myself by snoring—though I
don't believe I do snore, though that old Grumps always
declares I do. How tiresome to be awake, just when I
was so comfortable! However, I'll count my money now
and go to sleep again afterwards.

[*Draws the money bag forwards. Sings.*]

Gold! gold! gold! gold!
Bright and yellow, hard and cold.
Pounds and shillings, pennies too.
All for me, and none for you.

There don't seem to be as many as there were last time.
I believe Grumps has been taking some! I'll hang her
up to the top of the castle presently, if I remember it.
[*Makes a knot in nightcap.*] There, that will remind
me. [*Ties up bag.*] There—there are a great many
starving people in the world who would be glad to
have only a little of what that bag contains—Ha, ha!
they shan't have any of it—I'll keep it all for myself—
every bit! [*Puts money bag behind his chair, where it
rolls down.*] Now I'll see if I can't go to sleep again.
[*Music as before. Ogre snores. Jack comes out, and tries
to draw money bag—it is too heavy—at last he succeeds, but
rolls over with it. Ogre starts up. Jack lies down behind
the bag.*] Why, it's that stupid money bag that has rolled
over—stupid of me not to put it up safely! [*Going to*

sleep—Jack creeps out—Ogre starts up again—Jack goes back.] It's no use—I can't do it ! I'll make Mrs. Grumps come and play me to sleep. Here—Grumps ! Come ! [*Enter Grumps.*] Why don't you come more quickly ? Where are you ?

Grumps.   I was on the door mat, of course.

Ogre.   It's very kind of me to let you sit there—very kind, do you hear ?

Grumps.   I hear—yes.

Ogre.   Then don't presume to answer.   Take my fairy violin and play me to sleep, and mind you don't make any of those squeaks, or I'll wring your neck.

> [*Grumps plays. The Ogre hums the tune she is play-ing, and gradually goes off. She lays down the violin and makes a sign to Jack, he comes out quietly.*

Grumps (whispering).   Follow me quietly, and I will go on and open the doors.

> [*Takes big keys off Ogre's lap and exit.*

Jack (aside).   Yes—but I'll take a few of these things with me ! [*Pushes the money bag out of the window— takes the hen under one arm and the violin under the other.*] Now I'll make a rush past her and get down the beanstalk and take these home to my mother.

> [*Violin heard squeaking and calling 'Master ! master !' louder and louder.*

Enter Grumps.

Grumps.   Where is he ?   Quick, quick, you will have time to get away before he wakes.   Why, where is he ? Alas ! alas ! he is gone—the ungrateful little wretch—and he has taken everything with him.   Oh, what shall I do ?

> [*Violin heard calling.   Ogre wakes.*

Ogre.   What, why are all the noises in Christendom turned loose here to-day ?   What is all this ? [*Wakes quite up, and sees Grumps. She rushes out with a shriek.*] What is all this ? [*Puts his cap straight.*] Ha, what is this knot Ha -- I remember, Grumps !

[*Dashes out singing, ' Fee, fi, fo, fum !'*

Curtain.

ACT III.

Scene.—*Mrs. Brown's house. Mrs. Brown and Jack beautifully dressed.*

Jack. How comfortable we are, mother !

Mrs. Brown. Yes, and what beautiful clothes we have on !

Jack. It seems a great deal more than a week since I sold the cow, doesn't it ?

Mrs. Brown. Yes, indeed it does. I was quite in despair that day, till I saw you coming back again with the fairy hen, the money bag and the violin.

Jack. And ever since we have had everything we can wish for, and we have been able to feed all the poor people in the village besides.

Mrs. Brown. That reminds me—I said I would go out to see neighbour Hodge—but it is too muddy to walk, so I have ordered the carriage.

Jack. Which one ? The open one drawn by six cream-coloured horses ?

Mrs. Brown. No—I think it is too cold for that—I shall go in the shut glass coach, drawn by eight piebalds. I am so accustomed to driving now !

Jack. You see how right I was to climb up to the Ogre's castle and get all these things for you ! But, mother, I do wonder what he has done without them ! Don't you sometimes wonder how it is he has never come to look for them ?

Mrs. Brown. Oh—what a horrible idea ! Suppose he were to come !

Jack. I never thought of that—I almost think it would be safest to cut the beanstalk down, as then there will be no way for him to come.

Mrs. Brown. I think it would—but what a pity it seems—that dear beanstalk, to which we owe so much ! [*Gets up and looks out of window at it. She starts back.*] Jack ! Jack ! It is too late ! See—see—there is some one coming down it from the sky—a gigantic form— it must be the Ogre !

Jack. It is—it is the Ogre ! Where is my hatchet ? Quick !   [*Seizes hatchet and rushes out.*

Mrs. Brown. Stay—stay ! Jack ! Here ! Oh ! [*Then watching from window*]. The Ogre has reached the ground —he has drawn his sword—Jack has attacked him ! The Ogre has struck at him, Jack has jumped aside—he has cut off the Ogre's legs with his axe—the Ogre falls—Jack has cut off his head ! Ah—my brave boy !

Enter Jack with the Ogre's head.

Jack. There, mother—there is the monster's head, he will never trouble us any more—and as for poor Grumps, his companion, I believe he killed her the day I left the castle. So now we can be happy for the rest of our days.

[*They dance round it. As they leave off a knock is heard at the door.*

Mrs. Brown. Oh—who can that be—not another Ogre ?

Jack. No, I don't think that is very likely ! Besides, he'll soon go away when he sees that ! [*Pointing to head.*] Come in !

Enter Countryman, much better dressed.

Jack. Mr. Barleycorn !

Countryman. That is my name certainly, but I think

I must have made a mistake. [*Looking round.*] This is not the house that stood here before, surely ?

Mrs. Brown. Yes, it is only rather differently furnished !

Countryman (sees head and starts). That ornament is new, certainly, since I was here. Then you are the lady who wouldn't dance with me ?

Mrs. Brown. And you are the gentleman who bought my poor Brindle for some beans ?

Countryman. Exactly—I am, and a very good cow she was. I came to know if you could sell me another like her.

Mrs. Brown. Well, I must say I wonder you dare show your face here again after deceiving my innocent boy in the way you did about those beans !

Jack. Come, come, mother, after all you need not complain of the beans, for they have been the cause of all our good luck.

Mrs. Brown. It is quite true. (To Countryman) I forgive you, and I hope you have taken good care of my pretty Brindle.

Countryman. Indeed I have. She has brought me good luck, too—ever since I had her I have been growing richer and richer.

Jack. Then, you see, our bargain was a good one after all ! For if it had not been for you I should never have climbed up the beanstalk.

> Then there's my hand,
> My trusty friend,
> To fortune 'twas the way !
> We ne'er again
> Shall have, 'tis plain,
> The chance we had that day !
>
> [*Repeat together and dance.*

Curtain.

BEAUTY AND THE BEAST

A ROMANTIC DRAMA FOR CHILDREN IN SIX SCENES.

CHARACTERS.

ABOU CASSIM (a rich merchant).
ZULEIKA
AYESHA } (his daughters).
FATIMA
PRINCE FURRYSKIN.
MOLINKO (his servant).

SCENE I.—*Abou Cassim's house. Zu. and Ay. writing at different tables.*

Zul. What are you writing, sister Ayesha?

Ay. I'm making a list of all the things I want father to buy me when he is away. What are you writing, sister Zuleika?

Zul. I'm doing the same thing—but it is so tiresome, I can't remember any of the things I want.

Ay. Can't you? poor thing! I can. I've put down twenty-nine things on my list.

Zul. Twenty-nine? dear me! and I have only seventeen on mine! It is hardly worth while making a list at all!

> [*Abou Cassim heard calling outside*

Ab. C. Zuleika, Ayesha, Fatima!

Zul. and Ay. Yes, father.

Enter Abou Cassim, still calling.

Ab. C.   Zuleika—Ayesha—Fatima! where is every-body? why don't you answer when you are called? why don't you come and help me to pack my things?

Zul.   Oh, father, I am so sorry. I was just coming.

Ab. C.   Just coming—what's the good of that? I'm just going! you'll make me miss my camel! I said he was to be at the door at 3 o'clock, and it is now——[*Looks at the sun.*] I never can remember where the sun ought to be in the afternoon. I wish people used watches in Turkey.

Ay.   Oh, father, some day you must go a long way across the sea, to buy me a real gold watch, like the one you told me about once.

Ab. C.   I dare say! you think that your father has nothing to do but go shopping for you! Where is Fatima, my dear youngest girl? she is the only one that is any use to me when I am starting on my travels. Fatima – Beauty!
[*Goes up, C.*

Zul. (to Ay.)   It makes me sick to hear her called Beauty.

Ay.   So it does me. She's no more a beauty than we are!

Zul.   Not half so much.

Enter Fatima—she throws herself into Abou Cassim's arms.

Fat.   Dear, dear father! I wish you were not going away.

Ab. C.   Yes, my darling, so do I—never mind, I shall soon be back again.

Fat.   I've packed all your things, father, and got every-thing ready.

Ab. C.   There's a good little girl. [*Comes forward.*] Now, am I to bring you anything back this time?

Zul. and Ay.   Oh, yes, father !

Ab. C.   What would you like ?

Zul. and Ay. (unrolling lists).   We've made a list.

Ab. C. (horrified).   Made a list—upon my word, you have ! You don't expect me to bring back all those things, do you ? Why, I should have to buy two extra camels and hree ostriches, to carry the parcels across the desert.

Zul.   Oh, but I assure you, father, they are things we really want.

Ay.   That we couldn't possibly do without.

Zul. (reads).   An embroidered sash——

Ay. (reads).   A pair of golden slippers——

Zul.   A silk veil——

Ay.   A new turban——

Zul.   Some diamond earrings——

Ay.   A new-fashioned skirt——

Zul.   Some spangled muslin ——

Ay.   A tame monkey——

Zul.   A box of sweetmeats——

Ay.   A white ass——

Zul.   A gold necklace——

Ay.   A tall turban——

Ab. C: Stop, stop ! here, give me the lists, and if I can I will bring you each a present.   (To Fat.) And what would you like, my darling ?

Fat.   Oh, father dear, if you only come back safe I want nothing else.

Zul. (aside).   Little humbug !

Ab. C.   What, nothing at all ?

Fat.   Well then, bring me a rose —just one beautiful rose—nothing more.

Ab. C.   A red rose—very well, I will bring it.   Goodbye, then, my children.

[*Fat. dries her eyes—Zul. and Ay. crying loudly.*

Ab. C.   Why, what a fuss about nothing !   Is a man

never to go away from home on business without having all
his womankind boohooing like this?

Zul.　Oh, father, we're so afraid!

Ab. C.　Afraid of what? that I shall be lost in the
desert?

Zul.　No—that you will forget some of our commissions!

Ab. C.　Nonsense! I must be off.

Fat.　Take care of yourself, dear father.

Zul.　Don't mount your camel till he is kneeling.

Ay.　And don't fall off as he gets up again.

Finale.　Tune—'*My Maryland.*'

Fat.　Oh, come back to your daughters soon, dear papa,
　　　　oh dear papa.

Ay.　We don't like being left alone, dear papa, oh, dear
　　　　papa.

Zul.　When you are gone, we cry all day.
　　　　We don't know what to do or say.

Zul., Ay., and Fat.　We wish you would not go away,
　　　　dear papa, oh, dear papa.

Ab. C.　I'm sorry thus to cause you pain, your dear
　　　　papa, your dear papa.
　　　　I'll soon come back to you again, your dear
　　　　papa, your dear papa.
　　　　But I'm a merchant, as you know,
　　　　And that is why I travel so.
　　　　I buy and sell, I come and go, your dear papa,
　　　　your dear papa.

[*Exit Abou Cassim. Zul., Ay., Fat. sitting in a
row—Zul. R.—Fat. C.—Ay. L.*

Fat.　Oh dear, I wish father were not gone.

Zul.　Well, it is no use wishing—what shall we do to
amuse ourselves?

Ay.　Shall we go out?

Zul.　I don't care about going out—shall we stay in?

Fat. I don't care about staying in, unless we do something. Shall we make toffee ?

Ay. I don't care about making toffee. Shall we blow soap bubbles ?

Zul. I don't care about blowing soap bubbles. Shall we paint ?

Fat. I don't care about painting.　　　*[All sit silent.*

Ay. I have an idea.

Zul. and Fat. What ?

Ay. Let us dance !　　　　　　*[All clap hands.*

Zul. Oh yes !

Fat. Do let us dance !　　　　　　*[All dance.*

Curtain.

Scene II.—*Prince Furryskin's garden. Prince alone.*

Pr. Dear me—how tiresome it is to be a beast ! especially for a person who really ought to be a beautiful young prince, dressed in blue and silver, instead of having this horrid hairy skin on. I wish a wicked fairy had not enchanted me at my birth ! it is very inconvenient. And the worst of it is, that I shall never turn into a young prince again until a beautiful girl tells me she loves me—as if it were likely that a beautiful girl would say anything of the kind to me ! Well, well—it can't be helped, I suppose—I must try and amuse myself with my flowers, and see if I can't forget how ugly and hairy I am. [*Walks about.*] My pinks are looking very nice, certainly, and my Canterbury bells—and my dahlias are pretty good—but my roses have been very bad this year. However, I see there is one red rose on my favourite tree—I must tell the gardener not to gather it, I like seeing it grow on the tree best. This is certainly a very nice garden, and if I were not a beast I should enjoy it very much.

[*Gathers a pink. Strolls off, R.*

Enter Abou Cassim, carrying bundles.

Ab. C. Now I really think I have got as many things for those girls as I can well carry—I had to leave the rest in the desert. The only thing I have not yet got is the rose that Beauty asked me for—I came through this beautiful garden in hopes of finding one. Ha—there is exactly what I want.

Enter Prince, R. Ab. C. gathers rose. Pr. rushes at him.

Pr. Wretch! [*Seizes him by the collar. Ab. C. drops rose*] Who are you, who dare to pluck my favourite rose ?

Ab. C. I'm very sorry, I'm sure—I did not know it was your rose.

Pr. But you knew it wasn't yours, I suppose ?

Ab. C. Well, yes—I must confess I did.

Pr. Then if you knew it wasn't yours, you knew that you were stealing—and if you were stealing, you are a thief—and if you are a thief, you must have your head cut off !

Ab. C. Oh, sir —pray don't cut off my head—I couldn't see my way home if you did.

Pr. See your way home ? don't you wish you may get there ? Do you know who I am ?

Ab. C. I really can't say—I think I've seen some one very like you before, but perhaps it was at the Zoo. Are you a bear very like a man, or a man very like a bear ?

Pr. Never you mind which—it is just the same to you, as I'm going to kill you and eat you in about a minute and a half. Taking my rose that I loved so !

Ab. C. Oh, your lordship—your beastship, I mean—it was not for myself I took the rose—I took it for my daughter, my youngest daughter, Beauty, whom I love more dearly than you love your flowers.

Pr. (starts). Your daughter, did you say ? Is she beautiful at all ?

Ab. C. Very, very beautiful—she is considered particularly like her father.

Pr. Oh—indeed—she must be a beauty then! What will you give me if I spare your worthless life?

Ab. C. Anything you like to ask.

Pr. Well— promise to give me the first living thing you meet when you get inside your garden, and I will let you go free.

Ab. C. (kneeling). Oh, most generous beast! how can I thank you?

Pr. By getting up and taking yourself off, and not making marks on my gravel path. I'm very particular about my garden, as you may have observed.

Duet—Finale.

Pr. Now please walk out at my garden gate—
You'll find it is better for you not to wait,
In case I might take such a fancy to you
I might gobble you up in a minute or two,
And then of you there'd be nothing more,
So I think you had better get out of the door.

Ab. C. Very well, I'll walk out of your garden gate—
I think it is better for me not to wait,
In case you might take such a fancy to me
You might gobble me up in a minute or three,
And then of me there'd be nothing more,
So I think I had better get out of the door.

Curtain.

Scene III.—*Outside Abou Cassim's house.*

Ab. C. Not a dog or a cat to be seen! I promised that Beast, or Prince, or whatever he calls himself, to send him the first living thing I met on my way home—and I haven't seen so much as a spider since I got inside the gate!

[*Beauty runs out.*

Fat. Dear, dear father! how glad I am to see you!

Ab. C. Fatima, my child—alas! alas!

Fat. Why, father, are not you glad to see me? And I have been watching for you every day from the top of the house! and you've got my rose, too! thank you so much.

[*Smells it.*

Zul. and Ay. Oh, father! is it you? Have you brought our things?

Ab. C. I got them, yes—but there were so many of them that the camel who carried them died of fatigue in crossing the desert, and the eagles ate the camel and the parcels too—and so I have nothing.

Zul. Oh, father! how could you?

Ay. How couldn't you? [*Both sob.*

Ab. C. Parcels, indeed—as if that were all we have to care about. There's worse than that, I can tell you. I have—I have—— [*Sobs loudly.*

Zul., Ay., Fat. What, father, what?

Ab. C. I have sold my daughter to a beast!

Zul. Your daughter, which?

Ab. C. (covers his face with his hands and points to Fatima). That one!

Zul. and Ay. Thank goodness!

[*Fat. falls into her father's arms.*

Curtain.

SCENE IV.—*Prince Furryskin's dining-room.*

Pr. (calls). Molinko! Molinko! Where is that boy gone? I never knew such a tiresome servant! Molinko!

Mol. (behind.) What's the matter now?

Pr. Come here, directly.

Enter Molinko.

Mol. Well, here I am.

Pr. Didn't you hear me calling you?

Mol.   Of course I did.

Pr.   Then why didn't you come?

Mol.   Because I was waiting till you left off.

Pr.   Have you done all the things I told you?

Mol.   No.

Pr.   Didn't I tell you that I dreamt the merchant would bring his beautiful daughter here to-day? and that you were to get everything ready?

Mol.   Yes.

Pr.   And is it ready?

Mol.   No.

Pr.   Why not?

Mol.   Because it isn't.

Pr.   Now listen—you are to put lovely flowers in her room—silken sheets on her bed—embroidered curtains to her windows—all the most beautiful things you can think of.   Do you hear?

Mol.   Yes.

Pr.   And the dinner must be lovely too—all kinds of nice things to eat—sweetmeats—raisins—jam—fruits—chocolate——

Mol.   Yes.

Pr.   And lay the table for two—I will dine with her.

[*Exit Prince.*

Mol. (alone.)   [*Lays Table.*]   Why, there's nothing but work from morning till night here!

Song.   Tune—'So Early in the Morning.'

> I have to work so hard all day,
> That I have never time to play—
> I'm butler, groom, and housemaid too,
> I've got too much hard work to do.
> From early in the morning,
> From early in the morning,
> From early in the morning,
> Until the break of day.

Enter Fatima—looks round.

Fat. I thought I heard singing—was that you ?

Mol. Yes.

Fat. And who are you ?

Mol. I'm Molinko, the Prince's servant. And who are you ?

Fat. I'm Fatima, Abou Cassim's daughter.

Mol. Then you're the lady who is coming to dinner ?

Fat. I suppose so—is it ready ?

Mol. No, it isn't—nothing's ready.

Fat. Nothing ?

Mol. No, nothing—your bed isn't—nor your room, nor your curtains, nor your silk sheets, nor anything ! so now !

Fat. Well, well—don't be angry—I don't mind.

Mol. That's a good thing.

[*Repeats song—Fat. joins in chorus.*

Mol. I'll go and tell my master you are here.

[*Exit Mol.*

Fat. Alas—how strange to be here, away from all those I love. I wonder what they are doing in my home, my dear old home ?

Song.

Mid pleasures and palaces though we may roam,
Be it ever so humble, there's no place like home.
A charm from the skies seems to hallow us there,
Which seek through the world is ne'er met with
　　　elsewhere ;
　　Home, home, sweet, sweet home ;
Be it ever so humble there's no place like home.

Enter Prince. Fat. starts up.

Pr. Don't be frightened ! I'm not dangerous.

Fat. Are you sure ?

Pr. Quite. Beautiful damsel, are you Abou Cassim's daughter ?

Fat. I am—his youngest daughter.

Pr. His beloved daughter Beauty, of whom he spoke ?

Fat. The same.

Pr. He is right to call you Beauty—you are very beautiful.

Fat. I'm glad you think so.

Pr. But alas—I will not ask you if you think me beautiful.

Fat. No, I wouldn't, if I were you.

Pr. Am I too ugly for you to dine with me ?

Fat. Not if you have nice things for dinner.

Pr. You shall have the best of everything I can give you. Here Molinko !

Mol. (behind). Yes !

Pr. Be quick, lazy bones !

Enter Mol.

Mol. I'm being as quick as I can, long claws !

Pr. (to Fat). What may I give you—some Turkish delight ?

Fat. Please.

Pr. Oh, how Turkish delightful it is to see you eat it ! Have some lemonade ?

Fat. Please.　　　　　　　　[*They drink. Prince sings.*

Song.

Drink to me only with thine eyes,
　And I will pledge with mine—
Or leave a kiss within the cup,
　And I'll not ask for wine.
The thirst that from the soul doth spring,
　Doth ask a drink divine—
But might I of Jove's nectar sip,
　I would not change with thine.

Pr.   Beauty, you like me better now, don't you ?

Fat.   Oh, yes, much !

Pr.   Do you think you could say you loved me?

Fat.   Oh no—certainly not.   Now I should like to go back to my father again, please.

Pr.   What, and leave me ?

Fat.   Yes, please.

Pr.   Then I shall die of grief.

Fat.   Oh, no, you won't.

Pr.   You shall do as you like, Fatima, you shall not think me unkind as well as ugly—but first would you like to take a turn round the garden, and see if I can find another rose for you ?

Fat.   Yes, please.   [*Exeunt.*

Curtain.

Scene V.—*Same as Scene I.   Abou Cassim's drawing-room.   Zul. R.—Fat., Ay., Ab. C. L.   Smoking and reading.*

Zul.   Well, Beauty—well ? tell us all about it.

Ay.   What is the beast like ?

Fat.   He was very nice and kind.

Zul.   But what was he like to look at, I mean ?

Fat.   He is all over hair—and he has great furry ears, and I dare say he has claws too, but I didn't see them.

Ay.   And what did you have for dinner ?

Fat.   Oh, all kinds of nice things.

Zul.   I do wish we had been there ! why didn't you stay, you silly girl ?

Fat.   Because I wanted to come back and see you all again.

Ab. C.   Good girl, Beauty, very good girl, she likes her home best—that's what all good girls do.

Ay. And didn't he give you any presents ?

Ab. C. You think of nothing but presents.

Fat. Yes, he gave me this looking-glass.

Zul. Oh, delightful ! let me see.

Ay. And me !

> [*They take the glass and look at themselves in it —
> then turn away disappointed.*

Ay. Why, we can't see ourselves in it !

Fat. No — it's a fairy looking-glass.

Zul. What's the good of that ?

Fat. Nobody can see anything in it but me.

Ay. What a shame !

Fat. And I can't see anything in it but the Beast.

Zul. and Ay. Oh, how horrid !

Fat. By looking in this glass I can always see if he is well, when I am away from him. [*Starts.*] Oh, look — he is ill — he is dying — he is lying on the ground in the garden — I must go to him — quick — quick !   [*Runs out.*

Zul. Father, I should like to go too.

Ab. C. Go too ? nonsense, you're not wanted — mustn't go to places without being asked !

Ay. Oh, do let us go — it would be such fun.

Zul. Besides, perhaps the Beast is dead by this time, and then he won't mind.

Ab. C. Well, well, we'll see when I've finished my pipe — you must leave me in peace till then.

Ay. Come along, then, Zuleika, we'll go and put on our things.

Zul. Oh, what fun it will be !   [*Exeunt Zul. and Ay.*

Curtain.

SCENE VI.—*The Prince's garden.*

Fat. Where are you, my dear Beast? [*Starts.*] Oh, there you are! [*Kneels by him.*] Alas! I fear you are dead—I have killed you. Beast—wake up—I am here—it is Beauty come back to you! Dear Beast, I wish you would get up—I like you so much now—I'm very sorry I didn't say I loved you—I do really—I love you very much! [*The Beast springs up—his fur falls off.*

Pr. Beauty, my love! you have turned me into a prince again!

Fat. What! are you the same who was a beast?

Pr. Of course I am—and now I am never going to be a beast any more, but a beautiful young prince.

Fat. Oh, how nice!

Pr. And if you will marry me, you shall be a beautiful young princess!

Fat. That's nicer still! Of course I will, then!

Duet. Air—'Là ci darem.'

Pr.   Then I will be your husband,
      And you shall be my wife;
      We will love each other, and lead a happy life.

Enter Zul. and Ay., followed by Ab. C.

Zul. Why, what's all this about?

Ay. Who is this young man?

Pr. I'm Prince Furryskin, at your service.

Fat. And I'm going to be the Princess Furryskin.

Zul. (to Fat). Then why did you say he was a beast?

Ay. What horrid stories you told us!

Fat. I didn't tell stories—he was a beast—wasn't he, papa?

Ab. C. He certainly was the last time I saw him—a regular beast, I'll answer for that.

Pr.   Dear ladies, don't be angry—I will tell you how it was—a wicked fairy turned me into a beast, and said I shouldn't turn back into a prince again till a beautiful girl said she loved me.

Fat.   And so when I said I loved him, he jumped up and turned into a prince.

Pr.   And now you have all come, I hope you will stay to dinner.   (*Calls*) Here, Molinko ! where's the lazy beggar now ? here Molinko !

Enter Molinko.

Mol.   Yes !

Pr.   Is dinner ready ?

Mol.   No !

Pr.   We shall be six to dinner—can you manage that ?

Mol.   No.

Fat.   Oh, yes you can, dear Molinko—and we'll help you to get it ready—may we ?

Mol.   Yes.

Pr.   And then we'll be married.

Fat.   And I shall be a princess.

Zul. and Ay.   And we will be the bridesmaids.

Ab. C.   And I will be the father-in-law.

Mol.   And I'll eat the wedding cake.

Finale.   Tune—' The Young Recruit.'

And we'll be a merry party
  On this happy wedding day (*bis*) :
We will all be gay and hearty
  As we dance and sing and play.
      Tra la la la la, &c.

Curtain.

THE SURPRISE *

CHARACTERS.

DINAH.   PATIENCE.   EDITH.   JACK.
PEGGY.   DICK.   HAROLD.   LUCY.

Enter Dinah, on tiptoe.

Din. Nobody knows what I know.

Enter Harold.

Din. Hush, Harold, hush !
Har. What is it ?
Din. It's a surprise.
Har. A surprise ?
Din. Yes, we're going to be surprised.
Har. How do you know ?
Din. Because I saw the cage.
Har. The cage ! what cage ?
Din. The cage the hens are in.
Har. The hens ! which hens ?
Din. The hens mammy is going to give us.
Har. Is she going to give us some hens ?
Din. Yes ! and a cock !
Har. (clapping his hands). Oh !
Din. But mind you mustn't say a word about it—it's a great secret——
Har. Take care ! there's Lucy coming.

* The characters in this play can be acted either by girls or boys, the names being changed.

Enter Lucy.

Din. and Har.　Sh—sh !　Sh—sh !

Lucy.　What is it ?　Why are you saying 'Sh !' like that ?

Din.　We've got a secret.

Lucy.　A secret ! what sort of secret ?

Har.　A secret in a cage.

Din.　You naughty boy ! hold your tongue !

Lucy.　In a cage !　It's a bird, then !

Har.　Take care ! here's Edith !

Enter Edith.

Din., Har. and Lucy.　Sh—sh !!　sh—sh !!

Edith.　What is it !　what's the matter ?

Din.　We've got a secret.

Har.　You naughty girl ! hold your tongue !

Lucy.　They won't tell me what it is.　It must be a bird, because it's in a cage.

Edith.　In a cage !　It might be a wild beast.

Din. and Har.　A wild beast ! ha, ha !

Edith.　Well, how should I know what it is, if you don't tell me ?

Lucy.　Let's try to guess.

Har. (to Din.)　After all, if they guess right it won't be our fault.

Din.　No, that's true.

Edith.　Is it a bird !

Har.　Of course it's a bird, you stupid !

Edith.　I'm not stupid—it might have been a squirrel. Squirrels are in cages sometimes.

Har.　Of course, it *might* have been a crocodile, but it isn't.

Lucy.　Is it a canary ?

Har.　Bigger.

Edith.   A thrush ?

Din.   Bigger.

Har.   Take care ! there's Peggy.

Enter Peggy.

All.   Sh—sh ! sh —sh !

Peggy.   What is it ? what's the matter ?

Lucy.   We're guessing a secret.

Har.   Trying to guess it, you mean.

Edith.   It's something in a cage.

Peggy.   Oh, I'll guess too ! Is it a pigeon ?

Din.   Bigger.

Peggy.   What does it do ?

Din.   It surprises us.

Peggy.   I mean what noise does it make ?

Har.   It makes us say Sh—sh !

Edith.   Take care ! there's Dick coming !

Enter Dick.

All.   Sh—sh ! sh—sh !

Dick.   What is it ? what are you doing that for ?

Lucy.   We've got a secret.

Din.   A secret that we won't tell you.

Dick.   Then you're very rude indeed. I don't like rude people.

Ed.   Try and help us to guess it.

Dick.   What sort of a thing is it ? The last time we had a secret it was some knitted slippers for Pappy. Is this secret a pair of slippers, or a woollen comforter ?

Har.   Oh, you *are* a stupid child !

Din.   How could a pair of slippers get into a cage ?

Dick.   Quite easily, if anyone put them there.

Lucy.   Well, it isn't a pair of slippers.

Din.   Take care ! take care ! there's Jack !

Jack comes in mysteriously.

All. Sh—sh ! sh—sh !

Jack. What are you making that noise for ? Why are you all behaving like steam-engines in a station ?

Din. We've got a secret.

Jack. Have you ? So have I.

All. Have you ? What is it about ?

Jack. Ha ! I won't tell you.

Din. Then we won't tell you ours.

Jack. Is yours a nice secret ?

Har. Lovely !

Din. It's a surprise mammy's got for us.

Jack. It must be a good big secret if it takes so many of you to keep it.

Lucy. Do tell us yours, Jack !

Edith. There's a good boy !

Jack. Then you must tell me yours afterwards.

Din. Very well, we will.

Jack. All right, then, come here and I'll tell you.

[*Beckons them all round him mysteriously.*

Jack. You must know that as I went along the back passage I saw a curious-looking parcel.

All. A parcel !

Jack. So I bent down to look. I listened——

All. Listened !

Jack. And peeped.

All. Peeped !

Jack. There was a great flapping and pecking going on inside !

All. Flapping and pecking !

Jack. And then what do you think I heard ?

All. What ?

Jack. Cock-a-doodle-doo !

Peggy. A cock ?

Jack. Yes ! a cock and some hens.

Din. The cock and hens mammy is going to give us !

Dick. Is she going to give us a cock and hens ?

Din. Yes ! that was our secret too !

Har. That's the surprise !

Enter Patience.

Patience. Quick, quick, all of you ! Mammy wants you ! she's got a great surprise for you !

All. Oh, the cock and hens ! How nice !

Patience. Why, do you know what the surprise is already ?

Jack. It won't be much of a surprise if we all know what it is.

Din. What a pity ! What shall we do ? [*All reflect.*

Har. I have it ! Instead of mammy surprising us, we'll surprise her, by telling her we know her secret ! That will come to just the same thing.

Din. Oh, what a good idea !

All. Quick ! let's go and surprise mammy !

[*Exeunt, running.*

PRINTED BY
SPOTTISWOODE AND CO., NEW-STREET SQUARE
LONDON

Y

39 PATERNOSTER ROW, LONDON, E.C.

A SELECTION OF WORKS

IN

GENERAL LITERATURE

PUBLISHED BY

LONGMANS, GREEN, & CO.

MESSRS. LONGMANS, GREEN, & CO.

Issue the undermentioned Lists of their Publications, which may be had post free on application:—

1. MONTHLY LIST OF NEW WORKS AND NEW EDITIONS.

2. QUARTERLY LIST OF ANNOUNCEMENTS AND NEW WORKS.

3. NOTES ON BOOKS; BEING AN ANALYSIS OF THE WORKS PUBLISHED DURING EACH QUARTER.

4. CATALOGUE OF SCIENTIFIC WORKS.

5. CATALOGUE OF MEDICAL AND SURGICAL WORKS.

6. CATALOGUE OF SCHOOL BOOKS AND EDUCATIONAL WORKS.

7. CATALOGUE OF BOOKS FOR ELEMENTARY SCHOOLS AND PUPIL TEACHERS.

8. CATALOGUE OF THEOLOGICAL WORKS BY DIVINES AND MEMBERS OF THE CHURCH OF ENGLAND.

9. CATALOGUE OF WORKS IN GENERAL LITERATURE.

HISTORY, POLITICS, HISTORICAL MEMOIRS, &c.

Abbey and Overton's English Church in the Eighteenth Century. Cr. 8vo. 7s. 6d.

Abbott's Skeleton Outline of Greek History. Crown 8vo. 2s. 6d.

— **History of Greece.** Part 1, crown 8vo. 10s. 6d. Part 2, *in the press.*

Acland and Ransome's Handbook in Outline of the Political History of England to 1887. Crown 8vo. 6s.

Annual Register (The) for the Year 1889. 8vo. 18s. The Vols. for 1863–1888 can still be had.

Arnold's Lectures on Modern History. 8vo. 7s. 6d.

Ashby's English Economic History and Theory. Part 1, The Middle Ages. Crown 8vo. 5s.

Bagwell's Ireland under the Tudors. Vols. 1 and 2. 8vo. 32s. Vol. 3. 8vo. 18s.

Ball's Legislative Systems in Ireland, 1172–1800. 8vo. 6s.

— **The Reformed Church of Ireland, 1537–1886.** 8vo. 7s. 6d.

Boultbee's History of the Church of England, Pre-Reformation Period. 8vo. 15s.

Bowen's (Sir G. F.) Thirty Years of Colonial Government : a Selection of Official Papers. 2 vols. 8vo. 32s.

LONGMANS, GREEN, & CO., London and New York.

Bright's (J. Franck) History of England. Cr. 8vo. Vol. 1, 449–1485, 4s. 6d. Vol. 2, 1485–1688, 5s. Vol. 3, 1689–1837, 7s. 6d. Vol. 4, 1837–1880, 6s.

Buckle's History of Civilisation. 3 vols. crown 8vo. 24s.

Church (Sir Richard) : a Memoir. By Stanley Lane Poole. 8vo. 5s.

Cox's (Sir G. W.) General History of Greece. Crown 8vo. Maps, 7s. 6d.

Crake's History of the Church under the Roman Empire, A.D. 30–476. Crown 8vo. 7s. 6d.

Creighton's Papacy during the Reformation. 8vo. Vols. 1 & 2, 32s. Vols. 3 & 4, 24s.

Curzon's Russia in Central Asia in 1889. With Maps. Illustrated. 8vo. 21s.

De Redcliffe's (Viscount Stratford) Life. By Stanley Lane-Poole. 2 vols. 8vo. 36s. Abridged Edition, 1 vol. crown 8vo. 7s. 6d.

De Tocqueville's Democracy in America. 2 vols. crown 8vo. 16s.

Doyle's English in America : Virginia, Maryland, and the Carolinas, 8vo. 18s.
— — — The Puritan Colonies, 2 vols. 8vo. 36s.

Esssay Introductory to the Study of English Constitutional History. Edited by H. O. Wakeman and A. Hassall. Crown 8vo. 6s.

Ewald's Antiquities of Israel, translated by Solly. 8vo. 12s. 6d.
— History of Israel, translated by Carpenter & Smith. 8 vols. 8vo. Vols. 1 & 2, 24s. Vols. 3 & 4, 21s. Vol. 5, 18s. Vol. 6, 16s. Vol. 7, 21s. Vol. 8, 18s.

Freeman's Historical Geography of Europe. 2 vols. 8vo. 31s. 6d.

Froude's English in Ireland in the 18th Century. 3 vols. crown 8vo. 18s.
— History of England. 12 vols. crown 8vo. 3s. 6d. each.
— Short Studies on Great Subjects. 4 vols. crown 8vo. 24s.

Gardiner's History of England from the Accession of James I. to the Outbreak of the Civil War. 10 vols. crown 8vo. 60s.
— History of the Great Civil War, 1642–1649 (3 vols.) Vol. 1, 1642–1644, 8vo. 21s. Vol. 2, 1644–1647, 8vo. 24s.
— Student's History of England. Illustrated. (3 vols.) Vol. 1, crown 8vo. 4s.

Gibbs' England in South Africa. 8vo. 5s.

Greville's Journal of the Reigns of King George IV., King William IV., and Queen Victoria. Cabinet Edition. 8 vols. crown 8vo. 6s. each.

Harrison's The Contemporary History of the French Revolution. Cr. 8vo. 3s. 6d.

Historic Towns. Edited by E. A. Freeman, D.C.L. and the Rev. William Hunt, M.A. With Maps and Plans. Crown 8vo. 3s. 6d. each.

London. By W. J. Loftie.	Oxford. By the Rev. C. W. Boase.
Exeter. By E. A. Freeman.	Colchester. By the Rev. E. L. Cutts.
Cinque Ports. By Montagu Burrows.	Carlisle. By the Rev. M. Creighton.
	Winchester. By G. W. Kitchin, D.D.
Bristol. By the Rev. W. Hunt.	York. By the Rev. James Raine.

Hurlbert's France and her Republic : a Record of 1889. 8vo. 18s.

Jennings' Ecclesia Anglicana : a History of the Church of Christ in England. Crown 8vo. 7s. 6d.

Lecky's History of England in the Eighteenth Century. Vols. 1 & 2, 1700–1760, 8vo. 36s. Vols. 3 & 4, 1760–1784, 8vo. 36s. Vols. 5 & 6, 1784–1793, 36s. Vols. 7 & 8, 1793–1800, 36s.
— History of European Morals. 2 vols. crown 8vo. 16s.
— — — Rationalism in Europe. 2 vols. crown 8vo. 16s.

Leger's History of Austro-Hungary. Crown 8vo. 10s. 6d.

Lyde's Introduction to Ancient History. Crown 8vo. 3s.

LONGMANS, GREEN, & CO., London and New York.

Macaulay's Complete Works. Library Edition. 8 vols. 8vo. £5. 5s.
— — — Cabinet Edition. 16 vols. crown 8vo. £4. 16s.
— History of England :—
Popular Edition. 2 vols. cr. 8vo. 5s. | Cabinet Edition. 8 vols. post 8vo. 48s.
Student's Edition. 2 vols. cr. 8vo. 12s. | Library Edition. 5 vols. 8vo. £4.
People's Edition. 4 vols. cr. 8vo. 16s. |
Macaulay's Critical and Historical Essays, with Lays of Ancient Rome In One
Volume :—
Authorised Edition. Cr. 8vo. 2s. 6d. | Popular Edition. Cr. 8vo. 2s. 6d.
or 3s. 6d. gilt edges. |
Macaulay's Critical and Historical Essays :—
Student's Edition. 1 vol. cr. 8vo. 6s. | Cabinet Edition. 4 vols. post 8vo. 24s.
Trevelyan Edition. 2 vols. cr. 8vo. 9s. | Library Edition. 3 vols. 8vo. 36s.
People's Edition. 2 vols. cr. 8vo. 8s. |
Macaulay's Miscellaneous Writings. 2 vols. 8vo. 21s. 1 vol. crown 8vo. 4s. 6d.
— Miscellaneous Writings and Speeches :—
Popular Edition. Cr. 8vo. 2s. 6d. | Student's Edition. Cr. 8vo. 6s.
— Miscellaneous Writings, Speeches, Lays of Ancient Rome, &c.
Cabinet Edition. 4 vols. crown 8vo. 24s.
— Writings, Selections from. Crown 8vo. 6s.
— Speeches corrected by Himself. Crown 8vo. 3s. 6d.
Magnus's Outlines of Jewish History. Fcp. 8vo. 3s. 6d.
Malmesbury's (Earl of) Memoirs of an Ex-Minister. Crown 8vo. 7s. 6d.
May's Constitutional History of England, 1760–1870. 3 vols. crown 8vo. 18s.
Melbourne Papers (The). Edited by Lloyd C. Sanders. 8vo. 18s.
Merivale's Fall of the Roman Republic. 12mo. 7s. 6d.
— General History of Rome, B.C. 753–A.D. 476. Crown 8vo. 7s. 6d
— History of the Romans under the Empire. Cabinet Edition. 8 vols.
post 8vo. 48s. Popular Edition. 8 vols. 3s. 6d. each.
Murdock's Reconstruction of Europe, from the Rise to the Fall of the Second
French Empire. Crown 8vo. 9s.
Oman's History of Greece from the Earliest Times to the Macedonian Conquest.
Crown 8vo. 4s. 6d.
Porter's History of the Corps of Royal Engineers. 2 vols. 8vo. 36s.
Ransome's The Rise of Constitutional Government in England. Crown 8vo. 6s.
Rawlinson's The History of Phœnicia. 8vo. 24s.
Russell's (Lord John) Life. By Spencer Walpole. 2 vols. 8vo. 36s.
Seebohm's Oxford Reformers—Colet, Erasmus, & More. 8vo. 14s.
Short's History of the Church of England. Crown 8vo. 7s. 6d.
Smith's Carthage and the Carthaginians. Crown 8vo. 6s.
Stephens' (H. Morse) History of the French Revolution. 3 vols. 8vo. Vol. 1.
18s. Vol. 2, in the press.
Stubbs' History of the University of Dublin. 8vo. 12s. 6d.
Symes' Prelude to Modern History. With Maps. Crown 8vo. 2s. 6d.
Taylor's Manual of the History of India. Crown 8vo. 7s. 6d.
Toynbee's Lectures on the Industrial Revolution of the 18th Century in
England. 8vo. 10s. 6d.
Walpole's History of England, from 1815. Library Edition. 5 vols. 8vo. £4. 10s.
Cabinet Edition. 6 vols. 6s. each.

LONGMANS, GREEN, & CO., London and New York.

EPOCHS OF ANCIENT HISTORY.

Edited by the Rev. Sir G. W. Cox, Bart. M.A. and by C. SANKEY, M.A.

10 volumes, fcp. 8vo. with Maps, price 2s. 6d. each.

The Gracchi, Marius, and Sulla. By A. H. Beesly, M.A. With 2 Maps.
The Early Roman Empire. By the Rev. W. Wolfe Capes, M.A. With 2 Maps.
The Roman Empire of the Second Century. By the Rev. W. Wolfe Capes, M.A. With 2 Maps.
The Athenian Empire from the Flight of Xerxes to the Fall of Athens. By the Rev. Sir G. W. Cox, Bart. M.A. With 5 Maps.
The Rise of the Macedonian Empire. By Arthur M. Curteis, M.A. With 8 Maps.
The Greeks and the Persians. By the Rev. Sir G. W. Cox, Bart. · With 4 Maps.
Rome to its Capture by the Gauls. By Wilhelm Ihne. With a Map.
The Roman Triumvirates. By the Very Rev. Charles Merivale, D.D. With Map.
The Spartan and Theban Supremacies. By Charles Sankey, M.A. With 5 Maps.
Rome and Carthage, the Punic Wars. By R. Bosworth Smith. With 9 Maps.

EPOCHS OF MODERN HISTORY.

Edited by C. COLBECK, M.A. 19 volumes, fcp. 8vo. with Maps. Price 2s. 6d. each.

The Beginning of the Middle Ages. By the Very Rev. R. W. Church. With 3 Maps.
The Normans in Europe. By Rev. A. H. Johnson, M.A. With 3 Maps.
The Crusades. By the Rev. Sir G. W. Cox, Bart. M.A. With a Map.
The Early Plantagenets. By the Right Rev. W. Stubbs, D.D. With 2 Maps.
Edward the Third. By the Rev. W. Warburton, M.A. With 3 Maps.
The Houses of Lancaster and York. By James Gairdner. With 5 Maps.
The Early Tudors. By the Rev. C. E. Moberly, M.A.
The Era of the Protestant Revolution. By F. Seebohm. With 4 Maps.
The Age of Elizabeth. By the Rev. M. Creighton, M.A. LL.D. With 5 Maps.
The First Two Stuarts. By Samuel Rawson Gardiner. With 4 Maps.
The Thirty Years' War, 1618–1648. By Samuel Rawson Gardiner. With a Map.
The English Restoration and Louis XIV., 1648–1678. By Osmund Airy.
The Fall of the Stuarts. By the Rev. Edward Hale, M.A. With 11 Maps.
The Age of Anne. By E. E. Morris, M.A. With 7 Maps and Plans.
The Early Hanoverians. By E. E. Morris, M.A. With 9 Maps and Plans.
Frederick the Great and the Seven Years' War. By F. W. Longman. With 2 Maps.
The War of American Independence, 1775–1783. By J. M. Ludlow. With 4 Maps.
The French Revolution, 1789–1795. By Mrs. S. R. Gardiner. With 7 Maps.
The Epoch of Reform, 1830–1850. By Justin McCarthy, M.P.

EPOCHS OF CHURCH HISTORY.

Edited by the Rev. MANDELL CREIGHTON. 15 vols. fcp. 8vo. price 2s. 6d. each.

The English Church in other Lands. By the Rev. H. W. Tucker.
The History of the Reformation in England. By the Rev. George G. Perry.
The Church of the Early Fathers. By Alfred Plummer, D.D.
The Evangelical Revival in the Eighteenth Century. By the Rev. J. H. Overton
A History of the University of Oxford. By the Hon. G. C. Brodrick, D.C.L.
A History of the University of Cambridge. By J. Bass Mullinger, M.A.
The English Church in the Middle Ages. By Rev. W. Hunt, M.A.
The Arian Controversy. By H. M. Gwatkin, M.A.
Wycliffe and Movements for Reform. By Reginald L. Poole.
The Counter-Reformation. By A. W. Ward.
The Church and the Roman Empire. By the Rev. A. Carr.
The Church and the Puritans, 1570–1660. By Henry Offley Wakeman.
The Church and the Eastern Empire By the Rev. H. F. Tozer.
Hildebrand and His Times. By the Rev. W. R. W. Stephens.
The Popes and the Hohenstaufen. By Ugo Balzani.

LONGMANS, GREEN. & CO., London and New York.

BIOGRAPHICAL WORKS.

Armstrong's (E. J.) Life and Letters. Edited by G. F. Armstrong. Fcp. 8vo. 7s.6d.
Bacon's Life and Letters, by Spedding. 7 vols. 8vo. £4. 4s.
Bagehot's Biographical Studies. 1 vol. 8vo. 12s.
Carlyle's (Thomas) Life. By James A. Froude. Crown 8vo. 1795-1835, 2 vols.
7s. 1834-1881, 2 vols. 7s.
Clavers, the Despot's Champion. By A Southern. Crown 8vo. 7s. 6d.
Fox (Charles James) The Early History of. By Sir G. O. Trevelyan. Cr. 8vo. 6s.
Froude's Cæsar : a Sketch. Crown 8vo. 3s. 6d.
Hamilton's (Sir W. R.) Life, by Graves. 3 vols. 8vo. 15s. each.
Havelock's Life, by Marshman. Crown 8vo. 3s. 6d.
Macaulay's (Lord) Life and Letters. By his Nephew, Sir G. O. Trevelyan, Bart.
Popular Edition, 1 vol. cr. 8vo. 2s. 6d. Student's Edition, 1 vol. cr. 8vo. 6s.
Cabinet Edition, 2 vols. post 8vo. 12s. Library Edition, 2 vols. 8vo. 36s.
McDougall's Memoirs (Bishop of Labuan). By C. J. Bunyon. 8vo. 14s.
Mendelssohn's Letters. Translated by Lady Wallace. 2 vols. cr. 8vo. 5s. each.
Moore's Dante and his Early Biographers. Crown 8vo. 4s. 6d.
Newman's Apologia pro Vitâ Suâ. Crown 8vo. 6s. Cheap Edition, cr. 8vo. 3s. 6d.
— (Cardinal) Letters and Correspondence during his Life in the
English Church. 2 vols. 8vo.
Pasteur (Louis) His Life and Labours. Crown 8vo. 7s. 6d.
Shakespeare, Outline of the Life of. By J. O. Halliwell-Phillipps. Illustrated.
2 vols. royal 8vo. 21s.
Shakespeare's True Life. By James Walter. With 500 Illustrations. Imp. 8vo. 21s.
Southey's Correspondence with Caroline Bowles. 8vo. 14s.
Stephen's Essays in Ecclesiastical Biography. Crown 8vo. 7s. 6d.
Vignoles' (C. B.) Life. By his Son. 8vo. 16s.
Wellington's Life, by Gleig. Crown 8vo. 3s. 6d.

MENTAL AND POLITICAL PHILOSOPHY FINANCE, &c.

Adams' Public Debts ; an Essay on the Science of Finance. 8vo. 12s. 6d.
Amos' Primer of the English Constitution. Crown 8vo. 6s.
Bacon's Essays, with Annotations by Whately. 8vo. 10s. 6d.
— Works, edited by Spedding. 7 vols. 8vo. 73s. 6d.
Bagehot's Economic Studies, edited by Hutton. 8vo. 10s. 6d.
Bain's Logic, Deductive and Inductive. Crown 8vo. 10s. 6d.
PART I. Deduction, 4s. | PART II. Induction, 6s. 6d.
— Mental and Moral Science. Crown 8vo. 10s. 6d.
— The Senses and the Intellect. 8vo. 15s.
— The Emotions and the Will. 8vo. 15s.
Blake's Tables for the Conversion of 5 per cent. Interest from ⅛ to 7 per cent.
8vo. 12s. 6d.
Case's Physical Realism. 8vo. 15s.
Crump's Short Enquiry into the Formation of English Political Opinion. 8vo. 7s.6d.
— Causes of the Great Fall in Prices. 8vo. 6s.

LONGMANS, GREEN, & CO., London and New York.

Dowell's A History of Taxation and Taxes in England. 8vo. Vols. 1 & 2, 21s.
Vols. 3 & 4, 21s.
Green's (Thomas Hill) Works. (3 vols.) Vols. 1 & 2, Philosophical Works. 8vo.
16s. each. Vol. 3, Miscellanies. With Memoir. 8vo. 21s.
Hume's Essays, edited by Green & Grose. 2 vols. 8vo. 28s.
— Treatise of Human Nature, edited by Green & Grose. 2 vols. 8vo. 28s.
Ladd's Elements of Physiological Psychology. 8vo. 21s.
Lang's Custom and Myth : Studies of Early Usage and Belief. Crown 8vo. 7s. 6d.
Leslie's Essays in Political Economy. 8vo. 10s. 6d.
Lewes's History of Philosophy. 2 vols. 8vo. 32s.
Lubbock's Origin of Civilisation. Illustrated. 8vo. 18s.
Macleod's The Elements of Banking. Crown 8vo. 5s.
— The Theory and Practice of Banking. Vol. 1, 8vo. 12s. Vol. 2, 14s.
— The Theory of Credit. (2 vols. 8vo.) Vol. 1, 7s. 6d. Vol. 2, Part 1,
4s. 6d.

Manuals of Catholic Philosophy, crown 8vo. :—
Clarke's Logic. 5s.
Rickaby's First Principles of Knowledge. 5s.
— Moral Philosophy. 5s.
— General Metaphysics. 5s.
Maher's Psychology. 6s. 6d.
Boedder's Natural Theology. (In the press.)
Devas' Political Economy. (In preparation.)

Max Müller's The Science of Thought. 8vo. 21s.
Mill's (James) Analysis of the Phenomena of the Human Mind. 2 vols. 8vo. 28s.
Mill (John Stuart) on Representative Government. Crown 8vo. 2s.
— — on Liberty. Crown 8vo. 1s. 4d.
— — Examination of Hamilton's Philosophy. 8vo. 16s.
— — Logic. Crown 8vo. 5s.
— — Principles of Political Economy. 2 vols. 8vo. 30s. People's
Edition, 1 vol. crown 8vo. 5s.
— — Utilitarianism. 8vo. 5s.
— — Three Essays on Religion, &c. 8vo. 5s.
Monck's Introduction to Logic. Crown 8vo. 5s.
Mulhall's History of Prices since 1850. Crown 8vo. 6s.
Sandars' Institutes of Justinian, with English Notes. 8vo. 18s.
Seebohm's English Village Community. 8vo. 16s.
Sully's Outlines of Psychology. 8vo. 12s. 6d.
— Teacher's Handbook of Psychology. Crown 8vo. 6s. 6d.
Swinburne's Picture Logic. Post 8vo. 5s.
Thompson's A System of Psychology. 2 vols. 8vo. 36s.
— The Problem of Evil. 8vo. 10s. 6d.
— The Religious Sentiments of the Human Mind. 8vo. 7s. 6d.
— Social Progress : an Essay. 8vo. 7s. 6d.
Webb's The Veil of Isis. 8vo. 10s. 6d.
Whately's Elements of Logic. Crown 8vo. 4s. 6d.
— — — Rhetoric. Crown 8vo. 4s. 6d.

LONGMANS, GREEN, & CO., London and New York.

8

Zeller's History of Eclecticism in Greek Philosophy. Crown 8vo. 10s. 6d.
— Plato and the Older Academy. Crown 8vo. 18s.
— Pre-Socratic Schools. 2 vols. crown 8vo. 30s.
— Socrates and the Socratic Schools. Crown 8vo. 10s. 6d.
— Stoics, Epicureans, and Sceptics. Crown 8vo. 15s.
— Outlines of the History of Greek Philosophy. Crown 8vo. 10s. 6d.

CLASSICAL LANGUAGES AND LITERATURE.

Æschylus, The Eumenides of. Text, with Metrical English Translation, by J. F. Davies. 8vo. 7s.
Aristophanes' The Acharnians, translated by R. Y. Tyrrell. Crown 8vo. 1s.
Aristotle's The Ethics, Text and Notes, by Sir Alex. Grant, Bart. 2 vols. 8vo. 32s.
— The Nicomachean Ethics, translated by Williams, crown 8vo. 7s. 6d.
— The Politics, Books I. III. IV. (VII.) with Translation, &c. by Bolland and Lang. Crown 8vo. 7s. 6d.
Becker's *Charicles* and *Gallus*, by Metcalfe. Post 8vo. 7s. 6d. each.
Cicero's Correspondence, Text and Notes, by R. Y. Tyrrell. Vols. 1, 2, & 3, 8vo. 12s. each.
Harrison's Myths of the Odyssey in Art and Literature. Illustrated. 8vo. 18s.
Hellenica : a Collection of Essays on Greek Poetry, &c. Edited by Evelyn Abbott. 8vo. 16s.
Plato's Parmenides, with Notes, &c. by J. Maguire. 8vo. 7s. 6d.
Sophocles. Translated into English verse by Robert Whitelaw. Cr. 8vo. 8s. 6d.
Virgil's Works, Latin Text, with Commentary, by Kennedy. Crown 8vo. 10s. 6d.
— Æneid, translated into English Verse, by Conington. Crown 8vo. 6s.
— — — — — by W. J. Thornhill. Cr. 8vo. 7s. 6d.
— Poems, — — — Prose, by Conington. Crown 8vo. 6s.
— Eclogues and Georgics of Virgil. Translated by J. W. Mackail. Royal 16mo. 5s.
Witt's Myths of Hellas, translated by F. M. Younghusband. Crown 8vo. 3s. 6d.
— The Trojan War, — — Fcp. 8vo. 2s.
— The Wanderings of Ulysses, — Crown 8vo. 3s. 6d.
— The Retreat of the Ten Thousand, — Crown 8vo.

ENCYCLOPÆDIAS, DICTIONARIES, AND BOOKS OF REFERENCE.

Acton's Modern Cookery for Private Families. Fcp. 8vo. 4s. 6d.
Ayre's Treasury of Bible Knowledge. Fcp. 8vo. 6s.
Blake's Tables for the Conversion of 5 per Cent. Interest, &c. 8vo. 12s. 6d.
Chisholm's Handbook of Commercial Geography. 29 Maps. 8vo. 16s.
Gwilt's Encyclopædia of Architecture. 8vo. 52s. 6d.
Keith Johnston's Dictionary of Geography, or General Gazetteer. 8vo. 42s.
Longmans' New Atlas. 56 Maps. Edited by G. G. Chisholm. 4to. or imperial 8vo. 12s. 6d.

LONGMANS, GREEN, & CO., London and New York.

M'Culloch's Dictionary of Commerce and Commercial Navigation. 8vo. 63s.
Maunder's Biographical Treasury. Fcp. 8vo. 6s.
—   Historical Treasury. Fcp. 8vo. 6s.
—   Scientific and Literary Treasury. Fcp. 8vo. 6s.
—   Treasury of Bible Knowledge, edited by Ayre. Fcp. 8vo. 6s.
—   Treasury of Botany, edited by Lindley & Moore. Two Parts, 12s.
—   Treasury of Geography. Fcp. 8vo. 6s.
—   Treasury of Knowledge and Library of References. Fcp. 8vo. 6s.
—   Treasury of Natural History. Fcp. 8vo. 6s.
Quain's Dictionary of Medicine. Medium 8vo. 31s. 6d., or in 2 vols. 34s.
Rich's Dictionary of Roman and Greek Antiquities. Crown 8vo. 7s. 6d.
Roget's Thesaurus of English Words and Phrases. Crown 8vo. 10s. 6d.
Willich's Popular Tables, by Marriott. Crown 8vo. 10s. 6d.

NATURAL HISTORY, BOTANY & GARDENING.

Bennett and Murray's Handbook of Cryptogamic Botany. 8vo. 16s.
Hartwig's Aerial World. With 68 Illustrations. 8vo. 10s. 6d.
—   Polar World. With 93 Illustrations. 8vo. 10s. 6d.
—   Sea and its Living Wonders. With 315 Illustrations. 8vo. 10s. 6d.
—   Subterranean World. With 80 Illustrations. 8vo. 10s. 6d.
—   Tropical World. With 180 Illustrations. 8vo. 10s. 6d.
Lindley's Treasury of Botany. 2 vols. fcp. 8vo. 12s.
Loudon's Encyclopædia of Gardening. 8vo. 21s.
—   —   Plants. 8vo. 42s.
Rivers's Orchard House. Crown 8vo. 5s.
—   Miniature Fruit Garden. Fcp. 8vo. 4s.
Stanley's Familiar History of British Birds. Crown 8vo. 3s. 6d.
Wood's Bible Animals. With 112 Illustrations. 8vo. 10s. 6d.
—   Homes Without Hands. With 140 Illustrations. 8vo. 10s. 6d.
—   Insects Abroad. With 600 Illustrations. 8vo. 10s. 6d.
—   Insects at Home. With 700 Illustrations. 8vo. 10s. 6d.
—   Out of Doors. With 11 Illustrations. Crown 8vo. 3s. 6d.
—   Petland Revisited. With 33 Illustrations. Crown 8vo. 3s. 6d.
—   Strange Dwellings. With 60 Illustrations. Crown 8vo. 3s. 6d.

THEOLOGICAL AND RELIGIOUS WORKS.

Colenso on the Pentateuch and Book of Joshua. Crown 8vo. 6s.
De la Saussaye's Manual of the Science of Religion.
Hobart's Medical Language of St. Luke. 8vo. 16s.
Macdonald's (G.) Unspoken Sermons. First and Second Series. Crown 8vo. 3s. 6d.
each. Third Series. Crown 8vo. 7s. 6d.
—   The Miracles of our Lord. Crown 8vo. 3s. 6d.
Martineau's Endeavours after the Christian Life. Crown 8vo. 7s. 6d.

LONGMANS, GREEN, & CO., London and New York.

Martineau's **Hymns of Praise and Prayer.** Crown 8vo. 4s. 6d. 32mo. 1s. 6d.
— The Seat of Authority in Religion. 8vo. 14s.
— Sermons, Hours of Thought on Sacred Things. 2 vols. 7s. 6d. each.
Max Müller's **Origin and Growth of Religion.** Crown 8vo. 7s. 6d.
— — Science of Religion. Crown 8vo. 7s. 6d.
— — Gifford Lectures on Natural Religion. Crown 8vo. 10s. 6d.
Newman's **Apologia pro Vitâ Suâ.** Crown 8vo. 6s. Cheap Edition, cr. 8vo. 3s. 6d.
— The Arians of the Fourth Century. Crown 8vo. 6s. Cheap Edition,
crown 8vo. 3s. 6d.
— The Idea of a University Defined and Illustrated. Crown 8vo. 7s.
— Historical Sketches. 3 vols. crown 8vo. 6s. each.
— Discussions and Arguments on Various Subjects. Crown 8vo. 6s.
— An Essay on the Development of Christian Doctrine. Crown 8vo. 6s.
Cheap Edition, crown 8vo. 3s. 6d.
— Certain Difficulties Felt by Anglicans in Catholic Teaching Con-
sidered. Vol. 1, crown 8vo. 7s. 6d. Vol. 2, crown 8vo. 5s. 6d.
— The Via Media of the Anglican Church, Illustrated in Lectures, &c.
2 vols. crown 8vo. 6s. each.
— Essays, Critical and Historical. 2 vols. crown 8vo. 12s. Cheap Edition,
crown 8vo. 7s.
— Essays on Biblical and on Ecclesiastical Miracles. Crown 8vo. 6s.
Cheap Edition, crown 8vo. 3s. 6d.
— Present Position of Catholics in England. Crown 8vo. 7s. 6d.
— An Essay in Aid of a Grammar of Assent. 7s. 6d.
— Select Treatises of St. Athanasius in Controversy with the Arians.
Translated. 2 vols. crown 8vo. 15s.
Perring's **The 'Work and Days' of Moses.** 3s. 6d.
Reply to **Dr. Lightfoot's Essays.** By the Author of ' Supernatural Religion.'
8vo. 6s.
Roberts' **Greek the Language of Christ and His Apostles.** 8vo. 18s.
Supernatural Religion. Complete Edition. 3 vols. 8vo. 36s.

⁎ For other Works see Messrs. Longmans, Green, & Co.'s Catalogue of
Theological Works.

TRAVELS, ADVENTURES, &c.

Baker's **Eight Years in Ceylon.** Crown 8vo. 3s. 6d.
— Rifle and Hound in Ceylon. Crown 8vo. 3s. 6d.
Brassey's **Sunshine and Storm in the East.** Library Edition, 8vo. 21s. Cabinet
Edition, crown 8vo. 7s. 6d. Popular Edition, 4to. 6d.
— Voyage in the 'Sunbeam.' Library Edition, 8vo. 21s. Cabinet Edition,
cr. 8vo. 7s. 6d. School Edit. fcp. 8vo. 2s. Popular Edit. 4to. 6d.
— In the Trades, the Tropics, and the 'Roaring Forties.' Cabinet Edition,
crown 8vo. 17s. 6d. Popular Edition, 4to. 6d.
— Last Journals, 1886-7. Illustrated. 8vo. 21s.
Bryden's **Kloof and Karroo.** Sport, Legend, &c., in Cape Colony. 8vo. 10s. 6d.
Clutterbuck's **The Skipper in Arctic Seas.** Illustrated. Crown 8vo. 10s. 6d.
Coolidge's **Swiss Travel and Swiss Guide-Books.** Crown 8vo. 10s. 6d.

LONGMANS, GREEN, & CO., London and New York.

Deland's Florida Days. Illustrated. 4to. 21s.

Fronde's Oceana ; or, England and her Colonies. Cr. 8vo. 2s. boards ; 2s. 6d. cloth.
  —   The English in the West Indies. Crown 8vo. 2s. boards ; 2s. 6d. cloth.

Howitt's Visits to Remarkable Places. Crown 8vo. 3s. 6d.

James's The Long White Mountain ; or, a Journey in Manchuria. 8vo. 24s.

Knight's A Treasure Hunt. Crown 8vo.

Lees and Clutterbuck's B.C. 1887 : a Ramble in British Columbia. Cr. 8vo. 6s.

Nansen's The First Crossing of Greenland. 2 vols. 8vo. 36s.

Riley's Athos ; or, The Mountain of the Monks. 8vo. 21s.

Smith's The White Umbrella in Mexico. Fcp. 8vo. 6s. 6d.

Three in Norway. By Two of Them. Crown 8vo. 2s. boards ; 2s. 6d. cloth.

Willoughby's East Africa and its Big Game. 8vo. 21s.

Wolff's Rambles in the Black Forest. Crown 8vo 7s. 6d.

WORKS BY RICHARD A. PROCTOR.

The Orbs Around Us. With Chart and Diagrams. Crown 8vo. 5s.

Other Worlds than Ours. With 14 Illustrations. Crown 8vo. 5s.

The Moon. With Plates, Charts, Woodcuts, and Photographs. Crown 8vo. 5s.

Universe of Stars. With 22 Charts and 22 Diagrams. 8vo. 10s. 6d.

Light Science for Leisure Hours. 3 vols. crown 8vo. 5s. each.

Chance and Luck. Crown 8vo. 2s. boards ; 2s. 6d. cloth.

Larger Star Atlas for the Library, in 12 Circular Maps. Folio, 15s.

New Star Atlas, in 12 Circular Maps (with 2 Index Plates). Crown 8vo. 5s.

The Student's Atlas. 12 Circular Maps. 8vo. 5s.

How to Play Whist, with the Laws and Etiquette of Whist. Crown 8vo. 3s. 6d.

Home Whist : an Easy Guide to Correct Play. 16mo. 1s.

The Stars in their Seasons. Imperial 8vo. 5s.

Strength. With 9 Illustrations. Crown 8vo. 2s.

Strength and Happiness. With 9 Illustrations. Crown 8vo. 5s.

Rough Ways Made Smooth. Crown 8vo. 5s.

Our Place Among Infinities. Crown 8vo. 5s.

The Expanse of Heaven : Essays on the Wonders of the Firmament. Crown 8vo. 5s.

Pleasant Ways in Science. Crown 8vo. 5s.

Myths and Marvels of Astronomy. Crown 8vo. 5s.

The Great Pyramid : Observatory, Tomb, and Temple. Crown 8vo. 5s.

AGRICULTURE, HORSES, DOGS, AND CATTLE.

Fitzwygram's Horses and Stables. 8vo. 5s.

Lloyd's The Science of Agriculture. 8vo. 12s.

London's Encyclopædia of Agriculture. 21s.

Prothero's Pioneers and Progress of English Farming. Crown 8vo. 5s.

Steel's Diseases of the Ox, a Manual of Bovine Pathology. 8vo. 15s.
  —   —   —   Dog. 8vo. 10s. 6d.
  —   —   —   Sheep. 8vo. 12s.

Stonehenge's Dog in Health and Disease. Square crown 8vo. 7s. 6d.

Ville on Artificial Manures, by Crookes. 8vo. 21s.

Youatt's Work on the Dog. 8vo. 6s.
  —   —   —   — Horse. 8vo. 7s. 6d.

LONGMANS, GREEN, & CO., London and New York.

WORKS OF FICTION.

By H. RIDER HAGGARD.

She. 3s. 6d.	Maiwa's Revenge.
Allan Quater-	2s. bds.; 2s. 6d.
main. 3s. 6d.	cloth.
Cleopatra. 6s.	Colonel Quaritch.
Beatrice. 6s.	3s. 6d.

By H. RIDER HAGGARD & ANDREW LANG.
The World's Desire. 6s.

By the EARL OF BEACONSFIELD.

Vivian Grey.	Alroy, Ixion, &c.
Venetia.	Endymion.
Coningsby.	The Young Duke.
Lothair.	Contarini Fleming.
Tancred.	Henrietta Temple.
Sybil.	

Price 1s. each, bds.; 1s. 6d. each, cloth.
The HUGHENDEN EDITION. With 2 Portraits and 11 Vignettes. 11 vols. Crown 8vo. 42s.

By G. J. WHYTE-MELVILLE.

The Gladiators.	Kate Coventry.
The Interpreter.	Digby Grand.
Holmby House.	General Bounce.
Good for Nothing.	Queen's Maries.

Price 1s. each, bds.; 1s. 6d. each, cloth.

By ELIZABETH M. SEWELL.

Amy Herbert.	Cleve Hall.
Gertrude.	Ivors.
Ursula.	Earl's Daughter.

The Experience of Life.
A Glimpse of the World.
Katharine Ashton.
Margaret Percival.
Laneton Parsonage.
1s.6d. each, cloth; 2s.6d.each, gilt edges.

By Mrs. MOLESWORTH.
Marrying and Giving in Marriage. 2s. 6d.
Silverthorns. 5s. | Neighbours. 6s.
The Palace in the Garden. 5s.
The Third Miss St. Quentin. 6s.
The Story of a Spring Morning. 5s.

By MAY KENDALL.
Such is Life. 6s.

By Mrs. OLIPHANT.
In Trust. | Madam.
Price 1s. each, bds.; 1s. 6d. each, cloth.
Lady Car. 2s. 6d.

By G. H. JESSOP.
Judge Lynch. 6s.
Gerald Ffrench's Friends. 6s.

By A. C. DOYLE.
Micah Clarke. 3s. 6d.
The Captain of the Polestar, &c. 6s.

By G. G. A. MURRAY.
Gobi or Shamo. 6s.

By C. PHILLIPPS-WOLLEY.
Snap. 6s.

By STANLEY J. WEYMAN.
The House of the Wolf. 6s.

By JAMES PAYN.
The Luck of the Darrells.
Thicker than Water.
1s. each, boards; 1s. 6d. each, cloth.

By ANTHONY TROLLOPE.
The Warden.
Barchester Towers.
1s. each, boards; 1s. 6d. each, cloth.

By BRET HARTE.
In the Carquinez Woods.
Price 1s. boards; 1s. 6d. cloth.
On the Frontier. 1s.
By Shore and Sedge. 1s.

By ROBERT L. STEVENSON.
The Dynamiter. 1s. swd. 1s. 6d. cl.
Strange Case of Dr. Jekyll and Mr. Hyde. 1s. sewed; 1s. 6d. cloth.

By R. L. STEVENSON and L. OSBOURNE.
The Wrong Box. 5s.

By EDNA LYALL.
Autobiography of a Slander. 1s.

By F. ANSTEY.
The Black Poodle, and other Stories.
Price 2s. boards; 2s. 6d. cloth.

By Mrs. DELAND.
John Ward, Preacher. 2s. boards; 2s. 6d. cloth.
Sidney. 6s.

LONGMANS, GREEN, & CO., London and New York.

By the AUTHOR OF 'THE ATELIER DU LYS.'
The Atelier du Lys. **2s. 6d.**
Mademoiselle Mori. **2s. 6d.**
In the Olden Time. **2s. 6d.**
Hester's Venture. **2s. 6d.**
That Child. **3s. 6d.**
Under a Cloud. **5s.**
Fiddler of Lugan. **6s.**
A Child of the Revolution. **6s.**

By CHRISTIE MURRAY & HY. HERMAN.
Wild Darrie. **2s. bds   2s. 6d. cloth.**

By CHRISTIE MURRAY & HY. MURRAY.
A Dangerous Catspaw. **2s. 6d.**

By J. A. FROUDE.
The Two Chiefs of Dunboy. **6s.**

By Mrs. HUGH BELL.
Will o' the Wisp. **3s. 6d.**

By WILLIAM O'BRIEN, M.P.
When we were Boys. **2s. 6d.**

By the AUTHOR OF 'THOTH.'
Toxar. **6s.**

By JAMES BAKER.
By the Western Sea. **6s.**

By W. E. NORRIS.
Mrs. Fenton : a Sketch. **6s.**

By A. D. CRAKE.
HISTORICAL TALES, price 5s. each :—
Edwy the Fair. | The House of
Alfgar the Dane. | Walderne.
The Rival Heirs. | BrianFitz-Count.

By AGNES GIBERNE.
Ralph Hardcastle's Will. **5s.**
Nigel Browning. **5s.**

By JEAN INGELOW.
Very Young, and Quite Another Story.

By A. LEE KNIGHT.
Adventures of a Midshipmite. **5s.**

By L. T. MEADE.
The O'Donnells of Inchfawn. **6s.**
Daddy's Boy. **5s.**
Deb and the Duchess. **5s.**
House of Surprises. **3s. 6d.**
The Beresford Prize. **5s.**

By Mrs. O'REILLY.
Hurstleigh Dene. **5s.**
Kirke's Mill. **2s. 6d.**

By G. COLMORE.
A Living Epitaph. **6s.**

By L. N. COMYN.
Atherstone Priory. **2s. 6d.**

By C. M. YONGE, M. BRAMSTON, &c.
Astray : a Tale of a Country Town. **3s. 6d.**

POETRY AND THE DRAMA.

Armstrong's (Ed. J.) Poetical Works. **Fcp. 8vo. 5s.**
— (G. F.) Poetical Works :—
Poems, Lyrical and Dramatic. Fcp. 8vo. **6s.**
Ugone : a Tragedy. Fcp. 8vo. **6s.**
A Garland from Greece. Fcp. 8vo. **9s.**
King Saul. Fcp. 8vo. **5s.**
King David. Fcp. 8vo. **6s.**
King Solomon. Fcp. 8vo. **6s.**

Stories of Wicklow. Fcp. 8vo. **9s.**
Mephistopheles in Broadcloth : a Satire. Fcp. 8vo. **4s.**
Victoria Regina et Imperatrix : a Jubilee Song from Ireland, 1887. 4to. **2s. 6d.**

Arnold's (Sir Edwin) The Light of the World. Crown 8vo. **7s. 6d.** net.
Ballads of Books. Edited by Andrew Lang. Fcp. 8vo. **6s.**
Bowdler's Family Shakespeare. Medium 8vo. **14s.** 6 vols. fcp. 8vo. **21s.**
Clark-Kennedy's Pictures in Rhyme. With Illustrations. Crown 8vo.
Courthope's The Paradise of Birds. Illustrated by Lancelot Speed. Royal 8vo. **7s. 6d.**
Dante, Le Commedia di. A New Text, carefully revised. Fcp. 8vo. **6s.**
Deland's The Old Garden, and other Verses. Fcp. 8vo. **5s.**
Goethe's Faust, translated by Birds. Crown 8vo. Part I. **6s.** ; Part II. **6s.**
— — translated by Webb. 8vo. **12s. 6d.**
— — edited by Selss. Crown 8vo. **5s.**

LONGMANS, GREEN, & CO., London and New York.

Haggard's (Ella) Life and its Author. With Memoir, &c. Crown 8vo. 3s. 6d.
Ingelow's Poems. 2 Vols. fcp. 8vo. 12s.; Vol. 3, fcp. 8vo. 5s.
— Lyrical and other Poems. Fcp. 8vo. 2s. 6d. cloth, plain; 3s. cloth, gilt edges.
Kendall's (May) Dreams to Sell. Fcp. 8vo. 6s.
Lang's Grass of Parnassus. Fcp. 8vo. 6s.
Macaulay's Lays of Ancient Rome. Illustrated by Scharf. 4to. 10s. 6d. Bijou Edition, fcp. 8vo. 2s. 6d. Popular Edit., fcp. 4to. 6d. swd., 1s. cloth.
— Lays of Ancient Rome, with Ivry and the Armada. Illustrated by Weguelin. Crown 8vo. 3s. 6d. gilt edges.
Nesbit's Lays and Legends. Crown 8vo. 5s.
— Leaves of Life. Crown 8vo. 5s.
Newman's The Dream of Gerontius. 16mo. 6d. sewed: 1s. cloth.
— Verses on Various Occasions. Fcp. 8vo. 6s. Cheap Edit. cr. 8vo. 3s. 6d.
Reader's Voices from Flowerland: a Birthday Book. 2s. 6d. cloth, 3s. 6d. roan.
— Echoes of Thought: a Medley of Verse. Crown 8vo. 5s.
Rossetti's A Shadow of Dante: an Essay. Illustrated. Crown 8vo. 10s. 6d.
Smith's (Gregory) Fra Angelico, and other short Poems. Crown 8vo. 4s. 6d.
Southey's Poetical Works. Medium 8vo. 14s.
Stevenson's A Child's Garden of Verses. Fcp. 8vo. 5s.
Tomson's The Bird Bride. Fcp. 8vo. 6s.
Virgil's Æneid, translated by Conington. Crown 8vo. 6s.
— Poems, translated into English Prose. Crown 8vo. 6s.

SPORTS AND PASTIMES.

American Whist. Illustrated. By G. W. P. Fcp. 8vo. 6s. 6d.
Campbell-Walker's Correct Card, or How to Play at Whist. Fcp. 8vo. 2s. 6d.
Chetwynd's (Racing) Reminiscences, &c. 8vo.
Ford's Theory and Practice of Archery, revised by W. Butt. 8vo. 14s.
Francis's Treatise on Fishing in all its Branches. Post 8vo. 15s.
Hutchinson's Some Great Golf Links. Illustrated.
Longman's Chess Openings. Fcp. 8vo. 2s. 6d.
Pole's Theory of the Modern Scientific Game of Whist. Fcp. 8vo. 2s. 6d.
Proctor's How to Play Whist. Crown 8vo. 3s. 6d.
— Home Whist. 18mo. 1s. sewed.
Ronalds's Fly-Fisher's Entomology. 8vo. 14s.
Wilcocks's Sea-Fisherman. Post 8vo. 6s.

MISCELLANEOUS WORKS.

A. K. H. B., The Essays and Contributions of. Crown 8vo. 3s. 6d.

Autumn Holidays of a Country Parson.
Changed Aspects of Unchanged Truths.
Common-Place Philosopher in Town and Country.
Critical Essays of a Country Parson.
Counsel and Comfort spoken from a City Pulpit.
East Coast Days and Memories.
Graver Thoughts of a Country Parson. Three Series.
Landscapes, Churches, and Moralities.

Leisure Hours in Town.
Lessons of Middle Age.
Our Homely Comedy; and Tragedy.
Our Little Life. Essays Consolatory and Domestic. Two Series.
Present-day Thoughts.
Recreations of a Country Parson. Three Series.
Seaside Musings on Sundays and Week-Days.
Sunday Afternoons in the Parish Church of a University City.

'To Meet the Day' through the Christian Year. 4s. 6d.

LONGMANS, GREEN, & CO., London and New York.

Anstey's Voces Populi. Reprinted from *Punch*. With 20 Illustrations. Cr. 4to. 5s.
Armstrong's (Ed. J.) Essays and Sketches. Fcp. 8vo. 5s.
Arnold's (Dr. Thomas) Miscellaneous Works. 8vo 7s. 6d.
Bagehot's Literary Studies, edited by Hutton. 2 vols. 8vo. 28s.
Baker's War with Crime. Reprinted Papers. 8vo. 12s. 6d.
Blue Fairy Book (The). Edited by Andrew Lang. Illustrated. Crown 8vo. 6s.
Book (The) of Wedding Days. Illustrated by Walter Crane. 4to. 21s.
Comic (The) Birthday Book. Edited by W. F. March-Phillipps. 32mo. 1s. 6d.
Farrar's Language and Languages. Crown 8vo. 6s.
Henderson's The Story of Music. Crown 8vo. 6s.
Huth's The Marriage of Near Kin. Royal 8vo. 21s.
Jefferies' Field and Hedgerow : Last Essays. Crown 8vo. 3s. 6d.
Lang's Books and Bookmen. Crown 8vo. 6s. 6d.
— Letters on Literature. Fcp. 8vo. 6s. 6d.
— Old Friends : Essays in Epistolary Parody. Crown 8vo. 6s. 6d.
Lavigerie (Cardinal) and the African Slave-Trade. 8vo. 14s.
Mason's Steps of the Sun : Daily Readings of Prose. 16mo. 3s. 6d.
Matthews' (Brander) Pen and Ink. Reprinted Papers. Crown 8vo. 5s.
Max Müller's Lectures on the Science of Language. 2 vols. crown 8vo. 16s.
— — Lectures on India. 8vo. 12s. 6d.
— — Biographies of Words and the Home of the Aryas. Crown 8vo. 7s. 6d.
Moon's The King's English. Fcp. 8vo. 3s. 6d.
— The Revisers' English. Fcp. 8vo. 3s. 6d.
Mozley's Letters from Rome. 2 vols. crown 8vo.
Red Fairy Book (The). Edited by Andrew Lang. Illustrated. Crown 8vo. 6s.
Rendle and Norman's Inns of Old Southwark. Illustrated. Royal 8vo. 28s.
Shakespeare (The) Birthday Book. By Mary F. Dunbar. 32mo. 1s. 6d. cloth.
   With Photographs, 32mo. 5s. Drawing-room Edition, with Photographs,
   fcp. 8vo. 10s. 6d.
Strong and Logeman's Introduction to the Study of the History of Language. 8vo.
Wendt's Papers on Maritime Legislation. Royal 8vo. £1. 11s. 6d.

WORKS BY MR. SAMUEL BUTLER.

Op. 1. Erewhon. 5s.
Op. 2. The Fair Haven. 7s. 6d.
Op. 3. Life and Habit. 7s. 6d.
Op. 4. Evolution, Old and New. 10s. 6d.
Op. 5. Unconscious Memory. 7s. 6d.
Op. 6. Alps and Sanctuaries of Piedmont and the Canton Ticino. 10s. 6d.
Op. 7. Selections from Ops. 1–6. 7s. 8d.
Op. 8. Luck, or Cunning. 7s. 6d.
Op. 9. Ex Voto. 10s. 6d.
Holbein's 'La Danse.' 3s.

WORKS BY MRS. DE SALIS.

Cakes and Confections. 1s. 6d.
Entrées à la Mode Fcp. 8vo. 1s. 6d.
Game and Poultry à la Mode. 1s. 6d.
Oysters à la Mode. Fcp. 8vo. 1s. 6d.
Puddings and Pastry à la Mode. 1s. 6d.
Savouries à la Mode. Fcp. 8vo. 1s.
Soups and Dressed Fish à la Mode. Fcp. 8vo. 1s. 6d.
Sweets & Supper Dishes à la Mode. 1s. 6d.
Tempting Dishes for Small Incomes. 1s. 6d.
Vegetables à la Mode. Fcp. 8vo. 1s. 6d.
Wrinkles and Notions for Every Household. Crown 8vo. 2s. 6d

LONGMANS, GREEN, & CO., London and New York.

THE BADMINTON LIBRARY.

Edited by the DUKE OF BEAUFORT, K.G. and A. E. T. WATSON.

Crown 8vo. Price 10s. 6d. each Volume.

Hunting. By the Duke of Beaufort, K.G. and Mowbray Morris. With Contributions by the Earl of Suffolk and Berkshire, Rev. E. W. L. Davies, Digby Collins, and Alfred E. T. Watson. With Frontispiece and 53 Illustrations by J. Sturgess, J. Charlton, and Agnes M. Biddulph.

Fishing. By H. Cholmondeley-Pennell. With Contributions by the Marquis of Exeter, Henry R. Francis, M.A. Major John P. Traherne, G. Christopher Davies, R. B. Marston, &c.
Vol. I. Salmon, Trout. and Grayling. With 158 Illustrations.
Vol. II. Pike and other Coarse Fish. With 132 Illustrations.

Racing and Steeple-Chasing. Racing: By the Earl of Suffolk and W. G. Craven. With a Contribution by the Hon. F. Lawley. Steeple-chasing: By Arthur Coventry and A. E. T. Watson. With 56 Illustrations by J. Sturgess.

Shooting. By Lord Walsingham and Sir Ralph Payne-Gallwey. With Contributions by Lord Lovat, Lord Charles Lennox Kerr, the Hon. G. Lascelles, and A. J. Stuart-Wortley. With 21 Plates, and 149 Woodcuts, by A. J. Stuart-Wortley, Harper Pennington, C. Whymper, J. G. Millais, G. E. Lodge, and J. H. Oswald Brown.
Vol. I. Field and Covert. | Vol. II. Moor and Marsh.

Cycling. By Viscount Bury, K.C.M.G. and G. Lacy Hillier. With 19 Plates, and 61 Woodcuts, by Viscount Bury and Joseph Pennell.

Athletics and Football. By Montague Shearman. With an Introduction by Sir Richard Webster, Q.C. M.P. and a Contribution on 'Paper Chasing' by Walter Rye. With 6 Plates and 45 Woodcuts.

Boating. By W. B. Woodgate. With an Introduction by the Rev. Edmond Warre, D.D. And a Chapter on 'Rowing at Eton' by R. Harvey Mason. With 10 Plates, and 39 Woodcuts, by Frank Dadd.

Cricket. By A. G. Steel and the Hon. R. H. Lyttelton. With Contributions by Andrew Lang, R. A. H. Mitchell, W. G. Grace, and F. Gale. With 11 Plates and 52 Woodcuts.

Driving. By the Duke of Beaufort, K.G.; with Contributions by other Authorities. Photogravure Intaglio Portrait of his Grace the Duke of Beaufort, 11 full-page Illustrations, and 54 Woodcuts in the Text, after Drawings by G. D. Giles and J. Sturgess. Second Edition. Cr. 8vo .10s. 6d.

Fencing, Boxing, and Wrestling. By Walter H. Pollock, F. C. Grove, Camille Prevost, Maître d'Armes, E. B. Michell, and Walter Armstrong. With a complete Bibliography of the Art of Fencing by Egerton Castle, M.A. F.S.A. With 18 Intaglio Plates and 24 Woodcuts.

Tennis, Lawn Tennis, Rackets, and Fives. By J. M. and C. G. Heathcote, E. O. Pleydell-Bonverie, A. C. Ainger, &c. With 12 Plates and 67 Woodcuts, &c. by Lucien Davis and from Photographs.

Golf. By Horace Hutchinson, the Right Hon. A. J. Balfour, M.P. Sir Walter G. Simpson, Bart. Lord Wellwood, H. S. C. Everard, Andrew Lang, and other Writers. With 22 Plates and 69 Woodcuts, &c.

In Preparation.

Riding. By W. R. Weir, the Earl of Suffolk and Berkshire, the Duke of Beaufort, and A. E. T. Watson. With a Chapter on Polo, by Capt. Moray Brown.
[*In the press.*

Yachting.   ——   [*In preparation.*

LONGMANS, GREEN, & CO., London and New York.

THE SILVER LIBRARY.

Crown 8vo. price 3s. 6d. each.

	s. d.
Cardinal Newman's Apologia pro Vitâ Suâ	3 6
Cardinal Newman's Callista : a Tale of the Third Century	3 6
Cardinal Newman's An Essay on the Development of Christian Doctrine ..	3 6
Cardinal Newman's Essays, Critical and Historical 2 vols.	7 0
Cardinal Newman's The Arians of the Fourth Century	3 6
Cardinal Newman's Verses on Various Occasions ..	3 6
Cardinal Newman's Two Essays on Biblical and Ecclesiastical Miracles ..	3 6
She : a History of Adventure. By H. Rider Haggard. With 32 Illustrations	3 6
Allan Quatermain. By H. Rider Haggard. With 20 Illustrations	3 6
Colonel Quaritch, V.C. : a Tale of Country Life. By H. Rider Haggard. With Frontispiece and Vignette	3 6
Micah Clarke : his Statement. A Tale of Monmouth's Rebellion. By A. Conan Doyle. With Frontispiece and Vignette	3 6
Petland Revisited. By the Rev. J. G. Wood. With 33 Illustrations	3 6
Strange Dwellings : a Description of the Habitations of Animals, abridged from 'Homes without Hands.' By the Rev. J. G. Wood. With 60 Illustrations ..	3 6

	s. d.
Out of Doors : a Selection of Original Articles on Practical Natural History. By the Rev. J. G. Wood. With 11 Illustrations	3 6
Familiar History of Birds. By the late Edward Stanley, D.D. Lord Bishop of Norwich. With 160 Woodcuts	3 6
Rifle and Hound in Ceylon. By Sir S. W. Baker. With 6 Illustrations	3 6
Eight Years in Ceylon. By Sir S. W. Baker. With 6 Illustrations..	3 6
Memoirs of Major-General Sir Henry Havelock, K.C.B. By John Clark Marshman. With Portrait	3 6
Visits to Remarkable Places: Old Halls, Battle-fields, Scenes Illustrative of Striking Passages in English History and Poetry. By William Howitt. With 80 Illustrations..	3 6
Field and Hedgerow. Last Essays of Richard Jefferies. With Portrait	3 6
Story of Creation : a Plain Account of Evolution. By Edward Clodd. With 77 Illustrations..	3 6
Life of the Duke of Wellington. By the Rev. G. R. Gleig, M.A. With Portrait	3 6
History of the Romans under the Empire. By the Very Rev. Charles Merivale, D.C.L. Dean of Ely. 8 vols. each	3 6
Cæsar : a Sketch. By James A. Froude	3 6
Thomas Carlyle : a History of his Life. By J. A. Froude, M.A.	
1795-1835. 2 vols.	7 0
1834-1881. 2 vols.	7 0

LONGMANS, GREEN, & CO., London and New York.

Spottiswoode & Co. Printers, New-street Square, London.

25,000/11/90